Routledge Philosophy GuideBook to

Hume
on morality

'*Hume on Morality* is clearly written, well-organized, and especially admirable for the attention it gives to Hume's account of the passions and the importance of the general point of view to Hume's understanding of moral judgement.'

Geoff Sayre-McCord, University of North Carolina, Chapel Hill

'This is a lucid and well-organized introduction to Hume's moral philosophy. The book will prove particularly useful to students who are looking for a reliable account and review of Hume's central arguments. Baillie is careful to show how Hume's views on morality relate to his wider philosophical system.'

Paul Russell, University of British Columbia

David Hume (1711–76) is one of the greatest figures in the history of British philosophy. Of all of Hume's writings, the philosophically most profound is undoubtedly his first, *A Treatise of Human Nature*.

Hume on Morality provides us with a map to Books 2 and 3 of the *Treatise*, focusing on Hume's theory of the passions and morality. This book sets out its principal ideas and arguments of the *Treatise* in a clear and readable way and is ideal for anyone co *Treatise* for the first time. It also covers *An Enquiry Principles of Morals*, and there is a substantial secti 'Of the Standard of Taste'.

James Baillie is Associate Professor of Philosophy at t Portland. He is the author of *Problems in Personal Ide* editor of *Contemporary Analytic Philosophy* (1997).

Edited by Tim Crane and Jonathan Wolff
University College London

Hegel on History
Joseph McCarney

Hume on Knowledge
Harold W. Noonan

Kant and the *Critique of Pure Reason*
Sebastian Gardner

Mill on Liberty
Jonathan Riley

Mill on Utilitarianism
Roger Crisp

Wittgenstein and the *Philosophical Investigations*
Marie McGinn

Heidegger and *Being and Time*
Stephen Mulhall

Plato and the *Republic*
Nickolas Pappas

Locke on Government
D.A. Lloyd Thomas

Locke on Human Understanding
E.J. Lowe

Spinoza and Ethics
Genevieve Lloyd

LONDON AND NEW YORK

Routledge Philosophy GuideBook to

Hume

on morality

ROUTLEDGE

James Baillie

First published 2000
by Routledge
11 New Fetter Lane, London EC4P 4EE

Simultaneously published in the USA and Canada
by Routledge
29 West 35th Street, New York, NY 10001

Routledge is an imprint of the Taylor & Francis Group

Typeset in Times by Taylor & Francis Books Ltd
Printed and bound in Great Britain by Clays Ltd, St Ives PLC

British Library Cataloguing in Publication Data
A catalogue record for this book is available from the British Library

Library of Congress Cataloging in Publication Data
Baillie, James, 1957–
Hume on morality/ James Baillie.
(Routledge philosophy guidebooks)
Includes bibliographical references and index.
1. Hume, David 1711–1776–Ethics I. Series.

B1499.E8 B35 2000
170'.92–dc21
99-059823

ISBN 0–415–18048–1 (hbk)
ISBN 0–415–18049-X (pbk)

Contents

Acknowledgements

I am grateful to the University of Portland for granting me a term's sabbatical to work on this book. Many thanks to my colleague Jeff Gauthier for his careful reading of my first draft. I was also fortunate to receive many useful comments from Geoffrey Sayre-McCord and Paul Russell, who reviewed the manuscript for Routledge. Finally, thanks to Jonathan Wolff for inviting me to write the book, and for all his help during the process.

Abbreviations

Works by Hume referred to in the text:

T	*A Treatise of Human Nature*, ed. L.A. Selby-Bigge and P. H. Nidditch, Oxford: Clarendon, 1978. The *Treatise* is made up of three Books, which are in turn divided into Parts consisting of Sections. Hence, when I say '*T* 3/2/5', this refers to Book 3, Part 2, Section 5.
A	*Abstract* of the *Treatise*, in Selby-Bigge and Nidditch (1975).
1*E*	*An Enquiry Concerning Human Understanding*, in *Enquiries Concerning Human Understanding and Concerning the Principles of Morals*, ed. L.A. Selby-Bigge and P.H. Nidditch, Oxford: Clarendon, 1975.
2*E*	*An Enquiry Concerning the Principles of Morals*, in Selby-Bigge and Nidditch (1975).
ST	'Of the Standard of Taste', in *Essays, Moral, Political and Literary*, ed. E.F. Miller, Indianapolis: Liberty Classics, 1985.

Chapter 1

Introduction

Chapter 1

Life and times

David Hume was born in Edinburgh in 1711 into a distinguished but not particularly wealthy family whose estate was in Ninewells, Berwickshire, near the border with England. Records reveal that the family name had been typically spelled 'Home', which was pronounced the same as 'Hume', although those less bureaucratic times allowed many variations including 'Hoom' and 'Hum'. While the Homes had been in Berwickshire since at least the twelfth century, Hume's direct ancestors occupied Ninewells since the fifteenth century. After the death of his father, Joseph Home, in 1713, Hume was raised, along with an elder brother and sister, by his mother Katherine. In his biography, Ernest Mossner records that

> The family were Presbyterians, members of the established Church of Scotland. In politics they were Whigs, strongly approving the revolution of

> 1688, the Union of 1707, and the accession of the House of Hanover in 1714; and strongly disapproving all varieties of Jacobitism.
>
> (Mossner 1980: 32; unless otherwise stated, all page references in this section refer to Mossner)

Hume enrolled at Edinburgh University in 1722, alongside his brother John. This did not indicate precocity, since eleven was a typical age to enter a university, these being more akin to a modern day high school than a university as we know it. The core curriculum consisted of Latin, Greek, Logic, Metaphysics, and Natural Philosophy (i.e., Physics), with electives available in Mathematics and History. Hume left around 1726 without graduating, as was common in those days, and there is little record of his time there. In *My Own Life*, he merely notes that 'I passed through the ordinary Course of Education with Success' (1980: 40).

On leaving university, he was under some familial pressure to enter the legal profession, and entered into a period of private study within which law initially played a major part. His legal knowledge

> was thought sufficient...to gain him the commission of Judge-Advocate to a military expedition of 1746; and throughout his life it enabled him to draw up legal documents of many different types and to offer expert comment on matters pertaining to the law.
>
> (1980: 55)

Although he described himself as being 'religious when young', he parted company with it around this time, deciding that, as he later told Francis Hutcheson, 'I desire to take my Catalogue of Virtues from *Cicero's Offices*, not from the *Whole Duty of Man*' (1980: 64), the pietist tract of his boyhood. This seems to have been a period of extraordinary intellectual growth, since by 1729 he had reached the basic insights underlying his philosophical theory.

> After much Study, & Reflection on this [new Medium, by which Truth might be establisht], at last, when I was about 18 Years of

> Age, there seem'd to be open'd up to me a new Scene of Thought, which transported me beyond Measure, & made me, with an Ardor natural to young men, throw up every other Pleasure or Business to apply entirely to it. The Law, which was the Business I design'd to follow, appear'd nauseous to me, & I cou'd think of no other way of pushing my Fortune in the World but that of a Scholar & Philosopher.
>
> (1980: 65)

From 1729 till 1734, he pursued this new 'Scene of Thought' so single-mindedly as to affect his health, suffering depression, together with a variety of physical ailments including scurvy. His doctor eccentrically recommended a pint of claret each day, along with moderate exercise. Hume also came to the belief that 'Business and Diversion' would be the best cure for his state of mind, so he put his studies on hold and started work as a clerk for a sugar importer in Bristol. Around this time he changed the spelling of his name to Hume, since the English kept mispronouncing it. His business career was short-lived, being dismissed after incurring his employer's wrath for constantly correcting his grammar and literary style.

The *Treatise* was largely written in France between 1734 and 1737. Having a yearly allowance of around £50, he could not afford to live in Paris, his ideal choice of residence, and settled in La Fleche, Anjou. Apart from cheap lodgings, La Fleche had the advantage of a well-established Jesuit college (where Descartes had been educated) which included a substantial library.

Hume returned to London to find a publisher, staying there till early 1739. John Noon published Books 1 and 2 of the *Treatise* in January 1739, Book 3 being published by Thomas Longman in November 1740. He followed a common practice in publishing anonymously, and only explicitly admitted its authorship in posthumously published works. He chose to remove the most controversial section, a chapter on miracles, with the intention of avoiding the inevitable furore by 'enthusiasts' which would dominate discussion at the expense of the main theoretical considerations from which his theological views were consequent.

Hume judged this concession to have had no effect. While he

adapted Pope to lament that 'It fell *dead-born from the press*, without reaching such distinction, as even to excite a murmur among the zealots', there is much evidence to the contrary. Although initial sales were slow, the hostile reaction among excitable persons soon gathered such a momentum as to wreck his chances of an academic career, and he endured their attacks on his character, and misrepresentations of his work, throughout his life. Apart from a small circle of cognoscenti, which included members of the 'moderate' wing of the Church, he was 'Hume the Infidel' rather than 'le bon David'. Initial reviews were uniform in that (a) they focused almost entirely on Book 1; (b) they seriously misunderstood it; and (c) their tone was hostile and often insulting. There was no public response from those capable of understanding it, such as Berkeley or Hutcheson. His decision to publish an *Abstract* summarizing the argument of Book 1 had no effect. Disillusioned with his book's reception, he attempted to get his ideas across in the form of essays aimed at a general public. *Essays Moral and Political* was published in 1741, and was well received. Still, as late as 1766, Hume could sadly report that

> I cou'd cover the Floor of a large Room with Books and Pamphlets wrote against me, to none of which I ever made the least Reply, not from Disdain (for the Authors of some of them, I respect), but from my Desire of Ease and tranquillity.
>
> (1980: 286)

The first considered study of Hume's system was by Thomas Reid, who succeeded where Hume had not in becoming Chair of Logic at Glasgow. His *Inquiry into the Human Mind, on the Principles of Common Sense* came out in 1764, a quarter-century after the *Treatise*. However, even he seems not to have grasped Hume's intentions, failing to recognize many significant areas of agreement with his own work.

Within Hume's lifetime, his most famous critic was James Beattie, Professor of Moral Philosophy and Logic at Marischal College, Aberdeen. His book, *An Essay on the Nature and Immutability of Truth; in opposition to Sophistry and Scepticism*, appeared in 1770. Although an immediate popular success which was to go through five editions prior to Hume's death in 1776, it is now regarded as a work of little philosophical merit, with Beattie himself only remembered by Hume's epithet, 'That bigotted silly Fellow, Beattie'. While Hume never publicly countered Beattie, he was sufficiently stung to take the unprecedented step of adding a prefatorial 'Advertisement' to future editions of his works, denouncing the *Treatise* as a negligent and juvenile work, a judgement with which few would now concur.

Hume applied for the Chair of Ethics and Pneumatical Philosophy at Edinburgh University in 1745. Pneumatics referred not to the mechanics of gases, but consisted of Natural Theology and proofs of God's immortality, along with the study of immaterial beings and supposed 'subtle material substances' imperceptible to the senses. Hume complained that: 'The accusation of Heresy, Deism, Scepticism, Atheism &c &c &c was started against me; but never took, being bore down by the contrary Authority of all the good Company in Town' (1980: 156).

This is disingenuous to say the least, since opposition to his appointment included even Francis Hutcheson, a man who had probably done more than anyone else of his time to modernize and liberalize curricula at Scottish universities. Since 1690, all teachers at Scottish universities were required to subscribe to the Westminster Confession of Faith, something that Hume could surely not in all conscience do. As Alasdair MacIntyre has discussed at length, the Chair of Moral Philosophy at a Scottish university was unprecedented in its influence on general culture.

> For the task of a professor of moral philosophy in eighteenth-century Scotland came to be that of providing a defense of just those fundamental moral principles, conceived of as antecedent to both all positive law and all particular forms of social organization, which defined peculiarly Scottish institutions and attitudes. And in providing this kind of defense philosophy and especially moral philosophy assumed a kind of authority in Scottish culture which it has rarely enjoyed in other times and places.
>
> (MacIntyre 1988: 239)

The seriousness with which this role of defending and promoting Presbyterian theology was taken is shown by the fact that someone as devout as Hutcheson could be tried for heresy. Indeed, it was less than fifty years since a divinity student had been executed on such a charge. How Hume thought himself suited for such a job, or that he had any chance of getting it, is beyond me. It is hard not to agree with MacIntyre that

> Of Hume's unfitness to hold a chair which, for example, required its holder to give instruction in the truths of rational religion in a way that would be at least congruent with and supportive of the Christian revelation there can in retrospect be little doubt.
> (MacIntyre 1988: 286)

Around this time, Hume became tutor to the Marquess of Annandale, who professed himself an admirer of the *Essays*. The experience was not a happy one, since the Marquess was insane. Shortly after this fiasco, Hume was hired as military secretary for a projected expedition to Canada, which never took place. He was later seconded to embassies in Vienna and Turin.

There then followed an intensive period of writing, beginning with the publication in 1748 of the *Enquiry Concerning Human Understanding*, plus *Philosophical Essays*, which included 'On Miracles'. After returning to Ninewells in 1749, the next few years produced the *Enquiry into the Principles of Morals*, *Political Discourses*, and the posthumously published *Dialogues Concerning Natural Religion*. He also began research for his largest undertaking, the *History of England*. This was published in six volumes between 1754 and 1762, and was by far Hume's most successful book both financially and in terms of public acclaim, remaining the standard work in the field even into this century.

Hume was to make one more serious attempt at an academic career, applying for the Chair of Logic at Glasgow in 1751, after Adam Smith had vacated it to move over to the Chair of Moral Philosophy. As before in Edinburgh, his appointment was blocked by hostile clergy. By this point, it was not only the Presbyterians who were taking offence at his views. In 1761 he was flattered by having all his works placed on the Vatican's list of prohibited books.

On returning to Edinburgh in 1751, he became a central figure in elevating that city to a cultural centre second only to Paris. He was appointed Librarian to the Faculty of Advocates, a post he held for five years. While the salary was small, it placed him in charge of what was undoubtedly the best library in the country, which proved invaluable to his historical researches. He participated in many learned societies, and, as secretary to the Philosophical Society of Edinburgh, published Benjamin Franklin's paper on the lightning rod. These societies included many members of the 'Moderate' clergy, who were throughout his life to be among his strongest defenders against the wrath of their righteous brethren. For example, they were among his most prominent supporters in his struggle to obtain an academic position. Again, when the Evangelicals proposed excommunicating Hume from the Church, these friends patiently pointed out the absurdity of the suggestion, since 'it begins by alleging that the defender denies and disbelieves Christianity, and then it seeks to proceed against him and to punish him as a Christian' (1980: 347). While Hume's writings are full of disparaging remarks about the clergy, depicting them as hypocritical, conceited men whose zeal was fuelled by hatred and vengeance, it is obvious that he is talking primarily about the Evangelicals and other enthusiasts. Still, he should have been more careful, since his friends and allies included clergy who embodied more of his 'natural' virtues than the 'monkish' ones he so despised.

Hume spoke throughout his life with a strong accent, and his conversation was full of terms unique to Scots. This seems to have been a source of some embarrassment to him, as well as an inconvenience, since the English often had difficulty in understanding what he was saying. However, he paid serious attention to removing these 'Scotticisms' from his writings. In addition, he and his circle expended great energy in encouraging clear English pronunciation and prose in their fellows, going to the extent of establishing a Chair at Edinburgh University for that very purpose. This was judged necessary given the increasing numbers of Scots in positions of importance in London, following the Union of 1707.

In sharp contrast to his status in Britain, Hume was a celebrity in France. On arrival in Paris in 1763, as Private Secretary to the British Ambassador, he was immediately feted by the highest society, provoking the envy of Horace Walpole, who remarked that Hume 'is fashion itself, although his French is almost as unintelligible as his English' (1980: 445). He was at home in the leading salons, particularly that of the Comtesse de Boufflers, who was also, unfortunately for our hero, the mistress of the Prince de Conti. He remained in contact with her for the rest of his life.

Apart from high society, Hume was also in regular contact with leading French intellectuals including Baron d'Holbach, Diderot and D'Alembert. Voltaire, who called him 'my St David', was, to Hume's regret, then living on the Swiss border. Ironically, Hume's sceptical agnostic stance was as much at odds with the (what seemed to him) dogmatic atheism of 'les Philosophes' as it had been with the British theists.

It was at this point that Hume made the acquaintance of Jean-Jacques Rousseau. Rousseau's writings had made France a dangerous place for him, and his supporters enlisted Hume's help in relocating him to Britain. The result was by turns hilarious and grotesque, since the clinically paranoid Rousseau came to believe that Hume was at the centre of an international plot to ruin him. Although greatly angered at the time, Hume mellowed to sadly conclude that Rousseau was 'absolutely lunatic', and 'plainly delirious and an Object of the Greatest Compassion' (1980: 536). Conspiracy theories apart, it seems that Hume's habit of staring during conversation was too much for Rousseau's fragile psyche.

Towards the end of his life, Hume purchased a house in the New Town district of Edinburgh, where he lived with his sister Katherine until his death. His friend Nancy Ord (whom he seriously considered marrying around that time) nicknamed the street 'St David's Street', both in tribute to his good nature, and in ironic reference to his anti-clerical views. The name later became officially adopted.

By 1772 he fell gradually into the illness from which he never recovered. The 'disorder in my bowels', as he described in *My Own Life*, was probably either cancer or ulcerative colitis. He was able to work right until the end, and revised his published works and prepared his unpublished writings – notably the *Dialogues Concerning Natural Religion* – for posthumous release. On news of his impending demise, various persons visited in the hope of seeing Hume recant his sceptical views. They were disappointed, as he faced death with the same clarity and honesty with which he faced life. We are indebted to James Boswell for a record of Hume's last days, where we see his opinions unchanged:

> He said he had never entertained any belief in Religion since he began to read Locke and Clarke…He then said flatly that the Morality of every Religion was bad, and, I really thought, was not jocular when he said 'that when he heard that a man was religious, he concluded he was a rascal, though he had known some instances of very good men being religious'.
>
> (1980: 597)

Boswell was particularly disturbed by Hume's equanimity in rejecting belief in an afterlife, and regarding its absence as no more unsettling than the fact that he did not exist prior to his conception. As Boswell grudgingly admitted, 'It surprised me to find him talking of different matters with a tranquillity of mind and a clearness of head, which few men possess at any time' (1980: 598).

My Own Life was published in 1777, along with Adam Smith's letter to Hume's friend and literary executor William Strahan, in which he famously says: 'Upon the whole, I have always considered him, both in his lifetime and since his death, as approaching as nearly to the idea of a perfectly wise and virtuous man, as perhaps the nature of human frailty will admit' (1980: 604–5). Smith noted the hostility he met through praising the infidel:

> A single, and as I thought, a very harmless Sheet of paper, which I happened to write concerning the death of our late friend, Mr. Hume, brought upon me ten times more abuse than the very violent attack I had made upon the whole commercial system of Great Britain.
>
> (1980: 605)

Ironically, this illustrates the high level of the Scottish culture of the time, since it is hard to imagine too many people caring, let alone knowing, about what a philosopher says these days. Mossner assesses Hume's character by saying that

> The French learned to call him *le bon David*, but the epithet cannot readily be translated into one English word. To call Hume *good* would be misleading, for he was certainly no saint. In many ways, however, he *was* good; he was humane, charitable, pacific, tolerant, and encouraging of others, morally sincere and intellectually honest.
>
> (1980: 4)

I would go further and suggest that when judged against the virtues recommended by his own model of human nature, Hume was a very good man. He was not 'good' by the standards of the 'monkish virtues' of humility and self-denial. However, Hume hoped to radically reconstruct moral discourse, since it was all too apparent to him that those deemed 'good' in eighteenth-century Scotland were in fact the opposite, when assessed in terms of a viable theory of human nature.

Methods and aims

Hume's philosophical standing has fluctuated since his death, often due to factors irrelevant to his projects. It has to be remembered that Hume was writing before any strict distinction between science and philosophy was instituted. Thus, in the middle part of this century, when positivists and ordinary language philosophers were united only in viewing philosophy as an a priori practice of analysis, it seemed to many that much of the *Treatise* was not really philosophy at all, but an early form of empirical psychology. This attitude, probably more than anything else, was responsible for the highly selective reading of Hume's work that is still commonplace (for example, the passing over of most of Book 2), with the distortion that inevitably ensues. However, the pendulum has now swung in Hume's favour. In these Quinean times where naturalism is respectable and any strict demarcation of the nature of philosophy appears quaint, Hume looks more modern and relevant than ever.

The study of human nature, sometimes referred to as 'moral science', is to be distinguished from 'natural' science. While human beings can be considered as physical, chemical or biological systems, we can also be studied as intentional systems, as conscious purposeful agents, and it is under this latter aspect that Hume's investigations take place. So 'moral philosophy' or 'moral science' includes not only ethics, but takes in psychology, politics, social science, history and aesthetics. In attempting a *science* of human nature, Hume is explicitly treating mind as a purely natural phenomenon, regarding agents as part of the one same natural world, and therefore open to the same processes of empirically based investigation. The aim is the one at the heart of all sciences: to find the explanatory principles that produce order in diverse phenomena.

Hume stops at the *description* of these basic principles, from which everything else is *explained*. That is, he tries to discover *what* these principles are, not *why* they are. One reason for this is that any further investigation would belong to the natural sciences. Another, deeper reason is his belief that philosophy 'cannot go beyond experience; and any hypothesis that pretends to discover the ultimate original qualities in human nature, ought at first to be rejected as presumptuous and chimerical' (*Treatise* [*T*] xvii). However, he insists that stopping anywhere *before* a study of human nature affords an inadequate foundation.

> *There is no question of importance, whose decision is not comprised in the science of man; and there is none, which can be decided with any certainty, before we become acquainted with that science. In pretending therefore to explain the principles of human nature, we in effect propose a compleat system of the sciences, built on a foundation almost entirely new, and the only one upon which they can stand with any security.*
>
> (*T* xvi)

Hume consciously attempts to do for moral subjects what Newton did for the natural world, namely to provide an accurate classification of mental phenomena, and the principles underlying their activity. For example, parallel with Newton's physical atoms we find the mental 'atoms' of simple impressions and ideas; Newton's laws have their analogue in the principles of association (i.e., of attraction) among ideas, based upon the natural relations of resemblance, contiguity, and cause and effect. Hume thinks that a study of history, and an examination of all known societies, suggests that the principles of human nature are as universal and immutable as those governing the rest of the natural world. His wit is shown in a gentle dig at those who would construct elaborate philosophical systems on observably false theories of human nature:

> Shou'd a traveler, returning from a far country, tell us, that he had seen a climate in the fiftieth degree of northern latitude, where all the fruits ripen and come to perfection in the winter, and decay in the summer, after the same manner as in *England* they are produc'd and decay in the contrary seasons, he wou'd find few so credulous as to believe him. I am apt to think a traveler wou'd meet with as little credit, who shou'd inform us of people exactly of the same character with those in *Plato's Republic* on the one hand, or those in *Hobbes's Leviathan* on the other.
>
> (*T* 402)

In describing the development of his 'new scene of thought', he reports his surprise in discovering that

> the moral Philosophy transmitted to us by Antiquity, labor'd under the same Inconvenience that has been found in their natural Philosophy, of being entirely Hypothetical, & depending more on Invention than experience. Every one consulted his Fancy in erecting Schemes of Virtue and of Happiness, without regarding human Nature, upon which every Moral conclusion must depend. Therefore I resolved to make my principle Study, & the Source from which I wou'd derive every Truth in Criticism as well as Morality.
>
> (Mossner 1980: 72)

Hume aims to utterly dispose of any a priori preconceptions about the nature of man. In particular, he wants to dismantle the traditional conception of a rational animal whose capacity for abstract reasoning was identified with his true nature, and whose proper functioning demanded that reason subjugate the passions. Under such a conception, reason and passion were considered to be essentially in opposition, competing to control action, and a man acted in accordance with his true self by acting from rational rules totally untainted by passion. Hence, one's decisions and actions ought to ensue from pure abstract principles of rationality whose validity was independent of human nature.

One of Hume's greatest philosophical achievements was to destroy this false opposition between reason and passion, showing passion to penetrate to the very heart of the alleged activity of reason. Rather than seeing passions as irrational forces assaulting the mind, Hume relocates them as an essential part of human nature, and as potentially positive and beneficent. In this case, as throughout the *Treatise*, his tactic is to first undertake the 'negative' task of undermining the traditional position. He does this both in a direct manner by showing that it cannot accommodate undeniable facts, and more indirectly by destroying the original conception from the inside, following it through to reveal its false conclusions, proving it to be incapable of providing the results it is intended to describe and explain.

So, for example, Descartes regarded belief as being under control of the will. Hume counters that if the rational man requires strong reasons for believing anything, where this strength is objectively rooted in facts outside our minds, then *on his own assumptions* such a person could never be justified in believing anything, even under the most optimal conditions. Nor, therefore, could he ever have sufficient grounds for *doing* anything. But, of course, this is not what actually happens. Hume's conclusion is not that our beliefs are unjustifiable, but, rather, that this rationalistic model is untenable.

Hume was long interpreted as a sceptic, as one who followed empiricism through to its negative conclusions. Nowadays, due to the work of influential commentators such as Norman Kemp Smith and Barry Stroud, his naturalism takes precedence over his scepticism. It is now common to interpret him as showing that any attempt to found empiricism purely on principles of the understanding will fail. That is, the project of justifying beliefs in a causally structured world of mind-independent objects purely on the basis of sensory evidence, plus our capacities for deductive and inductive inference, will inevitably self-destruct in scepticism. However, far from endorsing this sceptical conclusion, Hume is now commonly read as rejecting the brand of empiricism that led to it.

He repeatedly denies interest in standard sceptical worries, seeing them as futile and 'idle', since they look in vain for justification for what are the non-negotiable assumptions of any enquiry. Since these basic beliefs are forced on us by our nature, they are not optional, and it is pointless to doubt them. This is his 'sceptical solution to the sceptical problem'. After proving that these sceptical worries can be settled neither by observation nor by demonstrative reasoning, Hume takes his task to be to explain how we actually come to believe in these things (and cannot fail to believe in them) despite the lack of such 'proof'.

> Nature, by an absolute and incontroulable necessity has determin'd us to judge as well as to breathe and feel; nor can we any more forbear viewing certain objects in a stronger and fuller light, upon account of their customary connexion with a present impression, than we can hinder ourselves from thinking as long as we are awake, or seeing the surrounding bodies, when we turn our eyes towards them in broad sunshine. Whoever has taken the pains to refute the cavils of this *total* scepticism, has really disputed without an antagonist, and endeavor'd by arguments to establish a faculty, which nature has antecedently implanted in the mind, and render'd unavoidable.
>
> (*T* 183)

So Hume is not sceptical about these basic beliefs themselves, but only about the prospects of philosophical projects aiming to objectively justify them. Nature ensures that we do believe these things in a purely automatic and unreflective manner that we can never escape. A justification for this practice is as unnecessary as it is impossible. Ultimately we have to say, with Wittgenstein, that 'this is how we do it'. In other words, Hume's scepticism is not about human knowledge, but about philosophical attempts to go beyond scientific evidence and ground our most basic beliefs in anything outside human nature and human practice. As mentioned before, his account of this bedrock level is purely descriptive: investigating the mechanisms and conditions under which we acquire these beliefs.

This acceptance of basic first-order beliefs, together with a critical attitude towards philosophical attempts to theorize about them, is a theme that will recur throughout the *Treatise*. For example, despite his having been often misrepresented as a moral sceptic, Hume regards ethical discourse itself as perfectly legitimate. That is, to *employ* moral concepts like right and wrong is not, in itself, to be guilty of metaphysical error. Hume must therefore be distinguished from the modern 'error theory' associated with J.L. Mackie (1977), who sees moral discourse as ontologically committing us to objective values, recognition of which automatically motivates us to act. Hume's view is that we, as human beings going about our business, are perfectly entitled to the use of moral terms. On the other hand, when we don our philosophers' caps to *theorize* about morality itself, we run the (avoidable) risk of falling into deep error, such as positing these mind-independent moral properties.

Hume's attitude to causation is the same. My claim that *x* caused *y* can be true. When it is wrong, then it would have been true to assert that something else, *z*, caused *y*. So causal discourse is fine, even though philosophical theorizing about the nature of causation itself may be prone to error, such as the attribution of mind-independent necessary connections between the causally related phenomena. Hume's account of causation will be discussed in the following chapter.

Moral sense

I will end this chapter with a few remarks locating Hume's moral theory within the context of its time. Philosophical taxonomists usually classify Hume as a *moral sense theorist*. This tradition originates with Lord Shaftesbury (Anthony Ashley Cooper, Third Earl of Shaftesbury), although its influence on Hume came primarily from the writings of Francis Hutcheson, then Professor of Moral Philosophy at the University of Glasgow.

Moral sense theory was an attempt to present an alternative to both *moral rationalism*, which claimed that virtue and vice could be ascertained by reason alone; and also to the radical *egoism* of Thomas Hobbes. Rationalists ascribed the major role in moral judgement to the intellect, which recognized a situation as being good, thereby generating a desire to achieve that good. So rationalism could be said to regard the passions as the 'slave' of reason. By contrast, moral sense theorists took moral judgements to be passions, species of pleasure or pain caused by exposure to or contemplation of character traits. These 'sentiments' correspond to judgements of virtue and vice respectively. Hutcheson's greatest influence on Hume was in this conception of moral judgements as being grounded in *feeling* rather than reason, and as lacking any rational justification or foundation independent of the moral sense. That is, the deliverances of the moral sense were held for no reason – not as a result of beliefs about the good – and were themselves the source of good. All 'exciting reasons', or motives for action, were seen as grounded in passions, which supply the ultimate end of action. Reason's function was restricted to providing information on the means to satisfy these ends. Second, Hutcheson insisted that 'justifying reasons', the approval or disapproval of action, require a moral sense. Reason can only justify an act in the sense of recognizing it as being a viable means to an end which is determined by the passions. It is highly probable that his appreciation of Hutcheson's views led Hume to his notorious claim that reason is the slave of the passions.

Moral sense theorists parted from Hobbes in denying that all motivating passions were self-interested, insisting that a full-blown egoism was inconsistent with observable facts, whether these be derived from introspection in one's own case, or by general study of human conduct. Hutcheson argued that a viable account of human behaviour had to posit a natural tendency towards *benevolence*, i.e., disinterested concern for others. The operation of the 'moral sense' consisted in the equally natural capacity to approve of such benevolent impulses, and condemn what was contrary to them. Hutcheson's theory of human nature had a theological foundation, in that our capacity for benevolent motives is the work of a benevolent Designer. By contrast, Hume's scientific enterprise takes his observations of human nature as basic facts, refusing to enter into what he regarded as futile speculations over their origin.

Like Hume, Hutcheson intended his moral psychology to be compatible with Locke's empiricism, which required that all mental representations ultimately derive from sense-experience:

> We are not to imagine, that this moral Sense, more than the other Senses, supposes any innate ideas, Knowledge, or practical Proposition: We mean by it only a Determination of our Minds to receive amiable or disagreeable Ideas of Actions, when they occur to our Observation, antecedent to any Opinions of Advantage or Loss to redound to our selves from them.
>
> (*Inquiry* 135)

The moral sense, along with the aesthetic sense, were considered as 'inner senses' whose impressions were dependent upon, and responsive to, the primary impressions delivered by the regular 'outer' senses. Moral approval is a response to the quality of goodness in certain traits, where this goodness is grounded in benevolence. Until recently, Hutcheson was taken to liken such a quality to Lockean secondary qualities such as redness or bitterness, ideas of which do not resemble qualities inherent in the object being considered. This interpretation is now greatly disputed (see Norton 1982).

Hutcheson predated Butler in saying that although moral approval is a form of pleasure, we do not choose such a state on account of its pleasure, and that the very capacity to do this 'plainly supposes a Sense of Virtue antecedent to ideas of Advantage, upon which this Advantage is founded' (*Inquiry* 152).

Hutcheson emphasizes the involuntary nature of moral judgements. We can no more will ourselves to see something that we regard as morally evil as being good, than we can deliberately turn the pain of a broken leg into a pleasure. This involuntariness is utilized against Hobbes: if the hedonic nature of the moral sentiments is 'hard-wired' into us by virtue of an unchangeable facet of human nature, and if the moral sentiments are essentially disinterested, then they cannot be deliberately modified to suit the aims of self-interest. One might put the point by saying that anyone who could be bribed to torture an innocent child probably would not need such an incentive.

Neither can education succeed in making any fundamental adjustment to these sentiments. The most it can do is extend these affective capacities, or adapt them to the contingencies and conventions of the time. One's ability to acquire more refined moral judgements presupposes the existence of the basic capacity. Someone lacking in a moral sense could no more benefit from a moral education than someone deaf from birth could develop the refined sensitivity to pitch of a piano tuner.

Space does not permit me to go into any detail over Hutcheson's influence on Hume, nor the extent to which the central themes of Humean moral psychology were predated in the work of Hutcheson. However, many feel sympathy with Norman Kemp Smith's famous claim that the core insight of Hume's 'new scene of thought' was to extend Hutcheson's doctrine of the primacy of passion over reason beyond the realms of aesthetics and morals, and applying it to all 'Matters of Fact and Existence', primarily the acquisition of belief.

Further reading

Ernest Mossner's *The Life of David Hume* is an entertaining and informative biography. Hume's two short autobiographical sketches, 'A Kind of History of My Life' (1734) and 'My Own Life' (1777), are included in *The Cambridge Companion to Hume*, edited by David Fate Norton (1993), an indispensable volume.

Of the many general discussions of Hume's philosophy, I particularly recommend Stroud (1977), Norton (1982) and Baier (1991). The journal *Hume Studies* is a regular source of high quality articles on all aspects of his work.

Stephen Darwall (1995) and J.B. Schneewind (1998) are two major scholarly works on the development of modern moral philosophy, and include chapters on Hume and his contemporaries and predecessors. Raphael (1991, vol. I) and Schneewind (1990, vol. II) contain selections from Shaftesbury and Hutcheson. Downie (1994) is a good affordable collection of Hutcheson's writings.

Chapter 2

Background on the understanding

Treatise, Book I

It goes without saying that a proper treatment of Hume's account of human understanding would take a book in itself, and several fine ones are available. However, Hume is an extremely systematic philosopher, such that no part of his philosophy can be understood apart from the whole. It follows that this book does not only concern 'Hume on morality'. It is about Hume's philosophy, but with an emphasis on his moral theory. Since I intend the book to be a self-contained volume, my aim in this chapter is to say just enough about the themes of Book 1 of the *Treatise* to prepare readers unfamiliar with Hume to understand his moral theory. Second, since no interpretation of Hume is uncontroversial, the chapter has the subsidiary function of stating the reading of Hume's metaphysics and epistemology that informs my take on his moral theory.

Impressions and ideas

Hume's generic term covering all mental states, or 'whatever can be present to the mind' (*Abstract* [*A*] 647), is 'perceptions'. Within these, the most basic distinction is between *impressions* and *ideas*. By 'ideas', he means what we would now call *thoughts* or *mental representations*. After initially dividing impressions into sensations, passions, and emotions, he generally distinguishes between *sensations* and *passions*, with emotions being subsumed within the latter category. In Book 1, he marks this distinction as between impressions of *sensation* and of *reflexion*, whereas Book 2 describes it as between *original* and *secondary* impressions. Whatever he calls it, the difference is between (1) sensory data such as colours, sounds and smells, together with internal bodily sensations such as pains, and (2) desires and affective states such as being happy, angry or afraid.

Since sensations 'arise in the soul originally, of unknown causes' (*T* 7), Hume takes them as basic data in his theory of human nature.

> As to those *impressions*, which arise from the *senses*, their ultimate cause is, in my opinion, perfectly inexplicable by human reason, and 'twill always be impossible to decide with certainty, whether they arise immediately from the object, or are produc'd by the creative power of the mind, or are deriv'd from the author of our being.
>
> (*T* 84)

While all ideas ultimately derive from sensations, the passions are 'derived in a great measure from our ideas'. First, a sensation (some species of *pain or pleasure*, such as heat or cold, thirst, hunger) generates a corresponding idea, which in turn leads to a passion such as desire or aversion, hope or fear. For example, seeing an apple may cause me to want to eat it. As with sensations, he regards the passions as 'a kind of natural instincts, derived from nothing but the original constitution of the human mind' (*A* 648).

Both impressions and ideas can be *simple* or *complex*. The criterion of simplicity is *indivisibility*, that is, that they 'admit no distinction or separation'. Complexes are made up of combinations of simples, such that, for example, an idea is complex if we can conceive of at least one of its aspects apart from the rest. Hume takes presentations of single colours, such as a patch of blue, as his paradigm of a simple impression, capable of yielding a simple idea. This picture has a surface plausibility that does not exist with the other senses, and it leads him to take simplicity to be a philosophically transparent notion. But what would count as a simple smell, for example? What about a simple sound?

Hume takes ideas to be *copies* of impressions. A straightforward case would be seeing my cat Mike chase a fly, then closing my eyes to form an almost exact replica of his futile enterprise in my 'mind's eye'. In such cases, the ideas are caused by the impressions they resemble. However, we can obviously consider things or situations of which we have never had an impression, nor are ever likely to. I can imagine myself winning the lottery, or holding a Chair at Princeton. In such cases, the faculty of *imagination* combines simpler ideas into new structures. The only requirement is that each idea will be based, *at some level*, on an impression. So the strict one:one correspondence between impressions and ideas is only required for *simple* ideas. With complex ideas, the only demand is that their constituent simple ideas satisfy this condition. Again, we can have 'secondary ideas, which are images of the primary', or in other words, thoughts about thoughts, which are traceable back to the same basis in sensory experience as the first-order thoughts they concern.

Hume proposes the general hypothesis: '*That all our simple ideas in their first appearance are deriv'd from simple impressions, which are correspondent to them, and which they exactly represent*' (*T* 4). His evidence is that in every case of which he is aware, a simple idea is predated by a corresponding simple impression. On this basis, he conjectures that anyone who has not had some particular simple impression cannot have a simple idea resembling it, nor any complex idea of which this is a part. For example, a blind man cannot conceive of redness.

Clearly, his thesis that all ideas are preceded by impressions is a *causal* claim. It is also the basis of a test for *meaningfulness*. As he says of himself in the *Abstract*:

> when he suspects that any philosophical term has no idea annexed to it (as is too common) he always asks *from what impression that pretended idea is derived?* And if no impression can be produced, he concludes that the term is altogether insignificant.
>
> (*A* 648–9)

One of Hume's most controversial claims is that impressions and ideas are distinguished only by 'the degrees of force and liveliness, with which they strike the mind'. Impressions are the more lively perceptions, whereas ideas are 'the faint images of these in thinking and reasoning'. Here, Hume is not merely saying that such a difference tends to hold, but making the stronger point that this difference is *constitutive* of being one or the other kind of perception.

However, he immediately undermines the distinction by acknowledging counter-examples to it. For example, an event that meant nothing at the time can seem with hindsight to be filled with importance, and be remembered with shocking vivacity far exceeding the original experience. By contrast, impressions can be so faint as to pass unnoticed. As we shall see, a crucial example of this latter phenomenon is the *calm passions*. The most charitable interpretation is to take him to be acknowledging, despite his 'official' theory, that this difference in vivacity is what we would now call a *ceteris paribus* law.

In fact, it is a curious part of Hume's literary style to first propose something as a general rule, and then immediately offer counter-examples to it. The most notorious example relates to the correspondence between simple ideas and impressions. He states that it is a strict rule which 'holds without exception', that 'every simple idea has a simple impression, which resembles it'. He then considers someone who has never seen a particular shade of blue, but who has seen various other shades, including those which would be contiguous to it on either side of a colour chart. Such a person, Hume concedes, would have the basis from which to imagine the missing shade. Even more strangely, he immediately dismisses this fabulous example as being of little theoretical importance, when in fact it clearly destroys the 'simple–complex' distinction on which his theory is based. It is just plain wrong to say that 'the instance is so particular and singular, that 'tis scarce worth our observing, and does not merit that for it alone we should alter our general maxim' (*T* 6). Not only could we run parallel examples about missing shades of red, yellow and so on, but on the other sensory modalities such as missing varieties of pain, of taste, of smell, and others.

As noted above, Hume regards impressions as differing from ideas only in their greater intensity. One might think that a more obvious way of drawing the distinction would be in terms of their different causal relationships. Thus, for example, we could define a sensation as the direct result of sensory stimuli. However, this approach is not open to Hume, since he regards an object's causal relations as being extrinsic to the thing itself, since we can conceive of it without considering its causes or effects. He is thereby forced to describe these perceptions purely in terms of their intrinsic properties. But since their only intrinsic properties are phenomenal ones, identifiable by introspection, he has little option but to indicate their difference in terms of 'force', 'liveliness' or 'vivacity', despite expressing some dissatisfaction over doing so. A second factor preventing a causally-based distinction is that in order to formulate his 'first general principle' that simple ideas are derived from simple impressions, he needs to be able to specify the nature of impressions and ideas independently of that principle, or else it will be a tautology.

Within the realm of ideas, he identifies the functions of *memory* and *imagination*. While distinguishing their outputs in terms of their respective force, he defines the capacities themselves in a functional manner. The difference is that memory 'replays' events in their original order and structure, whereas imagination can create new complex ideas by re-arranging components. 'The chief exercise of the memory is not to preserve the simple ideas, but their order and position.' By contrast, we have the principle '*of the liberty of the imagination to transpose and change its ideas*'. This functional distinction clearly relies on the simple–complex distinction, since 'Where-ever the imagination perceives a difference among ideas, it can easily produce a separation'. This highlights the point that his criterion of complexity is based on imagination: X is a complex idea if we can imagine two simpler ideas in which aspects of X are separated.

I was careful not to describe memory and imagination as *faculties*, since Hume opposes any appeal to faculties or powers, seeing no empirical grounds for a distinction between a power and the exercise of it. Likewise, no faculties of 'reason' or 'passion' exist over and above individual mental states or processes of reasoning and feeling, any more than a self exists over and above its perceptions. Any talk of faculties must therefore be taken as a convenient way of talking about the perceptions themselves. Another example of this metaphysical austerity comes in his moral theory. Despite his being tagged as a moral sense theorist, Hume's aim is to provide a causal account of moral evaluation without appeal to any *sui generis* moral sense. As we shall see, what I will call the 'moral stance' from which such evaluations emerge is the complex product of our rational and imaginative capacities modifying basic pre-moral tendencies to approve or disapprove of ourselves and each other.

The imagination flows from one idea to another via three principles of the association of ideas, 'RESEMBLANCE, CONTIGUITY in time or place, and CAUSE and EFFECT'. So two ideas or thoughts are either directly related in such ways, or via chains of such relations. As before, these principles can only be identified and described, and must be taken as explanatorily basic. While the *understanding* can be employed to actively form a far wider range of associations or connections between ideas, the imagination is responsible for the 'natural' movement of thought, when it is not deliberately controlled.

The introduction of these associative principles constitutes Hume's most significant development of the Lockean 'way of ideas'. While Locke acknowledged the association of ideas, he regarded it as a pathological phenomenon, an aberration from the real, rationally grounded 'connections' among ideas at the heart of proper reasoning. Hume, in sharp contrast, postulates principles underlying associative processes, and gives them foundational status in his science of mind.

Causation

Part 3 is devoted to answering the following questions:

> First, For what reason we pronounce it *necessary*, that every thing whose existence has a beginning, shou'd also have a cause?

> Secondly, Why we conclude, that such particular causes must *necessarily* have such particular effects; and what is the nature of that *inference* we draw from the one to the other, and of the *belief* we repose in it?
>
> (*T* 78)

He begins by presenting an exhaustive list of the seven 'philosophical relations' pertaining to ideas. *Philosophical* relations are contrasted with *natural* relations. Two ideas are naturally related when the thought of one leads to the other by natural associative principles, i.e., through the relations of resemblance, contiguity, or cause and effect. That is, natural relations describe the ways in which the *imagination* connects ideas in ordinary life-as-it-is-lived. On the other hand, we draw a philosophical relation between two items when engaged in theoretical reasoning, when the intellect actively and deliberately forms a connection between objects. He identifies seven philosophical relations, which include analogues to the associative principles. So resemblance, contiguity and cause and effect fall into both camps, being both natural principles of association and instruments of theorizing. I will bring out this difference by taking the example of resemblance.

Theoretical reasoning allows us to conceive of resemblances everywhere, given the trivial point that any two things have some similarity or some property in common. However, these need not generate a *natural* association in the mind. For example, Sting and I resemble each other in innumerable ways, such as being featherless, bipedal and born north of Watford. But since we share these traits with millions of others, the similarities will not be noticed, nor will lead us to be connected in someone's mind. By contrast, if I too were to be a blond Adonis with a keen interest in the Amazonian rain forest, meeting me might turn your thoughts towards Sting.

Hume makes a distinction within the class of philosophical relations, based on whether they 'depend entirely on the ideas, which we compare together, and such as may be chang'd without change in the idea' (*T* 69). The distinction appears to be between, on the one hand, cases in which the relation is internal to and constitutive of the idea, and cases in which the relation is separable in thought from the objects so related. In the first camp he places *resemblance*, *contrareity*, (that is, objects having incompatible properties), *proportions in quantity or number* (comparisons involving 'more or less' of a number of items) and *degrees in quality* ('more-or-less' comparisons applied to shared properties). These, 'depending solely upon ideas, can be the objects of knowledge and certainty' (*T* 70), since their denial is inconceivable.

Hume places the relation of *cause and effect* in the latter camp, alongside *identity* (taken as 'apply'd in the strictest sense to constant and unchangeable objects'), and *situations in time and space* ('which are the sources of an infinite number of comparisons, such as *distant*, *contiguous*, *below*, *before*, *after*, *&c.*'). He is thereby saying that any thoughts concerning an object's causal relationships are separable from the idea of the thing itself, at least in principle. In other words, we can theoretically conceive of any object without taking it to be the cause or effect of anything else. No causal relation between two objects X and Y can be demonstrated a priori, since its denial is not self-contradictory, and we can conceive of counter-examples to it. Knowledge of X's existence doesn't logically imply that X had *any* cause, nor can we deduce the existence of any *particular* cause or effect Y from it. Again, since we can imagine any object not existing at some time t_1 and coming to exist at a later time t_2 without adding the idea of a cause, it follows that the idea of any object X *per se* is separate from the idea of X *qua cause*, or *qua effect*. So considerations regarding relations of ideas give absolutely no warrant for the claim that all objects have a cause. (While Hume ascribes causal relations to objects, rather than to events as is now more common, it does no damage to his intentions to employ the latter terminology.)

Nor can the belief in the universality of causation be justified on empirical grounds. As we have seen, Hume's system demands that all ideas be ultimately derived from impressions. But we have no *sensory* impression of causation *per se*: that is, there is no distinct *quale* of cause or effect, since these relations are applicable to all objects and qualities. It follows that our idea of causation must derive from *observed relations between objects*. He notices only two common factors in individual cases where causal relationships are ascribed. First, the alleged cause is *temporally prior* to the effect; second, the cause and effect are *contiguous*, either directly or via an unbroken chain of intermediaries. Hume then makes a crucial move beyond these individual cases, adding that we ascribe a causal relationship in any case only when *similar* events have been observed to satisfy the first two requirements. He adds that this observed invariable connection or 'constant conjunction' of the appropriate kinds of events is also the basis of predictions of future events, and of general causal beliefs.

At this stage, then, the hypothesis under consideration is that we judge that X caused Y just in case (1) X occurs prior to Y, (2) X and Y are contiguous both spatially and temporally, and (3) past observations have revealed an impression similar to X to be always succeeded by one similar to Y. (He will offer a second 'definition' of cause shortly.) But what is the nature of such inferences? When we infer a causal relationship on the basis of this constant conjunction, does it come from the understanding or the imagination? Recall that reason consists in a conscious, reflective capacity for making inferences on the basis of evidence, whereas imagination is an automatic non-reflective capacity to move, by associative mechanisms, from impressions to ideas, or from one idea to another. So the question is 'whether we are determin'd by reason to make the transition, or by a certain association and relation of perceptions' (*T* 88–9). Hume will argue for the latter position.

Any *rational* grounds for the inference would require the general premise saying 'that instances, of which we have had no experience, must resemble those, of which we have had experience, and that the course of nature continues always uniformly the same' (*T* 89). Call this 'the uniformity of nature'. But such a premise could never be proven a priori, since it can be denied without contradiction. Hume makes this point in psychological fashion, in saying that its denial is conceivable and therefore, on his terms, possible. Secondly, any attempt to *inductively* prove the uniformity of nature would be circular. That is, to say that nature will continue to be uniform because it always has been so in the past would be an example of the form of inference needing to be justified. In fact, even if Hume were to grant, for the sake of argument, that the past conjunction of some A-events and B-events shows there to have been some 'power of production' connecting them, there could be neither a priori nor empirical grounds for believing in the *continuance* of that power.

Hume does not deny the existence of nomological necessities. Rather, he argues that belief in them cannot be rationally justified on empiricist principles, since it can be derived neither from observations nor demonstrative reasoning. That is, we cannot prove that any two objects or events are connected in any mind-independent way, nor infer the existence of one from the other. Nor does he deny that we have an *idea* of this necessary connection. Rather, he recognizes the need to explain the origin of this belief, since it seems to be a counter-example to his principle that all ideas originate in impressions.

So while we do in fact make a causal inference from X to Y after we have seen similar events constantly conjoined, he insists that this is not an action that we intentionally form for good reasons, or *any* reasons, for that matter. Since this is not something we choose to do, it is outside the realm of reasons and of rational justification, no more rational or irrational than breathing. Again, Hume is clear that any 'problem of induction' only exists for us as *philosophers*, not as *people*. That is, it only arises when we attempt a theoretical justification of what comes naturally, since these 'natural' beliefs cannot be justified in terms of some foundation independent of human nature and practice. They are purely a product of the custom and habit emerging from associative principles, and must be taken as basic. If no justification is possible, then none can be lacking.

After having shown that reason cannot ground causal inferences, his next task is to explain the ways in which the associative processes lead to the formation of causal beliefs. This leads him into an excursion on the nature of belief. Differences in 'force' or 'vivacity' hold not only between ideas and impressions, but also *within* either category. Thus Hume regards the difference between merely *conceiving* of some situation *p*, and *believing* that it has happened or will happen, as 'a new question unthought of by philosophers' (*A* 652). He proposes that this difference consists solely in the latter's greater vivacity, defining a belief as 'A LIVELY IDEA RELATED TO OR ASSOCIATED WITH A PRESENT IMPRESSION' (*T* 96). This distinction corresponds to a difference in their causes, since a belief derives from an impression, whereas any train of thought consisting only of conceptions can lead only to other such ideas. Since impressions and ideas differ only by the former's greater 'liveliness', this difference is transmitted to their effects. Hence a belief inherits its greater vivacity from the impressions it derives from.

Hume convincingly shows that the difference between believing and conceiving of some situation 'lies not in the parts or composition of the idea, which we conceive [but] in the *manner*, in which we conceive it' (*T* 95). Belief cannot consist in some generic ingredient that can be added to a conception to transform it into a corresponding belief. First, if a conception of *p* could be turned into a belief by adding some component to the conception itself, then the subsequent idea would no longer be of *p*. Hume recognizes the point, later emphasized by Frege, that when I believe some claim *p*, and you merely consider the situation apart from any question of its actual or potential occurrence, we both entertain the same thought, and take each other to do so. So the difference lies not in the content of the situation believed or considered, but in the mind's relation to that 'idea'. Second, if a conception could be transformed into a corresponding belief by adding something to the idea itself, then, given that the imagination can combine distinct items in any way it pleases, we would be able to believe absolutely anything by an act of will, something Hume rightly insists we cannot do. However, when these correct points are added to his insistence on distinguishing kinds of perceptions by their introspectively accessible properties alone, it severely limits what a difference in 'manner of conceiving' could consist in, and he is left with little but vivacity to fall back on. In doing so, he inherits the inadequacy of his original distinction between impressions and ideas.

Let us return now to the problem of causation. Hume thinks that his account of belief provides an explanation of why repeated experience of Xs being followed by Ys leads us to believe that X *causes* Y, where this belief is not just that Y *will*, but that it *must,* follow X. Granted, experiencing the constant conjunction of Xs and Ys gives no new kind of *sensory* impression, but just more of the same. However, the mere fact of their repeated co-experience leads the mind to naturally associate the two ideas, creating a new impression of *reflexion* (that is, a secondary impression) in the mind. This repetition literally causes a change in the mind, creating a natural tendency to associate the ideas, to move from the thought of X to that of Y. This is accompanied by an impression of reflexion, that of 'determination', and the subsequent *expectation* of the latter at the sight or thought of the former.

Compare our actual situation with one whose mind is a *tabula rasa*. That is, imagine someone possessing the full complement of natural human cognitive capacities, but who has never received any sensory impressions. Suppose him now to begin receiving these impressions. At the beginning, he would be totally lost, in that his initial impressions would not enable him to predict any others. For example, the first time he would see a material object released in mid-air, he would not know whether it would fall down, rise up, stay where it was or do a pirouette. Our difference from this unfortunate lies not in our having had any new kind of impression, but in having had far more of the same kinds, enabling us to recognize patterns among them, allowing the associative mechanisms to kick in.

This psychological determination is the root of our idea of physical necessity holding between objects. Hume suggests (*T* 167) that theorists ascribe a necessary connection between X and Y themselves by a projective error of moving from this *psychological* 'necessitation' to the ascription of some mind-independent necessity between the objects themselves.

He modifies his original claim that a belief is a 'lively idea related to a present impression', saying that a belief is caused not by a single impression taken as such, but only when it is considered in the context of a history of observed constant conjunctions of the relevant impressions. Thus, memory plays an essential role in generating beliefs, in supplying information about past impressions. He then makes a more significant amendment to his original theory, saying that the vivacity of an idea increases each time it is experienced, to the extent that mere repetition can be sufficient to 'enliven' it into a belief, even in the absence of a grounding impression. This explains how education can instill beliefs that are practically impossible to remove, even though their evidential basis is slight.

The vivacity of a causal belief, and the assurance with which it is held, depends on how extensive and how perfect is the constant conjunction of impressions grounding the belief. When this set is large, and there are no counter-examples, the belief is correspondingly strong. We have *proof* when it is believed with certainty. Below this are varying degrees of *probabilities*.

He concludes by offering two definitions of cause, corresponding to it considered as a philosophical or a natural relation:

> There may be two definitions given of this relation, which are only different, by their presenting a different view of the same object, and making us consider it either as a *philosophical* or a *natural* relation; either as a comparison of two ideas, or as an association between them. We may define a CAUSE to be 'An object precedent and contiguous to another, and where all the objects resembling the former are plac'd in like relations of precedency and contiguity to those objects, that resemble the latter'. [or, secondly] 'A CAUSE is an object precedent and contiguous to another, and so united with it, that the idea of the one determines the mind to form the idea of the other, and the impression of the one to form a more lively idea of the other'.
>
> (*T* 170)

So there is no truth to the common misconception that Hume denies the existence of causal relations. Rather, he sees himself as showing the flaws in a received view of what they consist in, and providing a corrective to it. If there really were no such things as causal relations, then, on his own assumptions, causal discourse would be meaningless; something that would invalidate the entire *Treatise*.

Denial of physical and mental substance

The previous discussion of causation took place under the assumption of a world consisting of temporally continuous objects, about which causal inferences were made by equally continuant persons. In Part 4, he acknowledges that this assumption is theoretically problematic. He stresses that it is a *problem* only for the philosophical project in which the understanding investigates its own functioning and foundations. Given that human nature has determined that we cannot help but believe in a world of temporally continuous objects existing distinct from our thought and perception, Hume takes the traditional sceptical worry of the existence of an external world to be an 'idle question', in that any argument about it is pointless: if the conclusion is negative, it will be literally unbelievable, and carry no force with us; if the conclusion is positive, it will be equally impotent, being utterly unnecessary. As with the case of causation, he chooses rather to trace the origin of our *idea of* and our *belief in* an external world, showing how they can come neither from the senses alone, nor reason as traditionally conceived of, but emerge from the associative principles governing the imagination.

It would be obviously contradictory to claim that the senses, by themselves, can deliver the idea of something *continuing* to exist when not sensed. Second, since the senses are only directly acquainted with impressions, which are essentially mind-dependent entities, they cannot yield the idea of objects existing *distinctly* of our perception. Turning to reason, Hume begins by noting that the common person's belief in a world of objects cannot rest on philosophical arguments of which he is unaware. As for philosophers themselves, since (1) he has already established the general thesis that any inference from an impression to a belief is a causal inference; and since (2) causal inferences from A to B require us to have observed a constant conjunction of events similar to A and B; and since (3) all we ever directly experience are impressions and ideas rather than objects, it follows that no causal inference from perceptions to such objects is rationally justified.

As with his discussion of causation, Hume surrenders the attempt to ground these basic beliefs in anything external to human nature and practice, turning away from the project of justification in favour of a detailed description of the practices themselves. That is, he looks for qualities *within* the impressions that are constantly conjoined with belief in objects. He identifies two such factors, namely *constancy*, or qualitative similarity between impressions, and *coherence*, or orderly and gradual changes.

Consider a case where I return to a scene after an interruption, such as when I leave my computer to refuel with more coffee. Call the two series of perceptions occurring before and after the interruption

S_1 and S_2. Any differences either *within* S_1 or S_2 are highly coherent, consisting mostly of a gradual addition of words on the screen. Any difference *between* S_1 or S_2 is negligible. Hume envisions that a subliminal tension is generated in the mind at this point: on the one hand, the strong constancy and coherence of these impressions inclines us to say they are the same; that is, numerically identical. On the other hand, our acknowledgement of the interruption rules this out. We resolve this tension, he says, by supposing an objective causal substratum involving mind-independent objects from which our interrupted series of impressions emerge. This projection is based on the previous and equally unwarranted move of taking even an *un*interrupted series of perceptions (such as S_1 or S_2) as a single unit, as being of one same object rather than a series of discrete momentary impressions. We have a natural tendency to mistake a series of discrete-but-similar impressions as being of one same continuous object. Note that Hume intends all this as a speculative account of what occurs in the natural scheme of things, not when we are deliberately theorizing. Nor is he claiming that we are consciously aware of any such thoughts.

Philosophers resolve the conflict by constructing a theory of 'double existence', whereby the perceptions are allowed to be mind-dependent and transitory, but are distinguished from an external world consisting of continuous objects. While Hume thinks that such a theory cannot be rationally supported on its own terms, he thinks that abstract reasoning will inevitably lead to it, and to the scepticism that follows. Our human predicament is that while nature ensures that we cannot help believing in a world of objects, we also have a natural tendency to philosophize, to devise explanations in an attempt to make sense of our experience. Hume's distinction from his peers and predecessors is that he gives no special status to the latter natural impulse.

In the same way that we naturally believe in a world of mind-independent objects, we also take it that each of us is a unit of *mental substance*, a *self* that continues as one same simple thing underlying all our perceptions, and being the source or container of them. But the senses cannot justify belief in a *temporally continuous* self, one same thing existing over time, since they only reveal a sequence of discrete momentary impressions.

> From what impression could this idea be deriv'd?...But self or person is not any one impression, but that to which our several impressions and ideas are supposed to have a reference. If any impression give rise to the idea of self, that impression must continue invariably the same, thro' the whole course of our lives; since self is suppos'd to exist after that manner. But there is no impression constant and invariable.
>
> (*T* 251)

As with the previous case of material objects, Hume diagnoses that we naturally (mis)take a highly constant and coherent series of momentary perceptions for a continuous mental substance. We confuse a succession of distinct yet related perceptions for one same simple thing that *has* these perceptions. But introspection reveals nothing but this sequence of perceptions:

> For my part, when I enter most intimately into what I call *myself*, I always stumble on some particular perception or other, of heat or cold, light or shade, love or hatred, pain or pleasure. I can never catch *myself* at any time without a perception, and never can observe any thing but the perception.
>
> (*T* 252)

This leads Hume to reluctantly end Book 1 with what is now called a reductionist theory of personal identity in which the self is nothing more than the set of perceptions themselves. As he puts it in the Appendix, 'When I turn my reflexion on *myself*, I can never perceive this *self* without some one or more perceptions; nor can I ever perceive any thing but the perceptions. 'Tis the composition of these, therefore, which forms the self' (*T* 634). He notoriously concludes that 'I may venture to the rest of mankind that they are nothing but a bundle or collection of different perceptions, which succeed each other with an inconceivable rapidity, and are in perpetual flux and movement' (*T* 252).

As with the case of material objects, we generate the idea of a mind or self when the mind naturally glides to it from a set of perceptions exhibiting a high level of constancy and coherence. These relations are rooted in the associative principles of resemblance and causation. (Spatial contiguity does not apply here, and temporal contiguity is covered by causation.) The key to their operation in this case is memory. Of course, given Hume's denial of mental or physical substance, he needs to reconstrue the nature of memory. 'Remembering an event' cannot consist in having some permanent representation in the mind, but only a sequence of highly constant ideas which resemble an initial impression, having been originally caused by it. Recall that I naturally assume that my computer is still there when I am making my coffee. In a similar way, when our thoughts are interrupted by sleep, we are irresistibly led to 'fill in the gap' and assume that something persisted through that time. We 'feign the continu'd existence of the perceptions of our senses, to remove the interruption; and run into the notion of a *soul*, and *self*, and *substance*, to disguise the variation' (*T* 254). In sum, not only do we perceive a mere sequence of perceptions (from which we invent a world of objects), but *what is doing the perceiving* is itself nothing over and above an orderly construct of discrete perceptions.

This reductionist theory reduces the idea of mental substance to absurdity. Traditionally, a substance was conceived of as something that could exist independently of anything else, including any properties. But, since all simple impressions are 'distinct existences', then all would qualify as substances, rendering the notion useless.

> But farther, what must become of all our particular perceptions upon this hypothesis? All these are different, and distinguishable, and separate from each other, and may be separately consider'd, and may exist separately, and have no need of anything to support their existence.
>
> (*T* 252)

Further reading

My presentation of Hume has focused exclusively on Parts 1, 3 and 4 of Book 1 of the *Treatise*. A simpler account of some of the same themes can be found in *An Enquiry Concerning Human Understanding*.

For a book-length discussion of Hume on the understanding, see Pears (1990). See also Stroud (1977: chs 1–6), Baier (1991: chs 2–6), and articles by John Biro, Alexander Rosenberg and Robert Fogelin, in Norton (1993).

For an exhaustive treatment of causation, see Beauchamp and Rosenberg (1981); for a recent controversial interpretation of Hume's views on this subject, see Galen Strawson (1989); for a clear commentary on that debate, see Simon Blackburn (1990).

Chapter 3

The passions

Treatise, Book 2, Parts 1 and 2; Part 3, Section 9

Chapter 3

The social self

An appreciation of Hume's views on personal identity cannot rest solely, nor even primarily, on the negative conclusions of Book 1, since that discussion was offered as an example of the understanding investigating itself. It assumed the essentially non-social and individualistic starting point of earlier empiricists, whereby the solitary thinker struggles to establish a world on the basis of sensory input. This process led quite literally to its own self-destruction, going beyond the more obvious danger of solipsism to the disintegration of the self.

By that point, Hume had already argued that our natural tendency to believe in a world of continuous independent objects could not be rationally justified, and that when non-naturalistic empiricism is pushed to its limits, it ends up positing nothing over and above a series of momentary perceptions, which the imagination assembles into a world. He is thus led to the barely intelligible conclusion that this process of world-making is not the work of a continuously existing mind which *has* thoughts and mental processes, but of something with the same ontological status as these perceptions themselves, such that all that exist are perceptions perceiving perceptions. Hence:

> The mind is a kind of theatre, where several perceptions successively make their appearance; pass, re-pass, glide away, and mingle in an infinite variety of postures and situations. There is properly no *simplicity* in it at one time, nor *identity* in different; whatever natural propensity we may have to imagine that simplicity and identity. The comparison of the theatre must not mislead us. They are the successive perceptions only, that constitute the mind; nor have we the most distant notion of the place, where these scenes are represented, or of the materials, of which this is compos'd.
>
> (*T* 253)

In the following books of the *Treatise*, Hume never directly refutes this denial of mental substance, nor does he explicitly challenge the view that each of us is no more than a 'bundle of perceptions'. Instead, he extends the conception of the perceiving subject to include the passions as well as the understanding. That this move utterly transforms the picture of self and identity should come as no surprise, given his insistence on the limitations of reason. Annette Baier puts it nicely:

> If reason is and ought to be the slave of the passions, it is not going to be able to get an adequate idea of the self, one of whose 'organs' it is, if it tries to abstract from the passions, those more vital and more dominant organs of mind and person.
>
> (Baier 1991: 130)

Where Book 1 showed reason being unable to discover a pure Cartesian ego, the self discovered in Book 2 is that of a being in the world. The key to its development lies in the passions. This socially constructed self, the object of reflexive concern, emerges alongside the capacity to feel the self-directed passions of pride and humility, which in turn require the capacity for love and hatred towards others. Social life is a hall of mirrors in which we symbiotically create ourselves and others through the endlessly reiterative reflection of each other's gaze. As Alasdair MacIntyre says:

> The passions of each person are therefore inescapably characterized in part as responses to others who are in turn responding to us. So in the reciprocities and mutualities of passion, whether harmonious or antagonistic, each self conceives of itself as part of a community of selves, each with an identity ascribed by others. Personal identity as socially imputed has emerged from the characterization of the passions, and so to that extent the way of ideas has been left behind.
>
> (MacIntyre 1988: 292–3)

As will be explained in this chapter, pride or humility result from pleasures or pains that are caused by seeing something (whether a material object, or a mental or physical skill or attribute) as *mine*, or as being in some relationship to oneself, and where this inference of the imagination is 'seconded' or reinforced by one's perception of the approval or disapproval of others on account of it. For the Humean persons described in Book 2, other people are a necessary condition for experiencing these self-regarding feelings of pride or humility, so the traditional sceptical problem of 'other minds' cannot get started. To feel pride is thereby to see oneself as the object of the love of others. In this sense, the self could be considered a special kind of non-individualistic secondary quality, since 'ourself independent of the perception of every other object is in reality nothing' (*T* 340).

The direct passions

Hume begins Book 2 of the *Treatise*, *Of the Passions*, by reviewing the psychological system which began Book 1. Every mental state is either an *impression* or an *idea*. The distinction between impressions of sensation and reflexion is recast as between *original* and *secondary* impressions. Bodily sensations and sense-impressions are 'original' in not resulting from prior perceptions, but rather 'without any antecedent perception arise in the soul', and so must be taken as explanatorily basic within psychology, since any investigation of their causes would belong to 'the sciences of anatomy and natural philosophy'. Hume's collective term for all secondary impressions is 'the passions'. This should be regarded as a term of art, so it is no criticism of Hume that it, or other theoretical terms, do not accord with ordinary usage (either of his time or ours). For example, it is of no import that many of these 'passions' do not seem particularly 'passionate'. Calling the passions *secondary* impressions indicates that they derive from original impressions. They are 'founded on pain and pleasure', either immediately, such as when a sensation of pain leads to a desire for it to stop, or via an idea, such as when the mere thought of pain can cause distress.

Hume divides the passions into two main classes, *direct* and *indirect*.

> By direct passions I understand such as arise immediately from good or evil, from pain or pleasure. By indirect such as proceed from the same principles, but by the conjunction of other qualities...under the indirect passions I comprehend pride, humility, ambition, vanity, love, hatred, envy, pity, malice, generosity, with their dependents. And under direct passions, desire, aversion, grief, joy, hope, fear, despair and security.
>
> (*T* 276–7)

Despite direct passions having a far simpler causal basis and psychological structure, Hume chooses to devote the first two Parts of Book 2 to the indirect passions, leaving his main discussion of the direct passions till near the end of Part 3. I will not follow this order of exposition.

The first thing one notices about his list of direct passions is that it consists of *pairs* of states where one is a species of pleasure, the other a form of pain. I will call such pairs 'hedonic opposites'. When the initial pleasure or pain strikes us as inevitable, we experience *joy* or *grief* respectively. When the prospects are less than certain, such that both are believed to be possible, we experience *hope* or *fear* depending on which outcome seems more probable. He describes these states as mixtures of grief and joy, produced by the mind's being unable to settle, fluctuating between the two potential outcomes. *Desire* and *aversion* are produced when pleasure and pain are 'consider'd simply', that is, when we think of a situation abstractly, without the idea that it might actually occur. So desire and aversion differ from the other direct passions in a way that corresponds to Book 1's distinction between merely *conceiving* of something and *believing* it.

Apart from pain and pleasure, direct passions can be generated by certain psychologically basic impulses directed towards other persons, including 'the desire of punishment to our enemies, and of happiness to our friends; hunger, lust, and a few other bodily appetites' (*T* 439). A certain degree of charity is needed to allow Hume a consistent position here. The passage above classifies the desires for the punishment of our enemies and the happiness of our friends as direct passions. But, as we shall see later in this chapter, his previous catalogue of *indirect* passions defined anger and benevolence respectively as the desires that harm befall one's enemies, and for the happiness of one's friends. Indeed, they were considered derivative forms of indirect passions, being the consequence of hatred and love. The only way to make Hume consistent here is to take him to be discussing different types of desire and aversion. So, one might say that the indirect passions of anger and benevolence are motivationally active, being desires to inflict this harm or help on particular persons, whereas the section on direct passions is discussing a more abstract form of desire, applying more to hypothetical situations rather than to concrete events and persons. It is noticeable that he places his description of desire and aversion beside that of the will, as if to contrast them: 'DESIRE arises from good consider'd simply, and AVERSION is deriv'd from evil. The WILL exerts itself, when either the good or the absence of evil may be attain'd by any action of the mind or the body' (*T* 439).

The will is directed towards pleasure considered as something that I might actively achieve, or pain that I could do something about avoiding. Either way, I see it as something immediately within my grasp. It has a very active feel, not merely '*thinking about* doing something', but intending to *do it* right now. So desire and aversion are experienced as passive states, as passions affecting me, whereas the impression of will has an active mode of presentation, in which I see myself as being the cause of immediately forthcoming events. I will return to the subject of the will in the following chapter. The rest of this chapter will be devoted to Hume's long discussion of the indirect passions.

Pride and humility

The indirect passions can be divided into basic and derivative states, the former being pride, humility, love and hatred. Notice that, like direct passions, they are divided into pairs of hedonic opposites. The derivative passions, such as benevolence, pity or malice, result from one of these initial four under certain circumstances. This basic/derivative distinction does not imply any difference in simplicity or complexity in the states themselves (since all are simple perceptions), but indicates that the basic ones are a causal precondition for the production of the others.

Pride and humility are essentially *self-directed* states in that I can only be proud or ashamed of something seen as being related to myself. Hume defines pride as 'that agreeable impression, which arises in the mind, when the view either of our virtue, beauty, riches or power, makes us satisfied with ourselves; and that by *humility* I mean the opposite impression' (*T* 297). So they are, respectively, pleasant or painful states involving thoughts about oneself, corresponding to good and low self-esteem. Love and hatred, by contrast, are parallel types of pleasant or painful states caused by reflecting on someone else. This can be displayed in a diagram:

	pleasant	*unpleasant*
self as object	pride	humility
other as object	love	hatred

I will follow Hume in focusing, for the moment, on pride and humility, returning to love and hatred later in this chapter. I will take pride as my exemplar of Hume's thesis that indirect passions are 'simple and uniform' impressions. He begins by stating that such impressions are unanalysable and thus indefinable, and that the most we can do is indicate them 'by an enumeration of such circumstances, as attend them' (*T* 277). On the other hand, any competent language user can 'form a just idea' of these words, which have a clear meaning and use within the language. However, he later goes on to specify pride in terms of its causal relations to other mental states. That is, 'by *pride* I understand that agreeable impression, which arises in the mind, when the view either of our virtue, beauty, riches, or power, makes us satisfied with ourselves' (*T* 297). In other words, pride is what is experienced on the contemplation of any intrinsically pleasing quality that I take myself to have.

Has Hume not thereby defined pride, something he has previously said to be impossible? No: when he says that pride is simple and unanalysable, he means that its *phenomenal* character is non-composite, and unimaginable by one who had never experienced it. When he says 'it is impossible we can ever, by a multitude of words, give a just definition of them' (*T* 277), he means that no reference to *other* passions that the hearer has experienced can enable him to know what the unfelt passion is like. The reason for this is that passions are simple impressions, not constructed out of other passions, and therefore not knowable by recombining familiar passions in thought. To put it in terms of Bertrand Russell's useful distinction, knowledge of the passions requires direct acquaintance with them, and no 'knowledge by description', such as verbal accounts or comparisons, will suffice.

However, recall that he ran a similar argument in Book 1, in the case of primary impressions such as colours. Recall also that he then shot a hole in his own thesis, pointing out that someone who had never seen a particular shade of blue, but who had seen other shades contiguous to it, could on that basis form an accurate idea of what the missing shade was like. One might object that a similar manoeuvre is possible with the passions, through comparison with other hedonically similar impressions.

But to repeat, when Hume says that passions are indefinable, he is taking the Cartesian position that what makes a particular mental state the kind of passion it is, is its possessing a specific sort of qualitative 'feel' which can only be known by acquaintance. Thus, what makes something a case of pride is the unique aspect of *what it feels like* to be proud. By contrast, when he describes pride in terms of its relations to the self, etc., he intends neither to give an *analytic definition* of the term, nor to say what pride itself *is*. Rather, his aim is to give an account of the *causal conditions of its production*. The crucial point is that he sees these two factors as non-identical: to say how something *is caused* is not to say what it *is*. So Hume is saying that no reductive analysis of an impression's *subjective* qualities, of 'what it is like', is possible. We can, however, give a descriptive account of its causal relations, since these are *objective* properties.

Confusion may arise from the fact that many contemporary philosophers *do* equate these two factors. Functionalism, the dominant position in philosophy of mind in recent decades, defines mental properties in terms of their relationships to other mental states, along with relations to perceptual input and to subsequent behaviour. While not denying that different kinds of states might have distinctive qualia, these are not regarded as determining its nature; that is, they do not count in making something the kind of state it is.

Hume is often accused of inconsistency in saying that each passion is a unique and simple kind of impression, while also making use of the notion of *similarity* between passions. One might object that two things can be similar only if they have some property in common. It would then follow that if two different kinds of passion had a shared property, they cannot both be simple because the difference between them can only be due to a *second* property that only one of them has.

However, Hume rejects the claim that similarity requires a shared property. As he says in the Appendix:

> 'Tis evident, that even simple ideas may have a similarity or resemblance to each other; nor is it necessary, that the point or circumstance of resemblance shou'd be distinct or separable from that in which they differ. *Blue* and *green* are different simple ideas, but are more resembling than *blue* and *scarlet*, tho' their perfect similarity excludes all possibility of separation or distinction.
>
> (*T* 637)

If Hume were wrong about similarity not requiring a shared property, conceding this point would do little real harm to his theory. He could grant that every passion is either pleasant or unpleasant, so that two impressions which are unique in every other way can share a hedonic resemblance. This would allow him to maintain that each would still have its own *sui generis* feel, which mere comprehension of its general pleasurableness would be insufficient to convey prior to the experience. He could also grant that distinct passions can be similar in the sense of sharing components of their causes, in the way that love and pride share the property of being caused by an intrinsically pleasing quality. This line would tie in nicely with his regarding the concept of pleasure as what we now call a 'family resemblance' term, a loose collective term covering a number of different types of impression: 'under the term *pleasure*, we comprehend sensations, which are very different from each other, and which have only such a distant resemblance, as is requisite to make them be express'd by the same abstract term' (*T* 472).

One other qualification must be made to Hume's presentation. His view of pride as a simple impression cannot be taken to imply that all cases of pride are indistinguishable. As Donald Davidson says, 'This would certainly be wrong, since it would provide no way of distinguishing being proud that one is clever and being proud that one is kind to kangaroos' (Davidson 1980: 278). We can come to Hume's assistance here by granting that there is a subjective difference between the experience of those two passions, deriving from a difference in their causes, namely the respective *beliefs* that one is clever and kind to kangaroos. Second, there would be another experiential difference between being *proud* that one is clever and being *ashamed* of it, a difference stemming from the passions themselves.

Object and cause

Hume distinguishes between the *object* and the *cause* of an indirect passion, 'betwixt that idea, which excites them, and that which they direct their view, when excited' (*T* 278). The object of pride or humility is *oneself*, and that of love or hatred is *someone else*. Thus Hume's use of 'object' corresponds roughly to 'intentional object', that to which the passion is directed. My pride or humility always primarily concern *me*, with anything else featuring only insofar as it relates to me. So I might be proud of *my* guitar playing, or ashamed of *my* obnoxious remark to a colleague. Although Hume does not explicitly say so, it is clear that he takes such states to have what some now call a *first-personal mode of presentation*, in that my pride is always felt because of something that *I* have done, rather than something *Jim Baillie* has done.

The *cause* of pride or humility can be either a mental characteristic, a bodily attribute, or even a material object connected to oneself, such as through the relation of property.

> Every valuable quality of mind, whether of the imagination, judgment, memory, or disposition; wit, good-sense, learning, courage, justice, integrity; all these are the causes of pride; and their opposites of humility. Nor are these passions confin'd to the mind, but extend their view to the body likewise. A man may be proud of his beauty, strength, agility, good mien, address in dancing, riding, fencing, and of his dexterity in any manual business or manufactures. But this is not all. The passions looking farther, comprehend whatever objects are in the least allay'd or related to us. Our country, family, children, relations, riches, houses, gardens, horses, dogs, cloaths; any of these may become a cause either of pride or humility.
>
> (*T* 279)

Within the cause, Hume distinguishes between 'that *quality*, which operates, and the *subject*, on which it is placed' (*T* 279). So if I am vain about my new guitar, the *object* of the vanity is myself, the *cause* is the guitar, within which the *quality* may be its design or its beautiful tone, and the *subject* being the guitar considered as *my* guitar. A beautiful guitar *per se* might evoke pleasure (that is, joy) in me, but not pride. We can see a close connection between the subject/quality distinction and the direct/indirect distinction: something causes love or pride through possessing a quality which would evoke the direct passion of joy, regardless of any indirect passions it might cause. The cause/object distinction allows us to see more clearly why pride and humility are an opposing pair of impressions. They are *opposites* hedonically, one being pleasant, the other painful; they are an opposing *pair* through having the same object.

However, this account seems to commit Hume to be taking the self as part of the *content* of a state of pride or humility, since something can cause me to feel these passions only by its being considered *in relation to me*. This clashes with the notorious claim commonly attributed to him, that passions lack any intentional content whatsoever. I will argue that if he did make this claim, it was an oversight, and must be rejected to preserve the overall integrity of his system.

I emphasize that my pride is caused when *I regard* some pleasant quality as being related to me. An *actual* connection is neither necessary nor sufficient to generate pride. For example, it could be caused by my delusion that such a relation exists, through misreading others' attitudes towards me. It could also occur through correctly interpreting others who are as deluded as I regarding my gifts. We all know of celebrities whose egos extend far beyond what their talents justify. Again, by contrast, I might do something which ought to have evoked pride but did not because I failed to appreciate my achievement.

It is important to keep in mind that the form of pride discussed in Book 2 is a pre-moral psychological reaction, which must be distinguished from pride the moral virtue, as discussed in Book 3. This latter is a *corrected* pride, and therefore a *justified* pride, and is felt only when one considers one's traits in an impersonal manner, from the 'general point of view'. Hence the only way that my perception of others' approval can 'second' this corrected pride is if I regard them as coming from this same general viewpoint.

So in Book 2, Hume the social scientist is merely describing conditions under which a feeling of positive self-esteem is felt. At this stage, there is no attempt to evaluate such responses. He is well aware that this pre-moral form of pride can be felt towards something that would be repugnant from the moral point of view. For example, a homophobic thug might feel pride in the admiring gaze of his fellow brutes on account of his leading role in a successful night of 'queer-bashing'.

While the distinction between cause and object is perfectly coherent, some of Hume's arguments for it leave much to be desired. For example, he says that proof of the opposition of pride and humility lies in the fact that ''Tis impossible a man can at the same time be proud and humble' (*T* 278). Now this is true in one sense, and false in another. While one cannot be simultaneously proud and ashamed of one and the same thing, it is possible to be proud of one aspect of an event, while ashamed of another. A thief might admire the panache with which a robbery was carried out, while regretting the hardship he caused by it. Second, he argues that we cannot identify the object with the cause of pride because pride and humility are opposites, and the same cause cannot be responsible for opposite effects:

> For as these passions are directly contrary, and have the same object in common; were their object also their cause; it cou'd never produce any degree of the one passion, but at the same time it must excite an equal degree of the other.
>
> (*T* 278)

This argument seems to depend on taking the self as a simple indivisible substance, which Hume of course denies. But if it is no more than a bundle of perceptions, then different constituents of that bundle could contribute (serially or even simultaneously) to the production of pride and humility.

He describes the contrasting roles of cause and object in the following manner:

> Pride and humility, being once rais'd, immediately turn our attention to ourself, and regard that as their ultimate and final object; but there is something farther requisite to raise them: Something, which is peculiar to one of the passions, and produces not both in the very same degree. The first idea, that is presented to the mind, is that of the cause or productive principle. This excites the passion, connected with it; and that passion, when excited, turns our view to another idea, which is that of self. Here then is a passion plac'd betwixt two ideas, of which the one produces it, the other produc'd by it. The first idea, therefore, represents the *cause*, the second the *object* of the passion.
>
> (*T* 278)

This confusing passage highlights a tension in Hume's theory over the status of the phenomenal and intentional aspects of the passions. It seems to say that pride or humility can exist distinctly and independently of any idea or impression of the self, since it 'turns our view to another idea, which is that of self'. This certainly looks like he is ascribing a *causal* relation between the passion of pride and the idea of oneself, and, as he tells us in Book 1, cause and effect are always 'distinct existents'. So this way of speaking makes self-directed content distinct from pride itself, since pride is raised prior to our attention being turned to ourself. However, it is surely built into the very idea of pride that it is about oneself. When I feel proud of a piece of music that I have written or performed, it is because the music is *considered as mine*. By virtue of that relation, the idea of myself is already contained in the mode of presentation of the music being considered.

That Hume sometimes views the relationship between pride and humility and the self as causal and contingent rather than constitutive is shown by his regarding the self's status as the object of pride and humility as being both a *natural* and an *original* fact. By 'natural', he means that it is part of human nature, and not chosen or created by any human artifice. He thinks that this natural status is confirmed by the lack of counter-examples, showing that he is proposing it as an inductively based empirical hypothesis. Its *originality* is shown by it being a basic unanalysable and inexplicable fact that these passions always concern oneself. The fact that pride is experienced as pleasant, and humility as painful, are equally original facts, and thus must be taken as basic in the science of man.

What Hume wants to say is something like this: I encounter some intrinsically pleasant quality; this causes *pleasure* (*joy*), which is transformed into *pride* due to its perceived relation to me. Hume misleadingly describes this process in a linear way: that is, pleasure → pride → idea of self. However, he surely means that the subject which *would have* caused me pleasure regardless of any perceived connection to me is a source of pride through the self-related way in which I see it. So its pleasure-giving capacity is separate from its pride-giving capacity. If I am proud of my car, it is due to it having some quality in it which raises this pride, a quality that is a source of pleasure *independent* of *my pride*, and which would cause me to still *admire* it even if it was not mine.

The root of all this trouble lies in two incompatible positions, both of which Hume seems committed to. On the one hand, he often writes as if passions were akin to primary impressions in being pure qualia without intentional content. On the other hand, his way of distinguishing these passions from each other employs the intentional idiom. Perhaps the most charitable response to this tension is to take the following line. One can grant that there is a semantic relation between the concepts of pride and self, and a logical connection between certain sentences involving them. But it can still be claimed that, in extensional terms, the impression that we call pride, is, as a purely contingent fact, caused by certain events involving reference to the self. It is therefore possible, but not actual, that this particular quale – this subjective feel – could have been felt towards others, for example had human nature been different. So, *qua pleasurable state* – without reference to content – this impression that we call pride could have had a different object.

Hume alleges that the causal mechanisms governing the indirect passions operate in all humankind. Human nature is universal and unchanging, both over time and across cultural divides. He takes this universality as strong evidence that the mechanism behind the causes of pride or humility is *natural*. On the other hand, the sheer variety of the causes themselves makes it improbable that they be *original*. That is, it is unlikely that nature separately pre-arranged that all these things cause us pleasure, particularly since they include new inventions or creations, that may come into existence after oneself. While the particular things that cause pride may change, the basic causal structure of the generation of the passions is the same, in that pride is evoked by some intrinsically pleasurable factor when seen as relating to me. While an attractive appearance is always a source of pride, what satisfies this criterion will vary. The purple velvet flares that admitted one to the in-crowd of 1967 London would only provoke snide comments in 1977. So there is not a specific mechanism for each thing which can cause pride, but one same mechanism, based on 'circumstances common to all of them, on which their efficacy depends' (*T* 282). This mechanism is the double relation of impressions and ideas.

The double association of impressions and ideas

Hume's most detailed explanation of the generation of indirect passions involves the *double association of impressions and ideas*. While *ideas* can be associated by resemblance, contiguity, or cause and effect, *impressions* can only be associated by the resemblance of their subjective qualities. When Hume introduces this theory, he focuses exclusively on hedonic resemblance, as is shown in the following passage:

> All resembling impressions are connected together, and no sooner one arises than the rest immediately follow. Grief and disappointment give rise to anger, anger to envy, envy to malice, and malice to grief again, till the whole circle be compleated. In like manner our temper, when elevated with joy, naturally throws itself into love, generosity, pity, courage, pride, and the other resembling affections.
>
> (*T* 283)

The cause of an indirect passion must have the capacity to produce a *direct* passion of pleasure or pain in observers, independently of whether it goes on to produce an indirect passion. If an indirect passion *is* produced, it must be hedonically similar to the direct passion. For example, if the cause of the passion is some property that causes *pleasure* in those who encounter it, then this limits the immediately consequent indirect passions to either pride or love. Likewise, if the causal property generates *unease* in observers, the indirect passions would be either humility or hatred, depending, of course, on whether the object of this passion is oneself or another. So, to repeat, the *association of impressions* consists in the hedonic similarity of the original direct passion and the subsequent indirect one.

The second condition for any indirect passion to be produced rests on the *association of ideas*, which demands that the independently pleasing or displeasing quality be seen in relation to some person. If that person is myself, then I feel *pride*; if it relates to someone else, then I feel *love* for that person.

> We may observe, that no person is ever prais'd by another for any quality, which wou'd not, if real, produce, of itself, a pride in the person possest of it…'Tis certain, then, that if a person consid-er'd himself in the same light, in which he appears to his admirer, he would first receive a separate pleasure, and afterwards a pride or self-satisfaction.
>
> (*T* 320)

In sum, the cause of the indirect passion must produce some pleasure or pain (to cause the association of impressions), and be related to oneself or another (to cause the association of ideas). So the initial pleasure gives rise to pride through (1) the hedonic similarity between the pleasure and pride, and (2) the causal relation between the subject and myself.

My Armani suit, when considered purely in itself, produces pleas-urable impressions in those who see it due to its superb cut and exquisite fabric. Thus, were I to consider it without reference to me, I would feel this pleasure. However, when I conceive of it not merely as *this* suit, but as *my* suit, an impression of myself is thereby generated as part of the mode of presentation of the garment, and the initial impression is transformed into the equally pleasurable state of pride.

At this stage, Hume is only describing the simplest and most basic cases of pride and humility. As we shall soon see, these passions can interact with other indirect passions to generate an array of complex interactive responses among persons. He is well aware that many people would not respond to my suit in the way I describe, but would regard me with hatred, envy or contempt on account of it. He knows that anyone in the grip of the 'monkish virtues' would regard me as indulging in the sin of vanity. For example, to take a contemporary variety of puritanism, those who see a shabby appearance as a sign of authenticity, and an aesthetic appreciation of clothes as indicating a shallow character, might despise me while feeling a glow of righteous pride. I will touch on these issues shortly.

Apart from our own traits, abilities and accomplishments, we can feel pride in the abilities of others with whom we are closely associ-ated. One obvious example would be the way in which parents glory in their children's achievements. In fact, pride can be felt even in the absence of any close connection to the person or event concerned. For example, I remember as a boy bursting with pride when Glasgow Celtic became the first British team to win the European Cup, in 1967. Even though I had yet to meet any of the eleven home-grown heroes, they were *my team*, and I felt a portion of their glory reflecting back on me. So pride can be felt in a stranger's achievement when it concerns something important to us, and where we can find some connection to it or to them, even if only by the veritable six degrees of separation.

Refinements to the rule

Hume has so far proposed the general rule that '*every thing related to us, which produces pleasure or pain, produces likewise pride or humility*' (*T* 291). That is, anything intrinsically pleasing causes me to feel pride when I see it in relation to myself. However, in *T* 2/1/6 he qualifies this claim, saying that other factors need to be in place before the transition will occur.

First, while mere exposure to something pleasing can cause 'joy' in all who experience it, pride requires me to see myself as having a closer relationship to the thing in question. Hume gives the example that while every guest at a feast will experience pleasure, only the host will feel pride. Second, it must be *rare*, as pride is proportional to peculiarity: 'the agreeable or disagreeable object be not only closely related, but also peculiar to ourselves, or at least common to us with a few persons' (*T* 291). In making an explicit connection between pride in some quality and its rarity, Hume appeals to the *principle of comparison*, whereby 'we likewise judge of objects more from comparison than from their real and intrinsic merit' (*T* 291). I am proud of my Armani suit not only because of its beautiful fabric and cut, or since it reveals my exquisite taste, or since it gives the illusion that I am a man of considerable means, but because it makes me stand out in the sartorial disaster area that is the typical university. By contrast, many things cause us joy without pride precisely because they are the norm. In a telling example, Hume remarks that one is not usually proud of good health, even though it is immeasurably more important than fine clothes. In fact, the only cases in which one will be proud of good health is when there is some unusual factor surrounding it. For example, a nonagenarian might feel this pride, as would a cancer survivor or organ recipient.

A third condition for the generation of pride is that the admirable quality be known not just to oneself but to *others*. 'We fancy ourselves more happy, as well as more virtuous or beautiful, when we appear so to others' (*T* 292). Hume was possibly the first to identify the complex symbiosis between one's self-image and the opinions of others, and I will return to it when I discuss the sympathy mechanism. While Hume would surely not deny that one can feel pride in a secret accomplishment, he would require that others *would* approve of it were they to learn of it. His deeper point is that the capacity to feel pride *at all* requires being able to conceive of oneself as the object of others' approval.

Fourth, pride requires that our relationship to the pleasing quality be relatively stable and long-lasting, since: 'It seems ridiculous to infer an excellency in ourselves from an object, which is of so much shorter duration, and attends to us during so small a part of our existence' (*T* 293). It would be odd to be proud of something that was a sheer 'fluke', or totally out of character. Suppose that a footballer is proud of scoring the winning goal in the Cup Final. While the specific event of scoring the goal lasted a matter of seconds, and the game less than two hours, pride is felt in this act because it is seen as a manifestation of, or the crowning achievement of, enduring traits which are the real source of pride. This lays the ground for an important theme of Book 3, that the primary subject of moral praise or blame is the character of persons, and that actions are praise or blameworthy only to the extent that they emerge from settled character traits.

A fifth limitation is the influence of 'general rules'. The particular qualities that will generate pride will vary, to a significant extent, between cultures. One reason for this is that what is rare in one place may not be in another. It follows that someone outside that culture cannot ascertain, a priori, all the features in which pride is located. Hume adds that even someone with full knowledge of human nature could not manage it. This, as we shall see, is proof that an element of convention is involved. In an example more suited to love and hatred rather than pride or humility, he says that one who has come to generally associate wealth with pleasure, and therefore with love and pride, may hold someone in high regard due to his wealth, even if such a person takes no pleasure in his position.

Of the three sources of qualities that can elicit pride, namely pleasant mental characteristics, bodily attributes and material goods, the first is by far the most important. Within the class of mental traits, the most prominent cause of pride is recognition of our *virtues*. In Book 2, Hume does not use 'virtue' and 'vice' as *moral* terms, but only in the natural pre-moral sense in which a virtue is a character trait which is a source of pleasure. These virtues extend beyond those usually classified as moral, including 'any other thing that has a connexion with pleasure and uneasiness', such as 'our wit, good humour, or any other accomplishment' (*T* 297). In a similar manner, 'vice', in this context, is roughly synonymous with 'defect'.

Turning to bodily attributes, Hume states that we can be proud of anything that is 'either useful, beautiful, or surprising' (*T* 300). This appeal to use and beauty reiterates his position that we naturally approve of anything that is either intrinsically pleasing, or is a reliable means for achieving such a thing. Since surprise is defined as 'nothing but a pleasure arising from novelty' (*T* 301), his claim is not that *any* unusual physical trait can cause pride, but only those which satisfy one of the other two criteria. Any equally rare trait that was displeasing or useless would cause humility. So the Elephant Man, for example, would fall in the latter camp, since the only pleasure that anyone could derive from his wretched appearance would be of the malicious kind stemming from the principle of comparison.

In the case of material objects, pride is evoked 'when external objects acquire a particular relation to ourselves, and are associated or connected with us' (*T* 303). This relation is either of causation or contiguity, since no resemblance can be the initial source of pride. For example, if I feel pride because of some resemblance to a great man, this resemblance is not the basis of my pride, since it presupposes that the resembling qualities are themselves worthy of pride.

> We can never have a vanity of resembling in trifles any person, unless he be possess'd of very shining qualities, which give us a respect and veneration for him. These qualities, then, are, properly

> speaking, the causes of our vanity, by means of their relation to ourselves.
>
> (*T* 304)

The most common way in which material things produce pride is through the relation of ownership. Hume's definition of property is explicitly causal: 'property may be defin'd *such a relation betwixt person and an object as permits him, but forbids any other, the free use and possession of it, without violating the laws of justice and moral equity*' (*T* 310). Since property itself is a source of pride, so also is the power to acquire property, as the thought of that power leads by association to the pleasure to be obtained by its exercise, and 'the anticipation of pleasure is, in itself, a very considerable pleasure' (*T* 315).

Sympathy

I mentioned at the start of this chapter that pride is dependent on the approval of others. The means by which this approval is transmitted is the mechanism of *sympathy*:

> But besides these original causes of pride and humility, there is a secondary one in the opinions of others, which has an equal influence on the affections. Our reputation, our character, our name are considerations of vast weight and importance; and even the other causes of pride; virtue, beauty and riches; have little influence, when not seconded by the opinions and sentiments of others.
>
> (*T* 316)

Sympathy consists in the empathic capacity to *detect* the mental states of other persons, and, as a result, to undergo an experience similar to that of the person being considered. A useful analogy is the way that the sitar has 'sympathetic strings' which are not touched, but resonate in response to the primary strings. So we can say that sympathy allows us to 'tune into' another's inner state. A sympathetic response can arise without actually seeing the sufferer, but merely contemplating the thought of him. This can even occur in reading fiction, although such cases presuppose a capacity for sympathetic response in the more basic cases.

> In general, we may remark, that the minds of men are mirrors to one another, not only because they reflect each other's emotions, but also because those rays of passions, sentiments and opinions may be often reverberated, and may decay away by insensible degrees.
> (*T* 365)

Sympathy is the capacity to simulate what others are experiencing, when we see or think of them. It is an operation of the *imagination* whereby a primary impression (such as behaviour indicating pain or pleasure) leads to an *idea* regarding the other's experience, which is transformed into an *impression* of pain or pleasure in correspondence with the observed state. Sympathy is not something we 'do' intentionally, but takes place involuntarily on the natural unreflective level. It is not a product of reason, such as the making of inductive inferences about someone's inner state on the basis of her behaviour, nor the deliberate manipulation of the imagination to put oneself in others' shoes. (Although, as we shall see, such processes have their place in the development of the *corrected* sympathy involved in the making of moral judgements.)

> When any affection is infus'd by sympathy, it is at first known only by its effects, and by those external signs in the countenance and conversation, which convey an idea of it. This idea is presently converted into an impression, and acquires such a degree of force or vivacity as to become the very passion itself, and produce an equal emotion, as any original affection.
> (*T* 317)

Consider a sympathizing with someone's emotional upset. The process goes something like this:

1 I see someone exhibiting behaviour that is a natural and reliable indicator of distress.

2 I form the idea of this state of mind.
3 At this point, the associative principle of resemblance enters the picture. All persons are highly similar to each other, purely by virtue of being of the same species. Since 'ourself is always intimately present to us' (*T* 320), seeing someone upset leads to the idea of *me* feeling this distress. That is, I am moved only because I am seeing *someone like me* in pain.
4 The additional pain caused by this thought 'enlivens' the original idea into an impression, so I come to feel a distress similar to what I originally perceived in the other person. 'In sympathy there is an evident conversion of an idea into an impression. This conversion arises from the relation of objects to ourself' (*T* 320).

However, sympathy is not an *impartial* mechanism. Although our similarity as human beings allows a basic degree of sympathy to extend to everyone, the extent to which it goes beyond this basis is proportional to the operations of the three associative principles. In other words, not only will sympathy more naturally flow to someone similar to oneself in some significant way, but also towards those related to us by contiguity and causation. The most obvious case of this will be how we are naturally more affected by the plight of our friends and family than of strangers on the other side of the world.

> The stronger the relation is betwixt ourselves and any object, the more easily does the imagination make the transition, and convey to the related idea the vivacity of conception, with which we always form the idea of our own person.
>
> Nor is resemblance the only relation, which has this effect, but receives new force from other relations, that may accompany it. The sentiments of others have little influence, when far remov'd from us, and require the relation of contiguity, to make them communicate themselves entirely. The relation of blood, being a species of causation, may sometimes contribute to the same effect; as also acquaintance, which operates in the same manner with education and custom.
>
> (*T* 318)

Sympathy is a mechanism by which perceptions (passions or opinions) can be communicated. In fact, Hume later refers to it as 'the principle of sympathy or communication' (*T* 427). It is not itself a passion, since it has no distinct quale of its own. So, as mentioned above, it cannot be confused with pity. Rather, the states it generates are pleasurable or painful depending on the state being communicated. The effect of sympathy on our *opinions* is shown by the phenomenon of peer group pressure, and the way in which our views are formed by repeated exposure to the views of those around us, such that it is extremely difficult to develop an independent viewpoint. However, the mechanism is most noticeable in cases of strong emotion, such as grief. For example, if you attended a funeral of someone you did not know particularly well, and news of whose death had not noticeably affected you, witnessing the grief of the deceased's family and friends would generate those same feelings in you. In other cases, the resemblance to the transmitted state will have a more restricted hedonic similarity. For example, if I witness a footballer breaking his leg, the nerves in my own limb will not send such violent impulses to my brain. While I may feel acute emotional distress, which could be intense enough to make me feel physically sick, my *leg* will not hurt.

A more complex and derivative sort of case may involve a hedonically opposed response. This occurs when the *principle of comparison* is involved. For example, being in the presence of a successful and highly capable person, I sympathetically pick up her self-esteem, which makes me feel bad when I compare myself to her. I will return to these cases shortly. However, the key to them lies in Hume's recognition that I do not just feel pride or humility from directly observing my own characteristics, but also from sympathetically perceiving others' feelings towards my character. A complex feedback mechanism operates in which each person's self-conception is constructed from, and transformed by (perceptions of) others' approval or disapproval. So, as Hume discusses in *T* 2/2/5, the effects of sympathy can echo: I may receive pleasure through sympathetically tuning into a rich person's enjoyment of his possessions; his pleasure and pride are increased by recognition of my pleasure and esteem/love. This, in turn, makes me put even more value on his wealth.

> 'Tis certain, then, that if a person consider'd himself in the same light, in which he appears to his admirer, he wou'd first receive a separate pleasure, and afterwards a pride or self-satisfaction, according to the hypothesis above explain'd. Now nothing is more natural for us to embrace the opinions of others in this particular; both from *sympathy*, which renders all their sentiments intimately present to us; and from *reasoning*, which makes us regard their judgment, as a kind of argument for what they affirm.
>
> (*T* 320)

I emphasize that the traditional sceptical 'problem of other minds' is not perceived as a genuine problem for Hume. Belief in the social world is just a fact of human nature, and thereby to be taken as theoretically foundational, being neither capable of nor in need of further justification. Through the mechanism of sympathy, I can detect or simulate others' thoughts and passions in me. While one might theorize that spectators can only observe others' *behaviour* directly, and not their *thoughts*, our natural experience is of a world of *people* who have thoughts, sensations, feelings, and so on.

Love and hatred

The structure and themes of Part 2 of Book 2 run directly parallel to those of Part 1. In the same way that pride and humility are pleasurable and painful passions whose object is oneself, love and hatred are specified as the hedonically correspondent passions directed at other persons. As with pride and humility, it must always be kept in mind that his names for indirect passions are technical terms, corresponding to high and low regard for persons, oneself or others. To love someone, in this sense, is to hold her in high estimation because of her personal qualities. As before, their simplicity makes it impossible to 'define' these impressions, enabling them only to be known by direct acquaintance, but such a verbal manoeuvre is unnecessary since they are 'sufficiently known from our common feeling and experience' (*T* 329). The causes of love and hatred are precisely the same qualities that produce pride and humility. Any character trait, bodily attribute or material item that would cause pride if it were mine would cause me to love anyone else who possessed it. In other words, the same process of the double relation of impressions and ideas is required to produce love and hatred, the only difference being the relation of ideas connects the relevant quality to someone other than oneself.

> As the immediate *object* of pride and humility is self or that identical person, of whose thoughts, actions, and sensations we are intimately conscious, so the *object* of love and hatred is some other person, of whose thoughts, actions and sensations we are not conscious.
>
> (*T* 329)

Hume offers a series of thought experiments to confirm his hypothesis of the double relation of impressions and ideas: that is, that the production of an indirect passion requires (a) that the cause must be in some close relation to the person concerned, and (b) that it be intrinsically pleasing or displeasing, regardless of any such relation.

1 Imagine that you and a stranger confront a stone or some other 'common object'. In such a case, no indirect passion will be produced since, first, the object bears no relation to either of us, so the association of ideas will not occur; second, the stone is too mundane an item to produce any feeling of pleasure or displeasure, so the association of impressions cannot even get started.

2 Now suppose the stone to belong to my companion or myself, and thus 'acquires a relation of ideas to the object of the passions' (*T* 334). However, the association of impressions is still a stumbling block, since the stone's inability to produce any direct passion prevents any indirect one from occurring.

3 Now reverse the situation: suppose we discover something beautiful, but which bears no relation to either of us. For example, we come across a waterfall. While this sight may evoke joy, the lack of any close relationship to either of us will prevent this direct pleasure being transformed into pride or love.

The second and third examples prove that neither the association of ideas nor that of impressions are *singly* sufficient to generate an indirect passion. The next experiment demonstrates that they are *jointly* sufficient.

4 Consideration of our *character traits* will generate the following results. First, suppose the trait to be a virtue:

(a) if it is mine, I will feel pride;
(b) if it is of my companion, I will feel love towards her.

Now suppose the trait to be a vice:

(c) if it is mine, I will feel humility;
(d) if it is of my companion, it will cause me to hate her.

This sequence of results is duplicated when the cause is a bodily attribute or material possession.

I will touch only briefly on the other experiments, which introduce ways in which these four 'basic' indirect passions interact with each other, particularly the conditions under which pride can result from love.

5 The next example supposes my companion to be no stranger, but someone 'closely related with me either by blood or friendship' (*T* 337). Suppose it to be my brother. Now consider an analogue of case 4b above. Here, the love I feel for my brother *because he is my brother* causes the love I feel for him *because of his virtuous trait* to generate pride. I am proud that *my brother* has this admirable quality. Here, the association of impressions between love and pride is based on their hedonic similarity, and the relation of ideas is grounded in the causal relationship between my brother and I. A parallel case can be drawn where the hatred I feel from my brother's vice leads me to feel humility.

> The person has a relation of ideas to myself, according to the supposition; the passion, of which he is the object, by being either agreeable or uneasy, has a relation to the impressions to pride or humility. 'Tis evident, then, that one of these passions must arise from the love or hatred.
>
> (*T* 338)

6 Hume now confronts an asymmetry, in that while love can lead to pride, and hatred to humility, such transitions tend not to occur in the reverse direction. For example, my pride in a virtue does not thereby yield an increase in the love I feel for my friends or family, yet my recognition of their virtues causes my self-esteem to rise. How can this asymmetry take place, when all the relations involved are symmetrical? (For example, if x is a blood relative of y, y is equally related to x.)

Hume attempts to explain this anomaly in terms of his associative principles. Since 'we are at all times intimately conscious of ourselves' (*T* 339), this self-awareness has greater vivacity than even the most powerful sympathy can convey regarding others. In other words, this direct awareness of our own perceptions means than anyone else, no matter how close the relation, is necessarily less contiguous to us than we are to ourselves. Since '*the imagination has difficulty passing from the contiguous to the remote*' (*T* 346), a thought of anyone related to me leads to a thought of myself far easier than vice versa.

> If a person be my brother I am his likewise: But tho' the relations be reciprocal, they have very different effects on the imagination. The passage is smooth and open from the consideration of any person related to us to that of ourself, of whom we are every moment conscious. But when the affections are once directed to ourself, the fancy passes not with the same facility from that object to any other person, how closely so ever connected with us. (*T* 340)

One apparent exception to the asymmetry between pride and love occurs when self-esteem is caused by recognizing that someone holds one in high regard. Then pride leads one to love this person, since they are part of the cause of the pride itself. Hume is satisfied that this is not really an exception to his system, but merely a special case of the general point that we like people to the extent that they make us feel good.

> Nothing is more evident, than that any person acquires our kindness, or is expos'd to our ill-will, in proportion to the pleasure or

> uneasiness we receive from him, and that the passions keep pace exactly with the sensations in all their changes and variations. Whoever can find the means either by his services, his beauty, or his flattery, to render himself useful or agreeable to us, is sure of our affections.
>
> (*T* 348)

One purported exception to the need for the 'double relation' in the generation of an indirect passion has already been briefly alluded to. This is where love for another, particularly a blood relation, can be caused purely by the fact of that relationship, and thereby from the association of ideas alone. The extent of this unconditional love will be proportional to the closeness of the relationship. Hence:

> the passion of love may be excited by only one *relation* of a different kind, *viz*. betwixt ourselves and the object;... Whoever is united to us by any connexion is always sure of a share of our love, proportion'd to the connexion, without enquiring into his other qualities.
>
> (*T* 352)

I agree with Ardal that Hume here seems to have forgotten that he has been using 'love' in a technical way, standing for a positive estimation of someone on account of his character or other attributes, and has reverted to the common meaning of 'love', in which we might love someone *regardless of their character*, purely on the basis of a familial or other close relationship.

Just as the presence or absence of 'power and riches' has a strong influence on our pride or humility, it is an equally salient cause of love or hatred for others: 'Nothing has a greater tendency to give us an esteem to any person, than his power and riches; or a contempt, than his poverty and meanness' (*T* 357). Hume considers three possible explanations for this correlation between love and social standing. The first is grounded in the 'agreeable' nature of certain possessions, which leads to approval for their owners by means of the 'double association'. The second theory proposes that our positive feelings for the rich and powerful derive from a hope or expectation that we might personally benefit from them in some way. The third theory is founded upon the *sympathy* mechanism.

Hume rejects the second theory for two reasons. First, we can have high regard for figures from antiquity, or other such persons from whom there is no possibility of personal gain. Second, he reminds us that any causal inference must be grounded in a constant conjunction of the features concerned; but since the rich are not in the habit of indiscriminately giving away all their goods, we will almost certainly have had little experience of such generosity, which rules out the possibility of such a naturally induced expectation. 'Of a hundred men of credit and fortune I meet with, there is not perhaps, one from whom I can expect advantage; so that 'tis impossible any custom can ever prevail in the present case' (*T* 362).

He grants, with the first thesis, that we experience pleasure on contemplating someone's property, and thereby extend our approval to him. However, he insists that the success of the double relation in such a case requires the operation of sympathy. *Our* pleasure is activated by our perception of *his* pleasure in his situation.

> Upon the whole, there remains nothing, which can give us an esteem for power and riches, and a contempt for meanness and poverty, except the principle of *sympathy*, by which we enter into the sentiments of the rich and poor, and partake of their pleasure and uneasiness. Riches give satisfaction to their possessor; and this satisfaction is convey'd to the beholder by the imagination, which produces an idea resembling the original impression in force and vivacity. This agreeable idea or impression is connected with love, which is an agreeable passion. It proceeds from a thinking conscious being, which is the very object of love. From this relation of impressions, and identity of ideas, the passion arises.
>
> (*T* 362)

Sympathy and comparison

Hume now turns to the 'compound passions', in which the four basic indirect passions are 'conjoin'd with' derivative ones. Calling these 'compound' is slightly misleading, since Hume insists that these passions are as *simple* as the basic ones. He compares passions to colours in this regard, in the way that red and yellow can mix to form the equally simple orange. One difference between pride and humility and love and hatred is that the former pair are 'compleated in themselves', being 'pure emotions in the soul unattended by any desire, and not immediately exciting us to action'. By contrast, love and hatred 'are not compleated in themselves, nor rest in that emotion, which they produce, but carry the mind to something farther'. Love naturally leads to *benevolence*, 'a desire of the happiness of the person belov'd, and an aversion to his misery', whereas hatred is constantly conjoined with *anger*, 'a desire of the misery of the person hated, and an aversion to his happiness' (all quotes from *T* 367). As before, the double association of ideas and impressions is behind these transitions. For example, love and benevolence share their object, and are hedonically alike as varieties of pleasure.

Benevolence and anger have 'counterfeits' in *pity* (also called *compassion*) and *malice*, the difference being that the latter pair do not derive from special relationships: '*Pity* is a concern for, and *malice* a joy in the misery of others, without any friendship or enmity to occasion this concern or joy' (*T* 369). Despite his claim that these passions 'may arise from secondary principles', pity is fully explicable in terms of sympathy alone, as deriving from the ground-floor empathy felt towards any person purely by virtue of our common humanity.

> We have a lively idea of every thing related to us. All human creatures are related to us by resemblance. Their persons, therefore their interests, their passions, their pains and pleasures must strike upon us in a lively manner, and produce an emotion similar to the original one; since a lively idea is converted into an impression. If this be true in general, it must be more so of affliction and sorrow. These have always a stronger and more lasting influence than any pleasure or enjoyment.
>
> (*T* 369)

By contrast, Hume's account of malice involves the principle of comparison in addition to sympathy. I will introduce the difference between these two processes by contrasting the ways in which they are both essentially partial and distorting. When sympathy transmits another's passions or attitudes to me, the object of my subsequent passion is that person, considered in a non-relational way. Although the extent to which this sympathy will operate, and consequently the intensity of my passion, will depend on the closeness of our relationship, I do not enter into the *content* of the passion itself. By contrast, the principle of comparison presents the other person specifically in terms of her relation to me. That is, to adopt Fregean terminology, I am included within the mode of presentation of the state itself, since she is thought of *in comparison to me*. That is, she is measured against me in some particular way, and the subsequent malice I feel towards her is through coming off second best. So now it seems that not only does Hume have to grant intentional content to the passions, but he has to make this content more 'fine grained' than mere reference will allow.

Hume's account suggests that the principle of comparison does not operate *instead of* sympathy, but *after* it, diverting or overruling it. In order to suffer through seeing oneself in comparison to someone else, one has to enter into their self-esteem, and compare it to one's own, in a way that requires sympathy. The idea seems to be that we naturally become aware of someone's inner state through sympathy, which results, via the intervention of comparison, in these negative derivative passions.

He compares this tendency to 'judge more of objects by comparison than from their intrinsic worth and value' (*T* 372) to perceptual illusions, where an object will seem to change size or shape when placed against different backgrounds; or how water will feel different to a hand that is already hot or cold. In the same way in which '*objects appear greater or less by a comparison with others*', malice is a reaction to the humility we feel when we come off badly in comparison to someone else:

> 'Tis evident we must receive a greater or less satisfaction or uneasiness from reflecting on our own condition and circumstances, in proportion as they appear more or less fortunate or unhappy, in proportion to the degree of riches, and power, and merit, and reputation, which we think ourselves possest of...The

> misery of another gives us a more lively idea of our happiness, and his happiness of our misery. The former, therefore, produces delight; and the latter uneasiness.
>
> (*T* 375)

He describes malice as 'a kind of pity reverst' (*T* 375), since, rather than empathically suffering alongside someone, I take pleasure in it. In fact, he could just as easily describe this as a case of what I might call 'pity usurp'd', since the original sympathetic response has been hijacked by the principle of comparison, which separates and divides persons as much as sympathy unites them.

The principle of comparison generates another state similar to malice, namely *envy*. The difference between them is that 'envy is excited by some present enjoyment of another, which by comparison diminishes the idea of our own: Whereas malice is the unprovok'd desire of producing evil to another, in order to reap a pleasure from the comparison' (*T* 377). So envy concerns events which have already occurred, whereas malice is future-directed and connected with action. Envy consists in a negative state of wishing for what someone else has, or resenting him for having it, whereas malice is actively wishing for some misfortune to befall him on that account. In both cases, these negative passions arise from the 'pain' of humility caused by comparing oneself to someone else and not liking what one sees.

Another pair of states generated through the principle of comparison are *respect* and *contempt*. These are 'mixed' states involving both sympathy and comparison:

> In considering the qualities and circumstances of others, we may either regard them as they really are in themselves; or may make a comparison betwixt them and our own qualities and circumstances; or may join these two methods of consideration. The good qualities of others, from the first point of view, produce love; from the second, humility; and from the third, respect; which is a mixture of these two passions. Their bad qualities, after the same manner, cause either hatred, or pride, or contempt, according to the light in which we survey them.
>
> (*T* 390)

In an interesting development, he remarks that one can even feel malice towards *oneself*, or, to be more precise, towards oneself at an earlier stage of one's life:

> Nor will it appear strange, that we may feel a reverst sensation from the happiness and misery of others; since we find the same comparison may give us a kind of malice against ourselves, and make us rejoice for our pains, and grieve for our pleasures. Thus the prospect of past pain is agreeable, when we are satisfy'd with our present condition; as on the other hand our past pleasures give us uneasiness, when we enjoy nothing at present equal to them.
>
> (*T* 376)

This 'malice against ourselves' does not refer to any indulgent dwelling on past troubles or triumphs for their own sake, but to the effects to our self-esteem caused by comparison to our present situation. So, in the former case, I can feel pride or relief in having overcome a difficult situation. In the latter case, I may become dispirited by how my fortunes have taken a downturn. I am unclear why he calls these cases of *malice*, since malice involves a desire for harm to come to the person considered; a desire that is absent here. In fact, '*envy* against ourselves' is closer to the mark.

Hume then notes that this discussion of pity and malice seems to have generated a counter-example to his associative principles:

> There is always a mixture of love or tenderness with pity, and of hatred or anger with malice. But it must be confess'd, that this mixture seems at first sight to be contradictory to my system. For as pity is an uneasiness and malice a joy, arising from the misery of others, pity shou'd naturally, as in all other cases, produce hatred; and malice, love.
>
> (*T* 381)

So love, benevolence and pity tend to be conjoined, as do hatred, anger and malice. The problem is that his presentation of the 'double relation' theory, up to this point, has only associated passions by their hedonic resemblance. Contrary to what this theory would predict, the pleasures of love and benevolence are connected with pity, a *pain* caused by appreciation of another's suffering. Again, the unpleasant passions of hatred and anger are conjoined with malice, a *pleasure* in another's misfortune. So malice and pity seem to be in the wrong place.

Hume's rather *ad hoc* solution is to introduce another principle governing the association of impressions, in addition to hedonic resemblance. He calls this principle the *parallel direction of impulses*. Although pity resembles hatred and anger in being a species of pain, it is similar to love and benevolence in exhibiting a positive attitude towards another's well-being; malice is likewise connected to hatred and anger by their attitude to harm befalling someone. He employs this parallel direction of impulses to explain the fact that 'benevolence and anger, and consequently love and hatred, arise when our happiness or misery have any dependence on the happiness or misery of another person, without any further relation' (*T* 382–3). He asks us to compare two cases in which you and another are in business; in the former case, he is in competition with you; in the latter, he is your ally. In the former case you will feel hatred and anger towards this man because your interests are opposed. In the latter case love and benevolence arise from the fact that his success is linked to yours. He interprets this correlation by saying that it is due to the 'parallel direction' of our interests.

Things get even more complicated when he notes that sympathy can have contrary effects, depending on the strength of its operation. The previous case, involving the parallel direction of interests, involves taking a long-term view of one's relationship to another. In a similar way, Hume now tells us that sympathy can transmit not only another's present state of mind, but also 'the pains and pleasures of others, which are not in being, and which we only anticipate by the force of imagination' (*T* 385). He refers to this as 'compleat' or 'extensive' sympathy:

> I have mention'd two different causes, from which a transmission of passion may arise, *viz*. a double relation of ideas and impressions, and what is similar to it, a conformity in the tendency and

> direction of any two desires, which arise from different principles. Now I assert, that when a sympathy with uneasiness is weak, it produces hatred or contempt by the former cause; when strong, it produces love or tenderness by the latter.
>
> (*T* 385)

When a sympathetic response is weak, we can feel hatred or contempt rather than compassion for a suffering person. Thus a sheltered suburbanite may turn up her nose at a homeless person on the street, reacting to his smelly unkempt appearance, and judging him to be a loser. At this stage, the degree of empathy is minimal, and overruled by the principle of comparison. Pity would only ensue from identifying with the other person, seeing similarity rather than difference, seeing a suffering person rather than an inferior. This more extensive sympathy would take one beyond an immediate reaction to the event, and into a wider view of the person concerned, which may lead to a desire to help him. So strong sympathy leads to love and benevolence or pity because it generates concern for the person as a whole – that is, his long-term interest – whereas weaker sympathy focuses only on his present painful situation, which causes hatred or contempt.

> A certain degree of poverty produces contempt; but a degree beyond causes compassion and goodwill... When the uneasiness is either small in itself, or remote from us, it engages not the imagination, nor is able to convey an equal concern for the future and contingent good, as for the present and real evil.
>
> (*T* 385)

> A strong impression, when communicated, gives a double tendency to the passions; which is related to benevolence and love by a similarity of direction; however painful the first impression might have been. A weak impression, that is painful, is related to anger and hatred by the resemblance of sensations. Benevolence, therefore, arises from a great deal of misery, or any degree strongly sympathiz'd with: Hatred or contempt from a small degree, or one weakly sympathiz'd with.
>
> (*T* 387)

One final complexity comes from the fact that once sympathy gets too strong, for example when one enters too fully into another's pain, the result is not pity but horror and revulsion. For example, when we see severe burn victims, our immediate reaction is for horror to overrule our sympathy.

> But tho' the force of the impression generally produces pity and benevolence, 'tis certain, that by being carried too far it ceases to have that effect...Thus we find, that tho' every one, but especially women, are apt to contract a kindness for criminals who go to the scaffold, and readily imagine them to be uncommonly handsome and well-shap'd; yet one, who is present at the cruel execution of the rack, feels no such tender emotions; but is in a manner overcome with horror, and has no leisure to temper this uneasy sensation by any opposite sympathy.
>
> (*T* 388)

Hume ends his discussion of the indirect passions just at the point at which his original quasi-Newtonian theory of the 'double association of impressions and ideas' is falling apart from the weight of counter-examples, shored up by auxiliary assumptions such as the 'parallel direction of interests' and the contrary effects of sympathy.

Further reading

Pall Ardal's ground-breaking study (1966, 2nd edn 1989) is still the best extended treatment of Hume's theory of the passions. See also Donald Davidson (1976) and John Bricke (1996: chs 1–2).

On the social construction of the self, see Amelie Rorty (1990), Baier (1991: ch. 6) and Pauline Chazan (1998: ch. 1).

Chapter 4

Motivation and will

Treatise, Book 2, Part 3; 1st *Enquiry*, Section VIII

Chapter 4

Freedom and the will

Hume locates his discussion of free agency in Book 2, Part 3, *Of the Will and Direct Passions*. While he admits that the will is not strictly a passion, he justifies placing it alongside the direct passions because, first, it resembles them in being an 'immediate effect of pain and pleasure'; and second, because he believes that an explanation of these passions requires an understanding of the will. I have not followed him in that belief, having covered the direct passions in the previous chapter.

As would be expected, Hume regards the will as 'impossible to define, and needless to describe any further' (*T* 399). But, as before, while the *impression* is simple and unique, we all understand the *expression* 'will' without the need for further analysis. Such an impression can be given a precise location on the mental map:

> I desire it may be observ'd, that by the *will*, I mean nothing but *the internal impression we feel and are conscious of, when we knowingly give rise to any new motion of our body, or a new perception of our mind.*
>
> (*T* 399)

The crucial word here is 'knowingly'. The will is a perception that immediately precedes either (1) any deliberate bodily movement, or (2) any thought that is actively generated. The fact that such events are systematically preceded by this kind of impression means that the will can be considered the *cause* of voluntary action, as the last link in the causal chain of mental events leading to action. Suppose I move my hand to switch on my computer. The desire to switch it on (plus the belief that moving my hand to press the button will do so) causes my volition to move my hand, which in turn (via a complex set of intermediary physiological processes) causes my hand to move.

Having given this initial description of the will, he endeavours to integrate an account of free action with his theory of causation. He begins by re-affirming his view that every event has a cause:

> 'Tis universally acknowledg'd, that the operations of external bodies are necessary, and that in the communication of their motion, in their attraction, and mutual cohesion, there are not the least traces of indifference or liberty. Every object is determined by an absolute fate to a certain degree and direction of its motion, and can no more depart from that precise line, in which it moves, than it can convert itself into an angel, spirit, or any superior substance. The actions, therefore, of matter are to be regarded as instances of necessary actions; and whatever is in this respect on the same footing with matter, must be acknowledg'd to be necessary.
>
> (*T* 399–400)

For present purposes, the most important part of this quotation are the last three lines, which set up his claim that whatever can be said about causation, necessity and liberty regarding matter applies equally to the mind. However, recall that Hume, as I interpret him, rejects any appeal to objective, mind-independent causal powers, operating under equally objective physical laws. Rather, our understanding of the concepts of cause and effect is acquired in the following way: various impressions get type-classified together on the basis of their resemblance; then, when we have repeatedly seen A-type events followed by B-type events, *our ideas of* A and B get associated in the mind. When this associative mechanism is established, we are led to anticipate B after seeing or thinking of A. Under these circumstances, we say that 'A causes B', although the only connection we know to exist is the association held between our ideas of A and B, rather than the objects we take these to be ideas *of*.

It is this view that Hume reaffirms when he asserts the universality of causal necessity, and which applies equally to our bodily processes and actions, and therefore to the moral realm:

> Are the changes of our body from infancy to old age more regular and certain than those of our mind and conduct? And wou'd a man be more ridiculous, who wou'd expect that an infant of four years old will raise a weight of three hundred pound, than one, who from a person of the same age, wou'd look for a philosophical reasoning, or a prudent and well-concerted action?
>
> (*T* 401)

So his thesis is that human behaviour is just as predictable and explicable as any other natural phenomenon, due to the observed constant conjunction between character and action:

> as the *union* betwixt motives and actions has the same constancy, as that in any natural operations, so its influence on the understanding is also the same, in *determining* us to infer the existence of one from that of the other.
>
> (*T* 404)

Notice that the inference can go both ways – from cause to effect and from effect to cause – if both have been repeatedly observed together. We form an opinion of someone's character when he behaves in ways commonly associated with certain traits and attitudes;

we can then take this assessment of his character as the grounds for both explaining and predicting other behaviour.

Hume's negative thesis is that introspection reveals no causal power linking the impression of willing and the subsequent action, any more than outwardly directed observation reveals objects to be so connected. I may be aware of having various beliefs and desires, over which I perform some means–ends calculations, leading to a decision to act, followed in turn by the appropriate action. But I am aware of no binding force connecting the volition to the action. His positive thesis is that actions are *constantly conjoined with* the appropriate volitions, alongside the preceding sequences of deliberations, making human behaviour as predictable as anything else in the natural world: 'For is it more certain, that two flat pieces of marble will unite together, than that two young savages of different sexes will copulate?' (*T* 402).

While acknowledging the undeniable 'capriciousness' of desires, and the less-than-perfect predictability of behaviour, he warns us not to overstate the case, since our capacity to make successful inferences about someone's behaviour based on past regularities is so common as to be taken for granted. While we do not have 100 per cent success in this enterprise, nor do we in our explanations of physical phenomena. However, in the latter case, our natural impulse is to take this uncertainty as showing our *incomplete knowledge* of the relevant causal factors, rather than the *absence* of such factors. Consistency requires that we take the same attitude to human behaviour. We make successful predictions about the movement of physical objects based on stable patterns observed in the past. In a similar way, human action is commonly predicted and explained by reference to 'moral evidence', that is, judgements about the person's stable character traits.

> There is no philosopher, whose judgment is so riveted to this fantastical system of liberty, as not to acknowledge the force of *moral evidence*, and both in speculation and practice proceed upon it, as upon a reasonable foundation. Now moral evidence is nothing but a conclusion concerning the actions of men, deriv'd from the consideration of their motivations, temper and situation. (*T* 404)

Recall that Hume's science of mind requires mental activity to display regularity and consistency in its operations. Accordingly, he will attempt to reframe the issue of human freedom, to show that any notion of liberty incompatible with this account is itself incoherent. It is undeniable that we do regularly and successfully appeal to another's specific beliefs and desires, or her character traits in general, to explain (or predict) her actions. To do so is thereby to acknowledge the causal connection (that is, the systematic correlation) between character and action. For example, suppose that I know that I am arriving back on a late flight, and do not want to pay the excessive cab fare, so I call a colleague and ask that he collect me from the airport. Given our friendship, and my estimation of his character, I predict that he will if he can; given his agreement, the same judgement of his character leads me to believe that he will do as he says.

Having shown how the notions of cause and necessity apply to the human mind, Hume then considers the objection that this is not 'real' causation or necessity. He counters that if someone wants to argue over semantics, the onus is on this person to justify his use of these terms in a legitimate way. In other words, if he insists on realistic construals of these terms, he has to show which impressions ground this usage. Hume predicts that any search for such a foundation will fail, and that his opponent will have to admit that his words have no meaning: 'Now I assert, whoever reasons after this manner, does *ipso facto* believe the actions of the will to arise from necessity, and that he knows not what he means, when he denies it' (*T* 405).

Hume backs up his thesis by observing that we can make use of moral evidence *in combination with* natural evidence to 'form one chain of argument betwixt them' (*T* 406). He considers the case of the prisoner who infers the inevitability of his impending demise, based as much upon the character of his guards as the physical conditions of his incarceration. For example, he sees that it is no more likely that these guards will relinquish the habits of a lifetime and secretly release him, than that the walls of his cell will suddenly collapse. The point here is that the forms of reasoning in both the 'moral' and the 'natural' cases are the same. If the notions of causation involved were different, they could not be combined in a single chain of inference to yield the conclusion. That is, unless persons are subject to the same laws of causation as the rest of the universe, any inference involving both forms of data would commit the fallacy of equivocation.

To explain Hume's position in greater detail, it will be helpful to have a little background on the venerable problem of freedom and determinism. The problem emerges from the apparent conflict between two beliefs, both of which are seemingly undeniable. First, we regard ourselves as being *free*; we see our future as 'open', such that what we choose can make a difference to what happens to us. Second, we believe that *every event has a cause*. Although this claim would not get the immediate and unanimous assent as the belief that we are free, it has seemed to most philosophers that anyone can be brought to accept it very quickly, by pointing out that its denial would make events *inexplicable*. This manoeuvre brings out the intimate connection between causation and explanation: explaining why something happened involves saying what caused it, and vice versa. As Hume correctly points out, when we cannot explain what is going on, we do not conclude that there is no cause for it, but merely that it has eluded us.

We want to say that our actions are caused, yet free, and the question is whether this combination is coherent. A way into the problem is via considering psychological explanation. We assume that our actions are caused by our mental states. That is, we act on the basis of a certain goal (or set of goals) and beliefs relating to the satisfaction of that end. On the basis of such deliberation, we form an intention to act, and, all things being equal, the action ensues. But our intentions, beliefs, desires, goals and so on are also events, and so, by our second assumption, have causes. By the same token, these causes themselves have causes, and so on. Given that causation is a transitive relation, we soon reach a point at which this causal chain predates our birth, so it looks like our actions were ultimately grounded in things outside our control, and our freedom dissolves before our eyes.

This belief that every event is the inevitable consequence of antecedent events, sometimes called the *Principle of Universal Causation* (PUC), arose in its modern form in the context of Newtonian science, and the conception of causation involved was non-Humean. The three standard philosophical responses to PUC are firstly from the 'hard determinists', who say that all events are governed by strict causal laws and, as such, there is no freedom; secondly from the libertarians, who say that our will lacks this causal determination, which shows PUC to be false; and thirdly from the 'compatibilists' or 'soft determinists' who regard determinism as true, yet compatible with a revised picture of freedom.

Hume is typically categorized as a compatibilist, and while this is correct, it must be kept in mind that his form of compatibilism is very different from the traditional one which (like hard determinism and libertarianism) is conceived in terms of the realist, mind-independent model of causation that he rejects. This orthodox compatibilism requires a non-Humean causal power linking *willing* and *action*, which is intended to allow a meaningful distinction between free and unfree actions, even though the universe is governed by strict deterministic laws, and every event is the inevitable consequence of preceding events. The ensuing dialectic rests on whether this relation can give us a sufficiently robust notion of freedom to satisfy our needs regarding the attribution of praise and blame, given that these acts of will are themselves determined by preceding events, and therefore resting on external factors outwith one's control.

In diagnosing why liberty has been commonly thought incompatible with causal necessity, Hume distinguishes the 'liberty of spontaneity' from the 'liberty of indifference':

> Few are capable of distinguishing betwixt the liberty of *spontaneity*, as it is call'd in the schools, and the liberty of *indifference;* betwixt that which is opposed to violence, and that which means a negation of necessity and causes. The first is even the most common sense of the word; and as 'tis only that species of liberty, which it concerns us to preserve, our thoughts have been principally turn'd towards it, and have almost universally confounded it with the other.
>
> (*T* 407–8)

He endorses the liberty of spontaneity, which presents a free action as being caused by one's desires and volition. An unfree action, on this conception, occurs when this transition from willing to action is interrupted or impeded by some external source. So if I decide to go out for a beer, and do so, then I act freely; my freedom would be prevented by, for example, my being locked up or banned from every bar in town. Hence, this freedom is not only *compatible* with causal necessity (as Hume understands that notion), but *requires* it. By contrast, the supposed liberty of indifference places the will outside any causal influence, as the uncaused cause of free actions. He acknowledges that 'from the inside', from the agent's own perspective, 'we feel that our actions are subject to our will on most occasions, and imagine we feel that the will itself is subject to nothing' (*T* 408), but insists that this appearance is false.

Failure to distinguish these two notions of liberty leads to confusion over the relationship between liberty and necessity. For example, while we grant that our actions 'were influenc'd by particular views and motives', we are not prepared to accept that they *necessitated* the action, such that we could not have done otherwise, as 'the idea of necessity seeming to imply something of force and violence, and constraint, of which we are not sensible' (*T* 407). In fact, not only do we feel no such 'necessitating force', but that 'there is a *false sensation or experience* even of the liberty of indifference; which is regarded as an argument for its real existence' (*T* 408). Given the absence of any causal power, it is not surprising that no feeling of necessitation is experienced. However, this leads us to falsely regard the will as being utterly disconnected from all prior mental events. Hume never explains the source of this error, perhaps because he takes it to be basic and inexplicable. As we shall see, we are most deeply afflicted by it as *agents* rather than as *theorists*.

Recall that libertarianism emerges from a background where non-Humean causal powers are assumed, and where free actions are taken to be *exceptions* to the causal order. On such a picture, since a free action is not necessitated by antecedent events, it requires that I could have done something else under exactly the same antecedent conditions. As critics have been quick to point out, it is hard to see how this can allow for a genuine notion of *action* at all, let alone *free* action.

> The constant and universal object of hatred or anger is a person or creature endow'd with thought and consciousness; and when any criminal or injurious actions excite that passion, 'tis only by

> their relation to the person or connexion with him. But according to the doctrine of liberty or chance, this connexion is reduced to nothing, nor are men more accountable for those actions, which are design'd and premeditated, than for such as are the most casual and accidental. Actions are by their very nature temporary and perishing; and when they proceed not from some cause in the characters and disposition of the person, who perform'd them, they infix not themselves upon him, and can neither redound to his honour, if good, nor infamy, if evil...According to the hypothesis of liberty, therefore, a man is as pure and untainted, after having committed the most horrid crimes, as at the first moment of his birth, nor his character concern'd in any way with his actions; since they are not deriv'd from it, and the wickedness of the one can never be us'd as a proof of the depravity of the other. 'Tis only upon the principles of necessity, that a person acquires any merit or demerit from his actions, however the common opinion may incline to the contrary.
>
> (*T* 411)

The traditional compatibilist objects to the liberty of indifference because any actions that lack a cause would thereby be random, so no one could be held responsible for them. It would follow, by this objection, that I can only be held responsible for my actions if there is a real connective power linking my intentions and actions. But this cannot be *Hume*'s main criticism of the liberty of indifference, since he rejects the conception of causal necessity within which the traditional dispute is framed. Still, he agrees that such a liberty of indifference would render human 'action' inexplicable. To be my *action*, rather than something that merely occurs in my body, such as my hair growing, it must proceed from reasons ensuing from my character. Second, he agrees that removing any connection between character and action would undermine the notion of moral responsibility that libertarians were trying to save. His difference from the traditional compatibilist position results from his need to reconceive the relationship between action and character in a way compatible with his reconstruction of the notion of causation. His crucial move is to step back from the first-person perspective of the agent herself, and adopt the third-person stance of the observer or interpreter. Consider the following passages:

> The necessity of any action, whether of matter or of the mind, is not properly a quality within the agent, but in any thinking or intelligent being, who may consider the action, and consists in the determination of his thought to infer the existence of some preceding objects: As liberty of chance, on the other hand, is nothing but the want of that determination, and a certain looseness, which we feel in passing or not passing from the idea of one to that of the other.
>
> (*T* 408)

> We may imagine we feel a liberty in ourselves; but a spectator can commonly infer our actions from our motives and character; and even when he cannot, he concludes in general, that he might, were he perfectly acquainted with every circumstance of our situation and temper, and the most secret springs of our complexion and disposition. Now this is the very essence of necessity, according to the foregoing doctrine.
>
> (*T* 408–9)

These quotations show that Hume has moved far away from his initial Cartesian position that all impressions are self-interpreting and transparent, open to the incorrigible eye of introspection. Now we see that introspection can actually mislead, as the absence of any sense of inner constraint on the will leads us to view it as self-generating. Second, we see an anticipation of the modern view that one's own motivation need not be self-evident, yet be clear to someone well acquainted with one's character and situation. This is a direct consequence of the theory of causation developed in Book 1, which denied that causation consists in what is *observed*, but is a feeling of expectation in the *observer*. In Pall Ardal's words,

> We only need to remind ourselves that necessity does not refer to a quality in the agent, but to a feeling in an observer, to see why

> one could not possibly prove the independence of causal necessity from one's feelings when doing something.
>
> (Ardal 1989: 88)

So Hume regards an action as free when it can be located within a coherent scheme in which behaviour systematically emerges from settled character traits. In other words, the attribution of free action requires that the agent's behaviour *as a whole* be intelligible to others by appeal to a stable set of beliefs and desires and other attitudes. Given that someone is only subject to approval or disapproval for actions deriving from her character, Hume is saying that the liberty of indifference would make one uninterpretable as an agent, and therefore not a moral subject. While Hume writes as if this interpretive strategy is primarily adopted towards someone else, it can also be applied to oneself. This issue will be relevant to Book 3, where the moral perspective is linked with the reflective calm passions of the ideal observer.

For Hume, the freedom of spontaneity is both necessary and sufficient to ground our moral practices, and their concomitant attribution of praise, blame, punishment and reward. Freedom of indifference is impossible, being contrary to the universality of causation. Rather than being a necessary foundation for moral practice, it is in fact incompatible with it, since any mind not governed by Humean necessity would be so unpredictable as to not afford the intrinsic connection between character and intentional behaviour that moral accountability requires. As we shall see in the following chapters, moral approval or disapproval can only be ascribed to character traits. Actions are merely indicators of them, as are volitions, which are closer links in the chain back to these traits. While volitions have no *causal power*, we look to them, together with actions, as reliable indicators of character.

Hume's claim that causal necessity, correctly understood, is a prerequisite of moral accountability is discussed again in the first *Enquiry*, where he adds some interesting comments on its consequences for religion. In the *Treatise*, he had assured his readers that his account of freedom and necessity was 'not only innocent, but even advantageous' (*T* 409) to religion and morality. In the *Enquiry*, he begins by noting that

> There is no method of reasoning more common, and yet none more blameable, than, in philosophical disputes, to endeavour the refutation of any hypothesis, by a pretence of its dangerous consequences to religion and morality. When any opinion leads to absurdities, it is certainly false; but it is not certain that an opinion is false, because it is of dangerous consequence.
>
> (1*E* 96)

As before, he insists that his theories are 'not only consistent with morality, but are absolutely essential to its support' (1*E* 97). However, as Paul Russell points out, he conspicuously avoids saying that it is consistent with *religion*. In fact, he goes on to show that his theories have serious consequences for a traditional Christian conception of God.

The problem goes back to the transitive nature of the causal relation. That is, if A caused B, and B caused C, then A is causally responsible for C. Given that Christians conceive of God as the First Cause, the Creator of the universe, the causal history of everything that has ever happened finally traces back to God. It would follow that since God is the ultimate cause of all human beings, he is equally responsible for all their actions, even those deemed evil. So the Christian is faced with a dilemma:

> Human action, therefore, either can have no moral turpitude at all, as proceeding from so good a cause; or if they have any turpitude, they must involve our Creator in the same guilt, while he is acknowledged to be their ultimate cause and author.
>
> (1*E* 100)

Hume dismisses the first option, seeing it as an example of theoretical speculation utterly at odds with lived experience properly understood. As we shall see in the following chapters, Hume offers a picture of morality as rooted in human nature, with moral judgements being the refined and corrected versions of initial responses to situations seen as pleasurable or painful. Any theory denying the reality of moral distinctions, as would the hypothesis under consideration, ought to be dismissed. Given the natural and unchangeable foundation of our moral responses, such 'remote speculations' could never be accepted once the theorist stepped out from his study. One can no more sincerely deny the existence of moral evil, than someone suffering from gout can be brought to accept that, from a broader perspective, his agonies play an indispensable role in the greater good, in this best of all possible worlds.

The second option fares no better. It suggests that if there is moral evil in the world, as there most certainly is, God must share in the blame for it. But it is surely incompatible with God's nature, as a being with omnipotence, omniscience and perfect moral goodness, to intentionally create evil. Since 'when any opinion leads to absurdities, it is certainly false', Hume must surely be read as saying that this 'problem of evil' refutes claims for the existence of a Christian God.

However, Hume regains his discretion by the end of the section, concluding that

> nor is it possible to explain distinctly, how the Deity can be a mediate cause of all the actions of men, without being the author of sin and moral turpitude. These are mysteries, which mere natural and unassisted reason is very unfit to handle; and, whatever system she embraces, she must find herself involved in inextricable difficulties, and even contradictions, at every step which she takes with regard to such subjects.
>
> (1*E* 103)

His recommendation, as consistent with all his writings, is that the philosopher should leave behind these 'obscurities and perplexities' and

> return, with suitable modesty, to her [i.e., philosophy's] true and proper province, the examination of common life, where she will find difficulties enough to employ her enquiries, without launching into so boundless an ocean of doubt, uncertainty and contradiction!
>
> (1*E* 103)

Reason cannot directly motivate action

Having explained the sense in which our actions are free despite being as causally explicable as anything else in nature, Hume goes on to establish two of his most famous and controversial theses:

1 The exercise of reason is insufficient to motivate action.
2 The notions of rationality and irrationality are not directly applicable to the passions.

From these he pronounces that 'Reason is, and ought only to be the slave of the passions, and can never pretend to any other office than to serve and obey them' (*T* 415). I will start with the first thesis, turning to the second in the following section.

The underlying target of Hume's attack is a picture of human nature, so deeply entrenched as to have been almost invisible, in which the faculties of reason and passion were regarded as essentially in combat with each other; in which virtuous action was seen as emerging from eternal principles of rationality which exist independently of human nature; and where reason functions to control the capricious and distorting passions which, being necessarily contrary to reason and hence to virtue, were seen as a threat to them.

> Nothing is more usual in philosophy, and even in common life, than to talk of the combat of passion and reason, to give the preference to reason, and to assert that men are only so far virtuous as they conform themselves to its dictates.
>
> (*T* 413)

Underlying this picture is the assumption that both reason and passion are, in themselves, sufficient to cause action. That is, they are taken to share a common capacity to control and initiate behaviour, and to be competing over its exercise. Hume denies this assumption, arguing that 'reason alone can never be a motive to any action of the will' (*T* 413), and that its role in the production of action is essentially subsidiary and supportive to that of passion. While it is equally true to say that *passion* alone cannot constitute a motive for action, he will argue that it holds all the executive power, with reason merely working to advise on its use.

As we have seen, the role of reason is to establish facts, whether through a priori demonstrative inferences involving relations of ideas, or by acquiring beliefs through causal inferences grounded in observation. While granting that demonstrative reasoning is *useful*, Hume insists that it cannot be the ultimate source of motivation. To call something useful is to imply the existence of something else that it is useful *for*. So, while a merchant certainly requires arithmetic in doing his accounts, this reasoning is purely a means towards paying his debts or ascertaining his chances of making a profit. Again, 'mechanics are the art of regulating the motions of bodies *to some design'd end or purpose*' (*T* 413–14). That is, reasoning provides the means for satisfying an end that has already been set, such as to build a bridge or a house. In conclusion, since the will is a *practical* capacity, essentially relating to action, whereas demonstrative reasoning deals only with relations between ideas, the only way in which such abstract considerations could influence the will would be by assisting causal inferences: 'Abstract or demonstrative reasoning, therefore, never influences any of our actions, but only as it directs our judgment concerning causes and effects' (*T* 414).

Turning to reasonings based on 'matters of fact', Hume reminds us of the previous conclusions of Book 2. The initial impulse to act is always the experience or anticipation of pain or pleasure. Reason operates only to determine the causal relations relevant to the issue concerned. For example, if I believe that my car engine is overheating, and that the best policy under such circumstances is to pull over and turn it off, then this is what I will do. These beliefs provide means for satisfying my goals, namely to avoid damage to the car, with the correlated danger and subsequent cost and inconvenience, all of which count as pain. In such cases, ' 'tis evident in this case, that the impulse arises not in reason, but is only directed by it' (*T* 414).

The mere recognition that my engine is overheating will not, by itself, motivate me to do anything about it. Even if we add the general knowledge that overheated cars are dangerous, and the inference that if I do not turn the engine off, I could get hurt or cause serious damage to the car, neither these facts nor this inference are sufficient to make me pull over. This requires my fear of an accident, or my desire to avoid unnecessary expense. It is important to note that not only is this causal interaction between my beliefs, desires and inference sufficient to *cause* the action, but that it also *rationalizes* the action. That is, what both causes and makes sense of an action is the interaction between two radically different types of mental states, namely passions and beliefs.

So it is not enough to know that if I do X, then Y will happen. The resulting Y must be seen as either involving or causally related to some actual or anticipated pain or pleasure. 'It can never in the least concern us to know, that such subjects are causes, and such others effects, if both the causes and effects are indifferent to us' (*T* 414). Mere recognition of some empirical fact will not produce any action. Rather, the situation must *matter to us*, either in itself, or as a means to something that does. Either way, it must concern something we want, or want to avoid. In drawing conclusions concerning the prospect of pain or pleasure, reason functions purely in the service of the passions, working out the probability of some goal that is already preordained by passion, or the best means to achieve it. While motivation of the will requires both beliefs and desires, and therefore input from both reason and passion, Hume's theory clearly gives desires a 'structural priority' over beliefs, in setting ends rather than means.

One refinement can be inserted at this point. In my example of the overheating car, you will notice that several desires are involved, some of which emerge in the process of reasoning. My wanting to pull over and turn the engine off is caused by my recognizing this to be the best policy for avoiding the imminent danger, damage and expense. But, in order to make sense of all this, we need to also ascribe long-standing tendencies holding prior to the entire incident, such as the general desire to avoid danger and the rest. Apart from desires emerging within the process of means–ends deliberation, some desires predate all practical reasoning and provide the grounds for it. In other words, even though some desires can be acquired on the basis of beliefs, these rest on other desires for which reasons cannot be given, being desired for their own sake.

Hume is arguing that our passions and reasoning powers are not and cannot be in competition, but play different yet compatible roles which are individually necessary and jointly sufficient for the willing of action. Despite this, he presents passion as having the dominant role, rather than as an equal partner in motivation. This dominance is trenchantly expressed in the *Treatise*, with the Second *Enquiry* and other later works describing the contribution of reason in a far more charitable light. It is still a matter of great controversy how much this is a difference of content or of emphasis. I tend towards the latter view. Once we get past the rhetoric, a careful and comprehensive reasoning of the *Treatise* shows that when Hume says (*T* 458) that reason is 'inert', he's not denying it *any* causal role in motivating the will. Nor, on the other hand, is he merely saying that reason alone is insufficient to cause action, since he clearly holds the same to be true of desire. Rather, he is making a claim about the *structure* of motivation, and denying reason the major role in the genesis of action. He emphasizes the priority of passion because it specifies the goal state, the end, the *point* of the action, regarding which factual knowledge and valid inference can provide the means towards achieving.

It is in this sense that 'reason is, and ought only to be the slave of the passions'. Note that, strictly speaking, the 'ought' clause is redundant in this famous quotation. Since 'ought' implies 'can', it makes no sense to say that one ought to do that which one can do nothing but. Perhaps Hume means something like this: being a good advisor to the passions is the *true function* of reason; that is all it *can do*, and, when functioning correctly, that is what it *does*.

I will close this section by commenting briefly on Hume's remark that not only can reason not motivate an action, but that 'it can never oppose passion in the direction of the will' (*T* 413). At first glance, this inference looks weak. Why does it follow that something cannot oppose an action just because it cannot initiate it? Counterexamples would seem to immediately come to mind. For example, censors cannot make movies, but they can ban them; goalkeepers do not score goals, but they can prevent them, and so on. But this would be to misunderstand Hume's point, which is that to oppose an action is to thereby initiate some other action. For reason and passion to come into conflict, they would both have to be independent sources of motivation, and reason cannot generate action but only *guide* it. Beliefs can therefore neither directly *compete with* nor *overrule* desires, since they lack any original or non-derivative causal power of their own.

In conclusion, by emphasizing the division of labour within the mechanism of motivation, Hume shows that reason and passion cannot be literally said to be in opposition, as competitors in the same line of business, both fighting it out for a prize that only one could win by vanquishing the other. It would make no more sense to say that a car's gas pedal and its steering wheel oppose each other. One's job is to make the car go, the other's job is to make it go in some particular direction, and both are needed to reach the intended destination.

However, the full picture has yet to emerge, since Hume is about to reveal various oblique and indirect strategies by which reason *does* oppose the passions in the direction of the will. The aim of the arguments described above is to show that it cannot do so *directly*. Recall that he views the will as a present-tense phenomenon, as the impression *immediately* preceding action. In the above remarks, Hume is saying that if I want to do X, and form a volition to do X, reason cannot block it with a command not to do X, where this veto would get its power purely from such a rational order. Rather, reason has to work indirectly, *via a change in the desires*. But in such cases reason is not 'working for itself', but only for the passions.

Passions as 'original existents'

Treatise 2/3/3 presents another argument intended to show the respective functions of reason and passion to be too different to allow any literal competition between them. This new argument is that the notions of being rational or irrational, reasonable or unreasonable, cannot literally apply to the passions, but only to beliefs, these being the product of the understanding. When functioning correctly in making good demonstrative and causal inferences, reason yields true conclusions on the basis of true premises. Passions, on the other hand, are neither true nor false, and so cannot conflict with the products of reasoning. This thesis is soon modified, allowing that passions can be considered irrational in a derivative way, when caused by *false beliefs*, whether through factual error or bad reasoning. These views are introduced in the following passage.

> A passion is an original existence, or, if you will, modification of existence, and contains not any representative quality, which renders it a copy of any other existence or modification. When I am angry, I am actually possest with the passion, and in that emotion have no more a reference to any other object, than when I am thirsty, or sick, or more than five foot high. 'Tis impossible, therefore, that this passion can be oppos'd by, or contradictory to truth and reason; since this contradiction consists in the disagreement of ideas, consider'd as copies, with those objects, which they represent.
>
> (*T* 415)

However, Hume is commonly read as making two distinct but related claims in this section, one of which is correct, the other mistaken:

1 Passions, as such, are not truth-evaluable.
2 Passions lack intentional content.

I will begin with the first of these claims, that passions can be neither true nor false, therefore neither rational nor irrational. Hume is right. While it can be true that I am angry, my anger itself cannot be true or false. My anger can, of course, *be caused by* something which is true or false, such as a belief. Since Hume defines reason as 'the achievement of truth or falsehood' (*T* 458), and thereby equates being evaluable as rational (or irrational) with being true or false respectively, it follows that the notion of rationality cannot apply to the passions. We will return to Hume's important amendment to this thesis shortly.

As mentioned above, Hume is typically taken to be making a second, far more controversial claim in this quoted passage, in denying intentional content to passions. (For a dissenting view, see Sayre-McCord 1997.) One thing is certain in this dispute, namely that if Hume *did* hold this position, he ought not to have done. Clearly, I am never just angry *per se* any more than I can have a belief *per se*. Rather, my anger is always directed: I am always angry *at someone*, or *about something*. This brings out a significant difference between primary and secondary impressions. For example, in a case of physical pain, an ache may be *in* my knee, but it is not *about* my knee; it may be *caused by* arthritis, but it is not *about* arthritis; whereas my frustrated anger at being in pain can be about arthritis.

Second, the denial of intentional content to passions is incompatible with the theory of the indirect passions that Hume has spent 125 pages painstakingly developing earlier in Book 2. Although his explicit, 'official' position takes a phenomenological view of these passions, in that they are considered primarily as impressions, and identified and individuated in terms of their 'subjective feel', it is clear when we examine what Hume actually says about these passions that they are states with intentional content. Without this we have no way of distinguishing between different tokens of the same passionate kind. Recall Davidson's remark on the clear difference between pride in my cleverness and in my kindness to kangaroos. So, to repeat, if Hume was denying intentional content to the passions, this claim should be regarded as an oversight, since not only is it incompatible with his general philosophical position, but it is clearly wrong in its own right when applied to the types of passions centrally implicated in his account of motivation.

The denial of content to passions would also be incompatible with Hume's theory of motivation, which requires relations among the contents of beliefs and desires. Although he never explicitly acknowledges this requirement (it being incompatible with parts of his 'official' view), it is clear from his examples. Recall Hume's merchant pondering his accounts. His merely believing that his calculations yield a certain result will not, by itself, motivate any action. Neither would the addition of causal inferences, such that if his expenditure and sales continue at their present rate he will go bust in a matter of months, be sufficient to motivate the will. However, if we add the input of particular passions, such as the desire for a thriving business, this may lead him to cut back on luxuries or, more likely, lay off some workers. Our knowledge of his desire that his business survive would allow us to both predict such actions, and also make sense of them. This example makes it clear that in order to make the behaviour explicable, the science of mind cannot stop at ascribing *just any* desire (or 'desire in general') to the person under scrutiny. The desire, the beliefs and the causal inference must be relevant to each other in a way that requires common content. The accounting, plus the aforesaid inferences, would not result in action when augmented with a desire for the resolution of the Middle East conflict, or for the end of the British monarchy. It has to be a *relevant* desire. *A fortiori*, Hume requires desires to have *some* content.

So, even though he does not (and, indeed, cannot) explicitly say it, it is clear that Hume takes a 'reason for action' as a complex state, involving (1) at least one passion, which sets the aim or purpose of the action, and (2) at least one informational state such as a belief, where these two states are related not merely causally, but via their content, such that the information represented in the belief is relevant to the attainment of the desire.

I now return to Hume's thesis that the passions are not truth-evaluable. As the reader will have come to expect, Hume immediately makes an important amendment to the basic claim. Loosely speaking, we can say that a passion is irrational when it is based on factual errors or faulty reasoning. Suppose I want to drink a six-pack every night because I believe that it will help me retain my trim, boyish waistline. Since it will actually give me a physique like the latter-day Elvis, my dietary regimen may be described as contrary to reason. Still, strictly speaking, it is my belief that is irrational, not the passion itself. Hume could, by the same token, say that passions are *rational* in the same loose derivative sense, if based on correct information and inference:

> passions can be contrary to reason only so far as they are *accompany'd* with some judgment or opinion. According to this principle, which is so obvious and natural, 'tis only in two senses, that any affection can be call'd unreasonable. First, when a passion, such as hope or fear, grief or joy, despair or security, is founded on the supposition of the existence of objects, which really do not exist. Secondly, When exerting any passion in action, we chuse means insufficient for the design'd end, and deceive ourselves in our judgment of causes and effects. When a passion is neither founded on false suppositions, nor chuses means insufficient for the end, the understanding can neither

> justify nor condemn it...In short, a passion must be accompany'd by some false judgment, in order to his being unreasonable; and even then 'tis not the passion, properly speaking, which is unreasonable, but the judgment.
>
> (*T* 416)

This seems to suggest that once I realized that drinking beer would not give me the intended result, my desire to drink would go.

> The moment we perceive the falsity of any supposition, or the insufficiency of any means our passions yield to our reason without any opposition. I may desire any fruit as of an excellent relish; but whenever you convince me of my mistake, my longing ceases.
>
> (*T* 416–17)

A little care has to be taken to preserve a true account here. On the one hand, it is right to say that my desire for beer, when seen as a weight-loss strategy, would cease. In other words, I would not drink *for that reason*. On the other hand, as a man once medically prescribed a pint of claret per day, Hume can comfortably concede that I can continue to desire to drink beer because I like the taste, or just like getting drunk.

We are now in a better position to see what is behind Hume's infamous remark that 'reason is, and ought only to be the slave of the passions'. This is a case where Hume has become the victim of his own literary skills, and his penchant for the memorable soundbite. People all too often focus on the attention-grabbing rhetoric, overlooking the nuances and contextualization behind the remark. The pejorative connotations of 'slave', and Hume's intention to totally undermine rationalism in ethics, have led many to forget his careful and detailed account of the indispensable role of reason in action. I will now propose another metaphor that corresponds better to the big picture that Hume is setting out. Consider the human agent as a company, with passion and reason respectively represented as executors and advisors. Passion (that is, the passions themselves) alone has executive authority to motivate the will and initiate action. However, it is incapable of determining the right thing to do. While it can 'press the button', supplying the final link in the causal chain leading to a volition to act, it relies on advice from a team of experts who can recommend the best way to satisfy its goals. Since a smart director takes the advice of his experts, they can make the executive directorship change its mind on what it wants. If reason tells passion that what it wants cannot be done, or can be done at too much cost, or that its plan is based on inadequate or false information, the executive will revise the plan of action. In other words, while reason *can* oppose passion in direction of the will by providing information that the desire is not viable, or is based on false information, it cannot do so *directly*, but only *via a change in the passions*. It can supply information that can lead to a desire ceasing, or being replaced by another contrary desire. But Hume's main point remains, that reason is relegated to a non-executive advisory role within the mechanics of motivation.

The reader will have noticed a certain awkwardness in my company analogy above, rooted first in Hume's view of the self, where he denied the existence of a permanent self-substance existing apart from patterns of perceptions; and secondly his opposition to any appeal to faculties or powers. No faculties of 'reason' or 'passion' exist over and above individual mental states or processes of reasoning and feeling, any more than a self exists over and above its perceptions, since there is no difference between a power and the exercise of it. So there is no overall 'managing director' in my analogy. Each of the two 'tiers' are collectives, and the bargaining strategy is correspondingly complex. In fact, this picture will need further revision in the light of Hume's account of the calm passions, as we shall see shortly.

Now let us turn to his notorious examples:

> 'Tis not contrary to reason to prefer the destruction of the whole world to the scratching of my finger. 'Tis not contrary to reason for me to chuse my total ruin, to prevent the least uneasiness of an *Indian* or person wholly unknown to me. 'Tis as little contrary to reason to prefer even my own acknowledg'd lesser good to my

> greater, and have a more ardent affection for the former than the latter.
>
> (*T* 416)

Hume does himself no favours with these examples, which do not bring out the strength of his general position, but divert attention from it. Bear in mind that in saying that these desires are 'not contrary to reason', he is not thereby implying that they are rational. As previous paragraphs indicate, he is saying that they are neither rational nor irrational, but *arational*. That is, they are not assessable in terms of truth and falsity, except in the loose and derivative sense discussed above.

It is hard to see how anyone could actually have these preferences without their being caused by some false belief. Try to imagine what would be involved in order to genuinely prefer that the world be destroyed, rather than receive a slight scratch. Ask yourself what it would take to *really mean it*, and not just be mouthing words to be controversial. For one thing, you would need to be able to *back it up* in some way, i.e., 'I prefer this because…' It is hard to see how the details could be filled in – at least within the limits of human psychology – without a plethora of false beliefs. Someone who would prefer global destruction to the receipt of a minor wound would have to believe he could exist apart from this world, such that he would remain unaffected, fingers and all, by its wholesale annihilation. When I imagine how someone could have such a preference, I can only see him as a madman, perhaps with Godlike fantasies. To say the least, such an individual would have rather a distorted perception of his place in the grand scheme of things.

These examples are also incompatible with a basic assumption of Humean psychology, namely that the motive for action involves avoidance of pain, or pursuance of pleasure. In saying that ''tis as little contrary to reason to prefer even my own acknowledg'd lesser good to my greater, and have a more ardent affection for the latter', Hume would seem to be denying the role of reason that he has just staked out. However, a more charitable interpretation might take him to be saying that any such irrationality would be derivative on false beliefs or bad inferences.

Several points must be kept in mind when interpreting these infamous passages. First, Hume regards each perception as a 'distinct existent'. Second, each passion is the particular kind of passion it is due to its 'qualitative feel' rather than due to any causal relations to other states. Although we have seen that he is ambivalent about these theses, his partial acceptance of them would explain why he would regard it as a logical possibility that any desire be causally related to any set of beliefs. While human nature will impose significant limits on which will actually be combined, these limits are contingent facts about us, and do not apply to all possible sentient creatures. So perhaps he is saying that no desire is *necessarily* contrary to reason, since any relation between beliefs and desires is contingent. Thus, with different desires, some creature might be able to will global destruction without falling into factual error or faulty reasoning.

Finally, we need to keep in mind that Hume's primary target is rationalistic ethics. He does not take it as a real possibility that anyone will actually have the strange preferences he describes, since human nature will take care of the slack left by the absence of a priori rules of morality or preference. His point is that these preferences are merely basic facts about the way we are, or the way we do things. They are not reflective of some grand cosmic order of objective mind-independent facts, nor can they be justified or grounded by appeal to any such facts.

A Humean account of motivation

Hume's arguments on the structure of motivation have stimulated as much debate in recent years as any part of the *Treatise*. I wish to briefly indicate how it has been the source and inspiration of recent work in philosophical psychology. While true to Hume's central claim that the role of reason is primarily instrumental and advisory, recent philosophers have excised some of the weaker accompaniments, such as the phenomenalistic and atomistic conception of the passions, or their supposed non-intentionality, leaving us with a powerful theory of motivation. While these amendments mean that this is not *Hume's* theory, it is a direct causal descendant of his work, and so deserves to be called *Humean*.

First, a word on terminology. I will use the expressions 'the Humean theory' and 'the belief-desire theory' interchangeably. They amount to the hypothesis that actions are both caused and explained by the presence of a connected set of beliefs and desires within the agent. Second, in accordance with common practice, I will use the terms 'belief' and 'desire' as exemplars for wide ranges of related states. Thus, the category of 'beliefs' should be understood as covering all informational states, such as of knowing, doubting, suspecting and so on. Likewise, states of hoping, fearing and so on count as desires. The theoretically important distinction is between (1) states that represent particular situations as holding in the world, and (2) goal-directed states; and where these are considered as irreducibly different and separate kinds of mental state.

It is now common to regard thoughts as complex entities made up of (1) a *proposition* and (2) an *attitude* taken to that bearer of content. The content of every proposition corresponds to a possible state of affairs. Beliefs and desires constitute the two most general forms of attitude that can be taken to a proposition. For example, I can *believe* that I will be promoted, and *hope* that this happens. But while a belief and a desire can share a common content, they differ in *how* they relate to this content.

The Humean theory employs a distinction (usually traced to Anscombe (1957)), between two different 'directions of fit' with regard to the world. Beliefs are described as having a *mind-to-world* direction: their job is, and their success depends on, accurately representing the way the world is. They say the world *is* a certain way, and succeed by being *true*; that is, if the world actually contains the state of affairs specified in the proposition believed. The functional role of beliefs in our cognitive system is to represent the world. A belief aims at truth, and a true belief is one that accurately represents the way the world actually is, in some respect specified in the content clause.

Desires, on the other hand, aim at changing the way the world is. They are said to have a *world-to-mind* direction of fit – their subjects want the world to change such as to fit the specified content – and they succeed if the world makes this change. That is, desires succeed not by being *true*, but by being *satisfied*. This distinction is often described as being between *taking* p to be true, and *wanting* p to be true. If I believe that I have won the lottery, my belief is true only if I am the winner; if I want to win the lottery, this desire will be satisfied only by my coming to win it. Whereas a belief is true if the world in fact *is* the way the belief asserts it is, a desire is not satisfied by the way the world is at the time of the desire, but by the world *changing* in some relevant way. Jonathan Dancy makes the same distinction without resort to the 'direction of fit' metaphor, by saying that 'a belief is a state which aims to be caused by the truth of its own content, while a desire is a state which aims to cause its own content to become true' (Dancy 1993: 28).

Michael Smith has developed a theory in which Hume's phenomenological model of the passions is replaced by a dispositional account of desire. On this conception, the different direction of fit between beliefs and desires consists in a difference in functional role:

> a difference in the counterfactual dependence of a belief that p and a desire that p on a perception with the content that not p: a belief that p tends to go out of existence in the presence of a perception with the content that not p, whereas a desire that p tends to endure, disposing the subject to bring about that p.
>
> (Smith 1994: 115)

Consider the difference between *believing* that I am wealthy, and *wanting* to be so. When faced with evidence to the contrary, such as my bank statement, my belief is cruelly shattered, but hope springs eternal in my continuing desire. So the 'direction of fit' metaphor can be cashed in by means of the different inferential relations entered into by a belief and a desire with the same content. If I perceive, and thereby come to believe that not p, I will (or ought to) cease to believe that p, but will not, nor ought not to cease desiring that p. In fact, desiring that p *requires* the belief that not p.

Calm passions

Having shown to his satisfaction that reason cannot motivate the will by itself, Hume acknowledges the need to explain how the contrary thesis has convinced so many able thinkers. He does so by means of the calm passions. Passions are either *calm* or *violent*, depending on their subjective intensity. While calm passions count as passions due to their affective nature, they have no discernible qualitative feel, and 'produce little emotion in the mind, and are more known by their effects than by the immediate feeling or sensation' (*T* 417). A *token* passion is calm if it has a low felt intensity; a *type* of passion is calm if its tokens are typically like this. However, a passion that is typically calm can, on occasion, be violent. For example, I can respond extremely intensely to music.

At the start of Book 2, Hume takes calm passions to include 'the sense of beauty and deformity in action, composition, and external objects', contrasting them with the violence of 'the passions of love and hatred, grief and joy, pride and humility' (*T* 276) and other indirect passions derivative from them. Now, in this later section, he describes them as 'either certain instincts originally implanted in our natures, such as benevolence or resentment, the love of life, and kindness to children, or the general appetite to good, and aversion to evil, consider'd merely as such' (*T* 417). The later discussion makes it clear that calm passions are to be regarded as general tendencies of character, and the suggestion is that these traits become invisible to consciousness by virtue of their sheer familiarity, like one's own smell.

The *violence* of a passion is not the same as its *strength*. While its violence consists in how intensely it is felt, its strength lies in how much it influences our behaviour, and a lack of violence need not imply a lack of strength. Violence is, at best, one dimension of strength, or one factor determining strength. While violent passions can have a strong *immediate* effect on the will due to the vivacity of the impressions involved, they can also be manipulated and diverted. Another more powerful factor in determining the motivating influence a passion may exert is the extent to which it is a settled and regular part of one's mental repertoire. That is, calm passions can overrule the 'momentary gust' of violent passion by virtue of their entrenchment as customs and habits, i.e., by being stable character traits.

> 'Tis evident passions influence not the will in proportion to their violence, or the disorder they occasion in the temper; but on the

> contrary, that when a passion has once become a settled principle of action, and is the predominant inclination of the soul, it commonly produces no longer any sensible agitation. As repeated custom and its own force have made every thing yield to it, it directs the actions and conduct without that opposition and emotion, which so naturally attend every momentary gust of passion. We must, therefore, distinguish betwixt a calm and a weak passion; betwixt a violent and a strong one.
>
> (*T* 418–19)

In this case as in many others, Hume's strategy is to agree with his rationalist opponents on the *phenomenology* of action, but to challenge their *theoretical interpretation* of that data. For example, he can agree that we feel what might be characterized as 'acting from duty', such as when we seem to overrule all our desires and 'do the right thing' not for long-term gain, but just because we regard it as being the right thing to do. Hume grants all this, and reinterprets it as being a case of a calm passion overruling a violent one. Of course, our rational capacities will be engaged in this process, but only in their usual advisory and non-executive role. There are therefore three distinct factors at work in these situations, namely the violent passions, reason and the calm passions. Because the calm passion is working 'behind the scenes', we give *all* the credit to reason, where it ought to be shared. Hume does not conceive of 'strength of mind' as a struggle between two distinct faculties, in which reason succeeds in constraining the desires. Rather, the major struggle takes place *within* the realm of passions (with reason potentially at the service of either), with strength of mind consisting in a settled tendency to act on the basis of calm passions. This adds a new twist to his dictum of reason not opposing the passions: what we falsely attribute to reason is in fact the operation of (calm) passion!

> Hence it proceeds, that every action of the mind, which operates with the same calmness and tranquillity, is confound'd with reason by all those, who judge things from the first view and appearance. Now 'tis certain, that there are certain calm desires and tendencies, which, 'tho they be real passions, produce little

> emotion in the mind, and are more known by their effects than by the immediate feeling or sensation…When any of these passions are calm, and cause no disorder to the soul, they are very readily taken for the determinations of reason, and are suppos'd to proceed from the same faculty, with that, which judges of truth and falshood. Their nature and principles have been suppos'd the same, because their sensations are not evidently different.
>
> (*T* 417)

As Ardal has suggested, our misinterpretation of calm passions may be a cause of the 'false impression of freedom' discussed earlier in this chapter: a violent passion may seem to have necessitating power, and so the absence of any such passion, or its being overruled, may lead us to conclude an absence of mental causation.

Hume's account of the calm passions highlights a deep tension in his theory. On the one hand, as we have seen, he needs the distinction between calm and violent passions in order to reinterpret what is going on when salient passions are overruled. On the other hand, in doing so he makes calm passions 'in a manner, imperceptible', thereby clashing with his 'official' phenomenological model of the passions, by which they are constituted by their subjective qualities. Hume would seem to need an *independent* way to show that calm passions exist, but it is hard to see how he can provide it in a way compatible with his official theory. First, he admits that introspection may not acquaint us with them. Second, his causal theory would seem to disallow any inference to their existence, since any causal inference to their presence on any particular occasion would require us to have had observed them being constantly conjoined with action in similar cases; but, as we have seen, this is what he cannot seem to say. Nor, of course, can their existence be demonstrated a priori.

In saying that calm desires 'are more known by their effects than by the immediate feeling or sensation', Hume looks to be making an *abductive* inference to the existence of calm desires; that is, an inference to the best explanation of the phenomenon of 'acting from duty', and so on. However, this invocation of 'inferred entities' is incompatible with the official line of Book 1, where he has limited himself only to deductive and inductive methods. On the other hand, since his writing is full of such abductive inferences, perhaps we should trust what Hume *does* with his theory, rather than what he *says* about it.

One way out for Hume would be to say that calm passions are *perceivable in principle* even when they are not actually noticed. That is, they are there to be perceived, to be explicitly attended to, in the same way that not everything in the visual field is consciously registered. This might fit well with a theme discussed in 'Of the Standard of Taste' regarding delicacy of sensory discrimination, in which he specifies a refined palate as one that discerns small amounts of some flavour that is mixed up with more prominent ones. So one might say in an analogous manner that the calm passions are there to be seen, but will only be noticed by a trained observer under certain conditions.

Further reading

Paul Russell (1995) is a useful extended treatment of Hume's theory of will in relation to moral responsibility. Francis Snare (1991) includes detailed but technical discussion of Hume's motivational arguments. Highly recommended is John Bricke (1996), particularly chapters 2 and 3. On the contemporary Humean theory of motivation, Michael Smith (1994) is the best entry into an often imposing area.

Chapter 5

Against moral rationalism

Treatise, Book 3, Part 1; 2nd *Enquiry*, Appendix 1

Chapter 5

Introduction

The aim of *Treatise* Section 3/1/1, the most famous of all Hume's writings on morality, is to show that moral distinctions do not derive solely from the understanding, but also require input from the sentiments. He argues that the making of moral judgements consists in the correcting, by reason, of natural sentiments produced via the mechanism of sympathy. I should point out from the start that my use of the expression 'moral judgement' is intended as neutral regarding the dispute between rationalists and moral sense theorists. I will use it interchangeably with 'moral evaluation'.

Given that nothing is 'present to the mind' but impressions and ideas, the question arises '*Whether 'tis by means of our ideas or impressions we distinguish betwixt vice and virtue, and pronounce an action blameable or praiseworthy?*' (*T* 456). How do we come to regard certain actions or character traits as instances of vice or virtue, and to morally condemn or endorse them? Hume fully accepted Locke's thesis that all ideas ultimately derive from impressions. We clearly have *ideas* of virtue and vice; that is, we constantly judge things to be right or wrong, and can no more desist from this practice than we can choose to stop breathing. The centrality of this practice is shown by our use of a well-developed moral vocabulary. Never does Hume suggest that moral discourse is *meaningless*, as his empiricist principles would force him to do if he were to be denying the reality of moral distinctions. But if words and sentences derive their semantic content from the ideas they stand for, the challenge is to locate the source of the meaning of moral judgements within this empiricist edifice. In other words, Hume has to give a causal account of the origin of our ideas of morality.

In line with his usual method, he reframes the issue by not directly inquiring into the nature of virtue and vice, but approaching it obliquely via a description of how we come to acquire the relevant ideas. He begins by asking whether *reason alone* could yield moral distinctions. His conclusion will be that the exercise of reason is necessary but not sufficient to account for the presence of these ideas. In fact, it is often overlooked that he draws the same conclusion regarding the passions. He will argue that the understanding, *if it were to function in isolation from the sensitive, affective aspects of our mental apparatus*, could detect no sensory impressions indicative of virtue or vice. Therefore, ideas of vice or virtue cannot be *directly* caused by sensory impressions in the way that, for example, the idea of a tree may be caused by a visual impression of one. He will also maintain that these moral ideas cannot derive from the exercise of pure demonstrative reason, in any way analogous to mathematical proof.

His positive thesis will be that moral distinctions are rooted in the presence of *secondary* impressions, that is, the *passions*. While these affective responses of pleasure or pain, like or dislike, are the ultimate *basis* of moral judgements, Hume does not adhere to any subjectivism that would seek to *identify* or *reduce* moral judgements to these feelings. Despite common misunderstandings and imaginative interpretations, he never claims that in making a moral judgement one is *reporting* or *expressing* an emotional reaction to events. Either of these responses would only be an initial step in the complex causal process that leads to moral judgement. Being part of the *cause* of moral judgement, they are of course distinct from it. As we shall see, Hume argues that specifically *moral* judgements result from the *correction* of these initial personal and partial responses, a process in which reason plays a number of crucial and essential roles.

I will hold off from a full consideration of Hume's positive theory until the following chapters, devoting the present one to his criticisms of his rationalist opponents. But before I do so, it is good sense to look at the kinds of theory that Hume was attacking, to give the reader a better chance of appreciating Hume's purpose in devoting time to refuting positions which can look arcane to the modern eye. Hence, I propose to make a brief examination of two leading rationalist philosophers, both of whom Hume explicitly identifies as objects of his critique. As we have seen, Hume limited the operation of reason to the making of demonstrative and causal inferences. The first of the two rationalists to be discussed, Clarke, attempts to ground moral distinctions on a priori relations of ideas. The second, Wollaston, tries to base them on empirical matters of fact.

Two rationalists: Clarke and Wollaston

Samuel Clarke (1675–1729) held that there exist certain 'necessary and eternal *different relations*, that different things bear to one another', which entail a '*fitness* or *unfitness* of the application of different things or different relations one to another', and which constitute an objective and categorically binding foundation for moral duties. In describing these relations as 'necessary and eternal', he explicitly compares them to logical or mathematical relations. Actions can be considered 'reasonable' or 'unreasonable' depending on whether this rational apprehension obliges us to practise or refrain from them.

> That there are differences of things, and different relations, respects or proportions, of some things towards others, is as evident and undeniable as that one magnitude or number is greater, equal to, or smaller than another. That from these different relations of different things there necessarily arises an agreement or disagreement of some things with others, or a

> fitness or unfitness of the application of different things or different things one to another, is likewise as plain as that there is any such thing as proportion or disproportion in geometry and arithmetic, or uniformity or disuniformity in comparing together the respective figures of bodies.
>
> Further, that there is a fitness or suitableness of certain circumstances to certain persons, and an unsuitableness of others founded in the nature of things and the qualifications of persons, antecedent to all positive appointment whatsoever; also that from the different relations of different persons one to another there necessarily arises a fitness or unfitness of certain manners of behaviour of some persons towards others, is as manifest as that the properties which flow from the essences of different mathematical figures have different congruities or incongruities between themselves; or that in mechanics certain weights or powers have very different forces and different effects upon one another, according to their different distances or different positions and situations in respect of each other.
>
> (Schneewind 1990: I, 295–6. All Clarke quotations are taken from this volume)

Clarke thought that these matters were self-evident and could not be denied by any honest person who had thought the issues through correctly.

> These things are so notoriously plain and self-evident that nothing but the extremest stupidity of mind, corruption of manners, or perverseness of spirit can possibly make any man entertain the least doubt concerning them. For a man endued with reason to deny the truth of these things is the very same thing as if a man that has the use of his sight should at the same time that he beholds the sun deny that there is any such thing as light in the world…
>
> (1990: I, 296–7)

Clarke's notion of the self-evidence of these fitnesses is subtle enough to avoid the more obvious objections to it, such as that they are not immediately assented to by everyone. To this he counters that even if entire societies were to be ignorant of them, this would no more refute them than would the ignorance of principles of mathematics by some primitive cultures cast any doubt on their necessary status. So he is not saying that these principles are innate, nor that they are immediately and automatically understood by everyone. Rather, he adheres to the Cartesian principle regarding clear and distinct ideas, that when someone takes the time and effort to think it all through – which may require proper instruction and plenty of practice – then he will see the truth with utter clarity. Any mentally competent adult who fails in this achievement has either not had the matter adequately presented to him, or is wilfully resisting acknowledgement through a perverse character.

Clarke opposes the voluntarist thesis that moral obligations originate in the will of God, insisting that both the relations and 'fitnesses' and subsequent obligations are independent of divine fiat. Such a voluntarism would be incompatible with the necessary and eternal nature of moral obligations, since it would make them contingent on divine decision; a decision which could not, without circularity, be morally evaluated. Clarke's position is rather that God, being omniscient and omni-benevolent, necessarily perceives and acts in accordance with these obligations of reason; and that what God necessarily does, we *ought* to do.

> These eternal and necessary differences of things make it *fit and reasonable* for creatures so to act; they cause it to be their *duty*, or lay an *obligation* upon them, so to do; even separate from the consideration of these rules being the *positive will* or *command of God*; and also antecedently to any respect or regard, expectation or apprehension, *of any particular private and personal advantage or disadvantage, reward or punishment*, either present or future; annexed either by natural consequence, or by positive appointment, to the practicing or neglecting of those rules.
>
> (1990: I, 295)

The necessary nature of moral obligation also precludes it from resting on contingent facts of our psychology, whether these be the self-interested impulses emphasized by Hobbes, or the more altruistic ones advocated by the moral sense theorists. Rather, we see these obligations as holding logically prior to any recognition of them. As we shall see, Hume can accept the moral phenomenology; he can agree with Clarke's observation that we feel the force of moral duties as being independent of all desires. He will grant that this is the way it *seems*, but insist that this cannot be the way it *is*. That is, he will offer theoretically compelling reasons for rejecting these appearances.

Hume's primary criticism of the analogies with arithmetic or geometry is that these deductions take place fully within the realm of mathematics. That is, given certain mathematical truths as axioms, other such truths necessarily follow. In the moral case, however, the inference goes from claims regarding abstract relations to a *practical* conclusion about what one *ought to do*. Hume highlights his disanalogy at the end of *T* 3/1/1, when he reports himself surprised to find 'that instead of the usual copulations of propositions, *is*, and *is not*, I meet with no proposition that is not connected with an *ought*, or an *ought not*' (*T* 469).

Clarke gives the example:

> that God is infinitely superior to men is as clear as that infinity is larger than a point, or eternity longer than a moment. And 'tis as certainly fit that men should honour and worship, obey and imitate God, rather than on the contrary in all their actions endeavor to dishonour and disobey him, as 'tis certainly true, that they have an entire dependence on him, and he on the contrary can in no respect receive any advantage from them.
>
> (1990: I, 296)

He thinks that we can see the superiority of God to man just as clearly as we can comprehend the difference between infinity and a point. To think about God is thereby to conceive of the supremely perfect being, who is therefore infinitely superior in all virtues to those that we imperfectly manifest. It is equally apparent, he thinks, that there is an asymmetrical relationship of dependency between God and ourselves: we are totally dependent on God, whereas God is complete in himself and requires nothing from us. He concludes that it self-evidently follows from these facts that we *ought* to worship God. So Clarke is arguing that demonstrative reasoning can both discover moral principles and provide motivation to act on them. Perception of fitness is intrinsically motivational.

However, it has to be said that Clarke's case consists more of assertion than of argument. It is one thing to draw an *epistemological* parallel between mathematical and moral insights in terms of their allegedly self-evident nature. It is quite another to explicitly show how these eternal obligations are *metaphysically* like the necessary truths of mathematics. It is hard to see a clear analogy between anything in moral reasoning or perception and the mathematical relationships of equivalence, proportion or entailment. For example, if the analogy between moral and mathematical axioms is as exact as Clarke says, then, Hume will respond, given that a contradiction results from the denial of certain mathematical inferences, a similar contradiction ought to emerge when someone grants that God exists, but questions whether we ought to worship him. But such a contradiction is not forthcoming. Despite Clarke's claim of self-evidence in this leap from an 'is' to an 'ought', an inference which has no equivalent in the mathematical case, there is no formal contradiction between the conjunction of any statement (like 'God is the creator of the universe') and the denial of an obligation.

Clarke goes on to say that in the same way that God should do what is best for his creation:

> In like manner, in men's dealing and conversing one with another 'tis undeniably more fit...that all men should endeavour to promote the universal good and welfare of all, than that all men should be continually contriving the ruin and destruction of all.
> (1990: I, 296)

This remark brings out Clarke's habit of framing judgements about the fitness of actions in comparative terms. That is, rather than saying that some action is fitting *per se*, he is more likely to compare two options, and claim it to be self-evident that one is more fitting than the other. Hume, as we shall see, would not deny that the promotion of universal welfare is 'reasonable' in the sense that our rationally tempered moral sentiments would approve of it. However, rather than being rooted in the necessary and eternal nature of things, he will argue that our preference for the well-being of ourselves and others is a consequence of basic and contingent facts about human nature, and, more importantly, that our acting on the basis of this judgement cannot be the result of reason alone.

Clarke then gives the 'three great and principal branches' from which all duties derive. The first is the duty to worship God; the second is proper maintenance of our own body and mind; the third concerns others, and focuses on *equity* and the Golden Rule:

> In respect to our fellow-creatures, the rule of righteousness is that in particular we deal with every man as in like circumstances we could reasonably expect he should deal with us; and that in general we endeavour, by an universal benevolence, to promote the welfare and happiness of all men. The former branch of this rule is equity; the latter, is love.
>
> As to the former, viz. equity: the reason which obliges every man in practice so to deal always with another as he would reasonably expect that others should in like circumstances deal with him, is the very same as that which forces him in speculation to affirm that if one line or number be equal to another, that other is reciprocally equal to it. Iniquity is the very same in action as falsity or contradiction in theory: and the same cause which makes the one absurd makes the other unreasonable. Whatever relation or proportion one man in any case bears to another, the same that other, when put in like circumstances, bears to him. Whatever I judge reasonable or unreasonable for another to do for me, that, by the same judgment, I declare reasonable or unreasonable, that I in the like case should do for him.
>
> (1990: I, 303–4)

In the case of equity, Clarke's mathematical analogy becomes more explicit, comparing the 'golden rule' that we should treat others in the same way as we ourselves would like to be treated in such a situation, to the logical relation of symmetry holding within ascriptions of exact similarity (for example, that if line *a* is the same length as line *b*, then line *b* is the same length as line *a*). The two cases are clearly disanalogous, since the moral example makes no appeal to symmetry, but to *consistency* between our own conduct and our expectations of others. Hume would have no quarrel with this 'golden rule', but would insist that both grasping and acting upon it would involve input from the passions as well as reason.

Always keep in mind that Hume can grant much of the moral phenomenology that rationalists stress. He agrees that we tend to act in the way that the rationalists' obligations require, that we have a capacity to step back from self-interest, to universalize judgements, and so on. His point is that in doing so, we go beyond what reason alone can do, and that what *appears* to be the purely cognitive recognition of objective obligations is really something else. Hume's negative tactic is to probe the rationalist claims deeper, and finds only error or obscurantism. For example, nowhere does Clarke explain, with the certitude of a mathematical proof, how obligation is a necessary consequence of certain facts or relations.

Clarke holds that the *will* can directly make us do what our reason tells us is obligatory, and suggests that this is the natural state of man, unless he is corrupted by 'negligent misunderstanding and wilful passions or lusts' (1990: I, 299). In the absence of these flaws, the mere recognition of these eternal relations will supposedly yield moral beliefs, such that we will see their obligatory nature in the very act of understanding them, and thereby come to act on them.

> And by this understanding or knowledge of the natural and necessary relations, fitnesses, and proportions of things, the wills likewise of all intelligent beings are constantly directed and must needs be determined to act accordingly, excepting those only who will things to be what they are not and cannot be; that is, whose wills are corrupted by particular passion or affection, or swayed by some unreasonable and prevailing passion.
>
> (1990: I, 299)

This claim is the target of Hume's deepest cut. The arguments denying the existence of these eternal relations, or on the obscurantism of the rationalist position, are secondary issues. His knock-down argument is to say that even if such necessary and eternal relations existed, mere recognition of them would be insufficient to motivate action. For that, we would need some *desire*, moral or otherwise. We have seen Hume's general theory of motivation in the previous chapter, and its application to morality will be discussed later in the present chapter.

Another rationalist, strongly influenced by Clarke, was William Wollaston (1659–1724). In his only published work, *The Religion of Nature Delineated* (1722), Wollaston attempts to prove the objective and eternal nature of moral obligation by basing the distinction between vice and virtue on that between truth and falsity. He starts off by giving a standard correspondence theory of truth, namely that a sentence is true if things are the way it says they are. Sentences have a specific content, or 'significance', and a sentence is true when the world accords with the content that is asserted to hold.

> *Those propositions are true, which express things as they are: or, truth is the conformity of those words or signs, by which things are expressed, to the things themselves*, Defin.
>
> (Raphael 1991: 240. All quotations from Wollaston are from this volume)

However, *actions* are also meaningful, and can therefore be true or false. The idea here seems to be that people, in performing some non-verbal actions, are asserting or 'saying' by their very performance that certain things are the case. For example, by taking your wallet and spending your money, I am thereby falsely 'saying', in this expanded sense, that this money is mine to spend. Likewise, if I attempt to purchase something using your credit card, I am 'saying' that I am you.

> *A true proposition may be denied, or things may be denied to be what they are, by deeds, as well as by express words or another proposition*...There are many kinds of *other* acts, such as constitute the character of a man's conduct in life, which have *in nature*, and would be taken by any indifferent judge *to have a signification*, and *to imply some proposition*, as plainly to be understood as

> if it was declared in words: and therefore if what such acts declare to be, is not, they must *contradict truth*, as much as any false proposition or assertion can.
>
> (1991: 240)

Omissions (that is, failures to act) can be equally granted content. Thus, if I promise to pay you back some money tomorrow, and then deliberately fail to show up, my absence is thereby 'saying' that this promise never took place. Similarly,

> should I, having leisure, health and proper opportunities, read nothing, nor make any inquiries in order to improve my mind, and attain such knowledge as may be useful to me, then I should deny my mind to be what it is, and that knowledge to be what it is.
>
> (1991: 247)

At times, Wollaston seems to go even further to suggest that actions are the primary bearers of meaning and truth, with that of sentences being derivative from them. His argument is that, '*Words* are but *arbitrary signs* of our ideas, or indications of our thoughts'. That is, the semantic properties of public language sentences are arbitrarily related to, and dependent on, the intrinsic content of thoughts. By contrast, the relationship between thought and action is not the conventional association between two distinct things, but rather a far more intimate relation, whereby the action is the thought made public, translated and embodied in behaviour: '*the thoughts themselves produced into act*; as the very conceptions of the mind brought forth and grown to maturity; and therefore as the most natural and express representations of them' (1991: 243).

Wollaston complicates his position in acknowledging that certain acts have their significance through human convention, accurately noting that the mark of such conventional acts is that some *other* practice could have worked just as well. For example, in Judaism it is regarded as a sign of worship for a man to wear a hat while in prayer; in Christianity this same respect is shown by being hatless. The idea is that Jews would be blaspheming through being men without hats in certain situations, and 'saying' by this bareheadedness the falsehood that God ought not to be worshipped. However, he concedes, the relation between this action itself and its meaning and subsequent falsity is grounded in human decision, and therefore on contingencies.

Still, Wollaston insists that there are other actions whose meaning is intrinsic, not mediated by convention, and the same in all societies. Such acts 'have an *unalterable* signification, and can by no agreement or force ever be made to express the contrary to it'. He never explicitly tells us his rule for distinguishing the two kinds of actions, sufficing with examples such as theft or the breaking of promises. Suppose I make a promise to repay you some money tomorrow. This puts me under an obligation to return the money. By not paying you, I deny my obligation to you. In being inconsistent with the fact of the obligation, my action constitutes a falsehood.

> If *A* should enter into a compact with *B*, by which he *promises* and engages never to do some certain thing, and after this he does that thing: in this case it must be granted, that his act *interferes* with his promise, and is contrary to it. Now it cannot interfere with his promise, but it must also interfere with the truth of that *proposition*, which says there was such a promise made, or that there is such a compact subsisting. If this proposition be true, *A made such a certain agreement with B*, it would be denied by this, *A never made any agreement with B*. Why? Because the truth of this latter is *inconsistent* with the agreement asserted in the former.
>
> (1991: 241)

Wollaston concludes by saying that

> I lay this down then as a fundamental maxim, *that whoever acts as if things were so, or not so, doth by his acts declare, that they are so, or not so*; as plainly as he could by words, and with more reality. And if the things are otherwise, his acts contradict *those propositions*, which assert them to be as they are…*No act* (whether word or deed) *of any being, to whom moral good and evil are imputable, that interferes with any true proposition, or denies any thing to be as it is, can be right*. [For] If that proposition, which is false, be wrong,

> that act which *implies* such a proposition, or is founded in it, cannot be right: because it is the very proposition itself in practice.
>
> (1991: 243–4)

The next stage in the argument is to claim that truth and falsity covary, respectively, with virtue and vice. '*Moral good and evil are coincident with right and wrong*', or in other words, expressing a falsehood is a necessary and sufficient condition for committing vice. Clearly Wollaston is placing the true–false dichotomy in the privileged position in this relationship: an action is wrong *because* it embodies or entails a falsehood.

Taking stock, we have the claim that certain actions are wrong because they 'say' or 'mean' something that is false. Hence my reneging on a promise is wrong because it falsely denies that I made the promise in the first place. But, one might object, all that this sort of case shows is an incompatibility between two actions, such that they cannot both be true. But if action Y is found vicious because it contradicts action X, then X must already be virtuous. Without this assumption, why assign the vice to one of the incompatible pair rather than to the other? In other words, to say that promise-breaking is wrong because it denies the making of a promise is to *presuppose* the morality of promise-keeping. Only if some actions are already virtuous can something else be wrong through being incompatible with them. But then what grounds this initial moral value? Hume makes this point in a footnote:

> Besides, we may easily observe, that in all those arguments there is an evident reasoning in a circle. A person who takes possession of another's goods, and uses them as his own, in a manner declares them to be his own; and this falshood is the source of the immorality of injustice. But is property, or right, or obligation, intelligible, without an antecedent morality? A man that is ungrateful to his benefactor, in a manner affirms, that he never received any favours from him. But in what manner? Is it because 'tis his duty to be grateful? But this supposes, that there is some antecedent rule of duty and morals.
>
> (*T* 462)

Another place where the question-begging nature of Wollaston's argument becomes apparent is when he acknowledges that truth and falsity are not subject to degrees. That is, he correctly holds that sentences are either true or false, but cannot be more or less true (or false) than another. His problem is that he also holds the plausible view that some actions are morally worse than others, such that 'the crimes committed by the violation of one of them may be equally said to be crimes, but not *equal crimes*'. This disanalogy would seem to create a serious problem for his attempt to ground the distinction between moral rightness and wrongness on that between truth and falsity. He attempts to deal with this anomaly by saying that some actions violate *more truths* than others; and that some actions violate *more important* truths than others. But, of course, to classify some truths as more important than others requires a criterion of importance which is separate from truth, and this Wollaston never provides.

It is at this point that we see the force of Hume's simple observation that culpability does not covary with falsehood, since there are many cases of error in which no vice is imputed. As I write this, I am making a number of errors, due to imperfect typing abilities and lack of concentration. That is why Divine Providence provided me with a spell-check program. But I am, according to Wollaston, thereby 'saying' that words are spelled in ways which they are not. However, even the most monkish of moralists would hesitate before condemning me for this. Hume places the burden on Wollaston to say *which* errors are blameworthy, and to do so in a way compatible with his original position of deriving immorality from error. In this criticism, Hume was following Hutcheson, who gently reminded his opponents of the blamelessness of one who elects 'to leave lights in a lodge, to make people conclude there is a watch kept' (1971: 143).

Hume also points out that Wollaston's view rests on the unargued assumption that there is something morally wrong with being in error in the first place. But anyone who holds this cannot, without begging the question, explain the immorality of falsity as being due to its falsehood. As Hume says in the same footnote,

> But what may suffice entirely to destroy this whimsical system is, that it leaves us under the same difficulty to give a reason why

> truth is virtuous and falshood vicious, so as to account for the merit or turpitude of any other action. I shall allow, if you please, that all immorality is derived from this supposed falshood in action, provided you can give me any plausible reason, why such a falsehood is immoral. If you consider rightly of the matter, you will find yourself in the same difficulty as at the beginning.
>
> (*T* 462)

Wollaston's account must be understood in its theological context. Consider the following passages, where he moves with astounding swiftness from truth-as-correspondence to a far stronger thesis whereby 'the nature of things' itself dictates that some actions are right, and others wrong, depending on whether they accord with these facts. He ends up saying that certain actions deny that things are the way they are (as in previous examples of theft or promise-breaking) and, in doing so, constitute a challenge to God himself, since everything that happens must accord with God's will.

> Those propositions, which are true, and express things as they are, express the *relation* between the subject and the attribute as it is: that is, this is either affirmed or denied of that according to the nature of *that relation*. And further, this relation is determined and fixed by the natures of the things themselves. Therefore nothing can interfere with any proposition that is true, but must likewise interfere with nature (the nature of the relation, and the natures of the things too), and consequently be *unnatural*, or *wrong in nature*...If there is a supreme being, upon whom the existence of the world depends; and nothing can be in it but what he either causes, or permits to be, then to own things *to be as they are* is to own what he causes, or at least permits, *to be thus caused or permitted*: and this is to take things as he gives them, to go into his constitution of the world, and to submit to his will, revealed in the books of nature. To do this therefore must be agreeable to *his will*. And if so, the contrary must be disagreeable to it, and since there is perfect rectitude in his will, certainly *wrong*.
>
> (1991: 244)

> As the owning of things, in all our conduct, *to be as they are*, is direct obedience: so the contrary, not to own things *to be* or *to have been* that are or *have been*, or not *to be what they are*, is direct rebellion against him, who is the Author of nature. For it is as much to say God indeed causes such a thing to be, or at least permits it, and it is; or the relation, that lies between this and that, is of such a nature, that one may be affirmed of the other, etc.; this is true, but yet *to me* it shall *not* be so.
>
> (1991: 245)

Be that as it may, we are still no farther along in determining the source of moral distinctions unless we know why God regards certain acts with approval, and not others. As before, if one says that some act is wrong because it contradicts or is incompatible with some natural facts, we still need to know why moral virtue is located in *these* facts rather than others. That is, we need to know precisely what it is about certain facts or relations that God, in his infinite wisdom, is responding to.

At times Wollaston comes closer to Clarke, as when he says that moral virtue and vice depend on their respective compatibility or incompatibility with axioms and 'eternal truths':

> Things cannot be denied to be what they are…without contradicting axioms and truths eternal. For such are these: *every thing is what it is*; *that which is done, cannot be undone*…If there are such things as axioms, which are and always have been immutably true, and consequently have always been known to God to be so, the truth of them cannot be denied in any way…but the truth of the divine knowledge must be denied too. Lastly, to deny things to be as they are is a transgression of the *great law of nature*, the law of reason. For truth cannot be opposed, but reason must be violated.
>
> (1991: 245)

However, it is hard to see why my stealing your wallet is more or less compatible with '*every thing is what it is*', or '*that which is done, cannot be undone*', than would be my returning it. Granted, everything is what it is; so stealing is stealing, and breaking a promise is breaking a promise. Agreed, what is done cannot be undone; but one can no more turn back the clock and erase the *keeping* of a promise than a *breaking* of it.

Wollaston runs into another objection when Hume points out that all his examples of non-conventional relations between actions and moral vice or virtue are, in fact, 'artificial', and grounded in convention. To take a more modern example, suppose I pass your credit card off as mine, and thereby 'say' that it is mine. Wollaston would seem to require the existence of facts, *in the nature of things*, such as that '*z* is *x*'s property', and prescriptions like 'if *z* is *x*'s property, *y* ought not to take *z* without *x*'s permission'. He needs to assume the necessary relationship between facts and obligations. If this were granted, then the individual obligations would follow, by virtue of their membership of that class of actions. As we shall see in the following chapter, Hume will show that any such facts, and subsequent obligations, require the intervention of a convention no less than the cases involving the wearing of hats in religious worship, or the avoidance of pork.

Finally, Wollaston's theory is clearly vulnerable to Hume's arguments concerning the nature of motivation, with the familiar point that the mere belief or recognition that an act is somehow imbued with falsity cannot by itself provide any motivating power to desist from it.

Morals and motives

One line of thought which Hume regards as sufficient to refute the grounding of morality in reason alone rests on the argument of *T* 2/3/3 that there is always a gap between cognitively *recognizing* some fact and coming to *act* on it. This gap cannot be filled by the presence of beliefs alone, but requires input from the passions. If this general argument is correct, it follows *a fortiori* that acting *morally* cannot be motivated solely by reason. Since moral considerations *can* motivate us to action, they cannot consist only of the materials that reason operates with. 'Morals excite passions, and produce or prevent actions. Reason of itself is utterly impotent in this particular. The rules of morality, therefore, are not conclusions of reason' (*T* 457).

Hume's target is any form of moral rationalism claiming that when we act from a sense of moral obligation – doing something because we judge it to be the right thing to do – our action is both caused and rationally explained by the presence of beliefs alone. For example, suppose I see your wallet falling out of your pocket, and return it to you. A rationalist might explain my action by saying that I believe that *stealing is wrong*, and that my holding onto your wallet would be a case of theft. By this account, my returning your wallet was both causally and rationally explained by the interaction of these two beliefs, and that what made my action *moral* was the presence of the former belief, with its explicitly evaluative content. Since, on this rationalist perspective, all the causal components leading to my action are beliefs, they are all either true or false. Assuming that it is true that stealing is wrong, were I to have stolen your wallet I would have failed to conform to a moral fact. The wrongness of stealing would be regarded as a rule from which it could be deduced that *my* stealing is wrong, and which would *oblige* me, and everyone else, not to steal. It is clear from this depiction that moral rationalism is committed to saying that moral features (for example, obligation) are objective, mind-independent properties of actions, but which are also practical. Moral rightness or wrongness consists in succeeding in or failing to conform to a moral truth.

As we have seen in many previous cases, Hume can grant that the phenomenology is on the side of the rationalist, since it often seems to us as if we act on the basis of such 'moral beliefs'. However, he is attempting a revision of common sense in the light of theoretical considerations, arguing that no mere intellectual recognition of morally relevant facts is sufficient to motivate action. He adds that since reason cannot *motivate* morality, neither can it *discover* what morality consists in: 'As long as it is allow'd, that reason has no influence on our passions and actions, 'tis vain to pretend, that morality is discover'd only by a deduction of reason. An active principle can never be founded on an inactive' (*T* 457).

One might reply that this last inference looks weak; after all, reason alone cannot motivate a student to do his algebra homework, but it does not follow that mathematical truths are not discovered by reason. However, such a response would miss the acuity of Hume's position, and the significant difference between the two cases. Hume is adopting what is now called *internalism*, the view that the making of a moral judgement, by its very nature, has some motivating influence on action. For example, one cannot genuinely accept some action is morally wrong without having some motive (which need not be overriding) to refrain from it. Since reason is motivationally inert, restricted to 'the discovery of truth and falsehood', whereas moral considerations are essentially motivational, the 'discovery of morality' cannot be the sole preserve of reason.

Hume then repeats his subsidiary argument from *T* 2/3/3 that passions are not the sort of thing that can be true or false, so cannot be related in any way that involves truth-values, such as contrariety, implication, and so on. This latter point, he says, proves directly what the previous argument proves more indirectly, that rightness cannot consist in conformity to reason.

> Reason is the discovery of truth and falshood. Truth or falshood consists in an agreement or disagreement either to the *real* relations of ideas, or to *real* existence and matter of fact. Whatever, therefore, is not susceptible of this agreement or disagreement, is incapable of being true or false, and can never be an object of our reason. Now 'tis evident our passions, volitions, and actions, are not susceptible of any such agreement or disagreement; being original facts and realities, compleat in themselves, and implying no reference to other passions, volitions and actions. 'Tis impossible, therefore, they can be pronounced either true or false, and be either contrary or conformable to reason.
>
> This argument is of double advantage to our present purpose. For it proves *directly*, that actions do not derive their merit from a conformity to reason, nor their blame from a contrariety to it; and it proves the same truth more *indirectly*, by shewing us, that as reason can never immediately prevent or produce any action by contradicting or approving of it, it cannot be the source of the distinction betwixt moral good and evil, which are found to have that influence. Actions may be laudable or blameable; but they cannot be reasonable or unreasonable. Laudable or blameable, therefore, are not the same with reasonable or unreasonable. The

> merit and demerit of actions frequently contradict, and sometimes control our natural propensities. But reason has no such influence. Moral distinctions, therefore, are not the offspring of reason. Reason is wholly inactive, and can never be the source of so active a principle as conscience, or a sense of morals.
>
> (*T* 458)

The Second *Enquiry* provides another angle on this argument. Hume has already shown that usefulness is a means–end relation, such that to call something useful commits you to regarding something else as valuable in its own right, and for which no justification can be given. For example, there is no reason *why* we want happiness, or do not like pain. Indeed, none would be intelligible.

> It appears evident that the ultimate ends of human actions can never, in any case, be accounted for by *reason*, but recommend themselves entirely to the sentiments and affections of mankind, without any dependence on the intellectual faculties. Ask a man *why he uses exercise*; he will answer, *because he desires to keep up his health*. If you then enquire, *why he desires health*, he will readily reply, *because sickness is painful*. If you push your enquiries farther, and desire a reason *why he hates pain*, it is impossible he can ever give any. This is an ultimate end, and is never referred to in any other object...It is impossible there can be a progress *in infinitum*; and that one thing can always be a reason why another is desired. Something must be desirable on its own account, and because of its immediate accord or agreement with human sentiment or affection.
>
> (Second *Enquiry* [2*E*] 293)

The foundations of virtue are equally basic: Why do we approve of things that are useful to ourselves? Why do we regard it as praiseworthy to be useful to others?

> Now as virtue is an end, and is desirable on its own account, without fee or reward, merely for the immediate satisfaction which it conveys; it is requisite that there should be some senti-

ment which it touches, some internal state or feeling, or whatever you may please to call it, which distinguishes moral good and evil, which embraces the one and rejects the other.

(2*E* 293)

Demonstrative reasoning cannot ground morality

The following two sections will elaborate on the critiques of rationalism touched on in the discussions of Clarke and Wollaston. Since the work of the understanding consists in either the comparison of ideas or in the discovery or inference of empirical facts, then, if reason were capable of discovering moral distinctions, 'the character of virtuous or vicious must either lie in some relations of objects, or must be a matter of fact, which is discovered by our reasoning' (*T* 463). Hume will show that neither possibility holds. This section will focus on attempts to ground moral distinctions in relations of ideas, leaving matters of fact to the next one. When Hume considers whether moral differences can be demonstrated a priori to be grounded in the 'eternal immutable fitnesses and unfitnesses of things', he concludes that no intelligible and correct reformulation of this obscurity can be provided. He ends by contrasting the clarity and checkability of his own theory. Any a priori foundation for moral differences would have to be based on *relations of ideas*, and Book 1 had claimed only four such demonstrable relations to exist, namely resemblance, contrariety, degrees of quality, and proportions in quantity and number. To prove an action immoral, the idea of vice would have to be deducible from some formal relation pertaining to the action itself. But this claim is at best vague, and at worst incomprehensible.

In the Second *Enquiry*, Hume describes an attempt to deduce the immorality of ingratitude from the relation of contrariety, showing that the mere fact that such a relation holds between actions is insufficient to locate vice or virtue. Suppose two actions to derive from the contrary character traits of good-will and ill-will. The problem is that contrariety is a symmetrical relation: if *p* is contrary to *q*, then *q* is contrary to *p*. Thus, merely knowing that two traits are contraries, and that one of them is vicious, cannot tell us *which* one; it does not enable us to attach the vice to *p* or to *q*.

> In the case stated above, I see first good-will and good-offices in one person; then ill-will and ill-offices in the other. Between these, there is a relation of *contrareity*. Does the crime consist in that relation? But suppose a person bore me ill-will or did me ill-offices; and I, in return, were indifferent towards him, or did him good offices. Here is the same relation of *contrareity*; and yet my conduct is often highly laudable. Twist and turn this matter as much as you will, you can never rest the morality on relation; but must have recourse to the decisions of sentiment.
>
> (2*E* 288)

Hume then confronts a problem affecting all four demonstrable relations, namely that the rationalist has no way to limit the application of moral attributes to rational beings. The same supposedly wicked relationships equally apply to events involving non-rational and non-sentient things, such as animals and plants, to which moral considerations surely cannot apply. Incest, for example, can occur between humans, non-human animals or inanimate life-forms such as trees. The point, of course, is that such relations among ideas are purely *formal*, with no intrinsic application to any particular subject-matter, and so can preclude none either. Thus, if vice consisted in the presence of that relation, then it must hold equally in *all* instantiations of that relation. However, such a result is preposterous, since we do not apply moral judgements to animals or plants, and therefore these formal relations cannot be the source of moral distinctions in the human case either.

> If you assert, that vice and virtue consists in relations susceptible of certainty and demonstration, you must confine yourself to those *four* relations, which alone admit of that degree of evidence; and in that case you run into absurdities, from which you will never be able to extricate yourself. For as you make the very essence of morality to lie in the relations, and as there is no one of these relations but what is applicable, not only to an irra-

> tional, but also to an inanimate object; it follows, that even such objects must be susceptible to merit and demerit. *Resemblance, contrariety, degrees of quality*, and *proportions in quantity and number*; all these relations belong as properly to matter, as to our actions, passions, and volitions.
>
> (*T* 463–4)

> Inanimate objects may bear to each other all the same relations which we observe in moral agents; though the former can never be the object of love or hatred, nor are consequently susceptible of merit or iniquity. A young tree, which over-tops and destroys its parent, stands in all the same relations with Nero, when he murdered Agrippina; and if morality consisted merely in relations, would no doubt be equally criminal.
>
> (2*E* 293)

The rationalist might then object that the moral difference between these cases is due to the fact that humans, unlike animals, can *perceive* or *discover* the wrongness of the act. Hume responds that such a response is inconsistent with the original rationalist premise that the immorality of incest was due to the relationship involved. Such an objection would tacitly concede Hume's point that the immorality cannot *consist in* the existence of the incest relation, since any talk of discovering or perceiving wrongness presupposes an independent criterion of the wrongness being perceived.

> If it be answer'd, that this action is innocent in animals, because they have not reason sufficient to discover its turpitude; but that man, being endow'd with that faculty, which *ought* to restrain him to his duty, the same action becomes criminal to him; should this be said, I would reply, that this is evidently arguing in a circle. For before reason can perceive this turpitude, the turpitude must exist; and consequently is independent of the decisions of our reason, and is their object more properly than their effect.
>
> (*T* 467)

If we say that animals are not to be blamed because they lack the reason with which to recognize the 'turpitude', then this is to assume that this turpitude exists to be discovered, independently of the detective capacities of reason. But then if it exists, the animals are guilty, despite not recognizing it. In sum, saying that reason discovers moral distinctions presupposes some other source of those distinctions, which reason then identifies. You can only discover something if it is already there to be discovered. The rationalists have yet to account for this prior existence. 'Their want of a sufficient degree of reason may hinder them from perceiving the duties and obligations of morality, but can never hinder these duties from existing; since they must antecedently exist, in order to their being perceiv'd' (*T* 468).

If, on the other hand, the rationalist claims that some *other* demonstrable relation grounds moral distinctions, then he must tell us what it is. However, he has his work cut out, since such a relation will have to be such as to apply only to rational agents, and would also have to be intrinsically motivational, so that any rational agent who grasps it will thereby be motivated by this understanding alone to act morally.

Hume argues that mathematical and moral reasoning are importantly disanalogous. For example, if I know that a figure comprises three straight lines enclosing a space, I can establish that the sum of the interior angles is 180 degrees. If I know that the square of the longest side is equivalent to the sum of the squares of the other two sides, then I can work out that one of the interior angles measures 90 degrees. In sum, mathematical facts generate other results of the same kind. By contrast, moral rightness or wrongness depends on *all* the natural facts – but once all these facts are in, and all the relations between them worked out, there is no more for reason to do. It would follow, then, that the final step in the production of a moral judgement comes not from reason, but from sentiment.

> A speculative reasoner concerning triangles or circles considers the several known and given relations of the parts of these figures; and thence infers some unknown relation, which is dependent on the former. But in moral relations we must be acquainted beforehand with all the objects, and all their relations to each other; and from a comparison of the whole, fix our choice

> or approbation. No new fact to be ascertained; no new relation to be discovered. All the circumstances of the case are supposed to be laid before us, ere we can fix any sentence of blame or approbation. If any material circumstance be yet unknown or doubtful, we must first employ our inquiry or intellectual faculties to assure us of it; and must suspend for a time all moral decision or sentiment.
>
> (2*E* 289)

Notice that Hume says that until that point, we 'must suspend for a time all moral decision or sentiment'. This illustrates how far he is from any simple subjectivism, since any basic untutored response is not the sort of thing that could, on principle, suspend itself. As we shall see, moral judgement can be suspended because of the involvement of reason in its creation, it being the last link in a complex chain of three-way interaction and readjustment between reason, imagination and passion.

The Second *Enquiry* draws an analogy between moral and aesthetic appreciation. While an object's beauty *depends* on its physical properties and relations, such as proportions, size, and so on, appreciation of this beauty does not consist in an intellectual grasp of these factors. Reason grasps the grounding features but not the beauty itself, which is felt as a consequence of this apprehension.

> This doctrine will become still more evident, if we compare moral beauty with natural, to which in many particulars it bear so near a resemblance. It is on the proportion, relation, and position of the parts, that all natural beauty depends; but it would be absurd thence to infer, that the perception of beauty, like that of truth in geometrical problems, consists wholly in the perception of relations, and was performed entirely by the understanding or intellectual faculties. In all the sciences, our mind from the known relations investigates the unknown. But in all decisions of taste or external beauty, all the relations are beforehand obvious to the eye; and we thence proceed to feel a sentiment of complacency or disgust, according to the nature of the object, and disposition of our organs.

> Euclid has fully explained all the qualities of the circle; but he has not in any proposition said a word of its beauty. The reason is evident. The beauty is not a quality of the circle. It lies not in any part of the line, whose parts are equally distant from a common centre. It is only the effect which that figure produces upon the mind, whose peculiar fabric of structure renders it susceptible of such sentiments.
>
> (2*E* 291–2)

Nothing can possess *only* the property of being beautiful. If I judge an object to be beautiful, then its beauty is dependent on its material and/or structural properties, and it could not be beautiful in the absence of *any* such properties of that kind. Another aspect of this dependency is that changes in these properties might result in an increase, decrease or removal of its beauty, at least in the estimation of some observer. Again, if I judge that some object is beautiful, I am committed to saying that any other object sharing all its material and structural properties is equally beautiful. All this is compatible with saying, as Hume would want to say, that I may judge something to be beautiful at one time, and later decide that it was not as good as I thought, despite its other properties remaining the same. This difference in judgement would be down to a change in my sensibility, which may have been due to some change in my reasoning.

Finally, even if these objections could be overcome, the rationalist would still face Hume's earlier point that even if we could perceive some rationalistic basis of moral distinctions, mere recognition of such facts would be insufficient to motivate action. So Hume is offering the reader a choice between, on the one hand, a clear and testable theory, and a rationalism cloaked in obscurity, advancing

> an abstruse hypothesis, which can never be made intelligible, not quadrate with any particular instance or illustration. The hypothesis which we embrace is plain. It maintains that morality is determined by sentiment. It defines virtue to be *whatever mental action or quality gives rise to a spectator the pleasing sentiment of approbation*; and vice the contrary. We then proceed to examine a plain matter of fact, to wit, what actions have this influence. We

consider all the circumstances in which these actions agree, and thence endeavour to extract some general observations with regard to these sentiments. If you call this metaphysics, and find anything abstruse here, you need only conclude that your turn of mind is not suited to the moral sciences.

(2*E* 289)

Factual error cannot be the source of immorality

In refuting the claim that moral culpability consists in factual error, Hume begins by simply pointing out that error is not *always* regarded as morally reprehensible, and that we sometimes *pity* people for error rather than blame them. So the rationalist needs to specify which kinds of error constitute immorality:

> 'tis easy to observe, that these errors are so far from being the source of all immorality, that they are commonly very innocent, and draw no manner of guilt upon the person who is so unfortunate as to fall into them. They cannot extend beyond a mistake of *fact*, which moralists have not generally suppos'd criminal, as being perfectly involuntary. I am more to be lamented than blam'd, if I am mistaken with regard to the influence of objects in producing pain or pleasure, or if I know not the proper means of satisfying my desires.
>
> (*T* 459–60)

Of course, Hume could admit that sometimes we do, and ought to, blame someone for their error, such as when negligence is involved. However, this condemnation would be because we believe that the person ought to have known certain factors of which they are ignorant. So, in such cases, the blame is not due to the mere fact of error, but to dereliction of duty.

Second, as mentioned in the discussion of Wollaston, Hume notes that the distinction between truth and falsity is strict, not subject to degrees, so that to call something 'partly true' is misleading. Granted, there is a loose sense in which one claim can be 'closer to the truth' than another; for example, if you say that 2 + 2 = 5, and I say that 2 + 2 = 6, then your answer was *closer to* the correct answer. Still, the first answer is no more true, since both are equally false. One could add that a *theory* can only be 'partly true' in the sense of comprising some true statements and some false ones. Hence, a theory can be 'more true' than another only in the above sense, or in that it contains more true statements (or less false ones) than its competitor. This result is bad news for the rationalist, since if the distinction between right and wrong actions were based on the true/false distinction, we would have the patently false result that all immoral actions, being equally false, would be equally wrong.

> And here it may be proper to observe, that if moral distinctions be deriv'd from the truth or falshood of those judgments, they must take place wherever we form the judgments, nor will there be any difference, whether the question be concerning an apple or a kingdom, or whether the error be avoidable or unavoidable. For as the very essence of morality is suppos'd to consist in an agreement or disagreement to reason, the other circumstances are entirely arbitrary, and can never either bestow on any action the character of virtuous or vicious, or deprive it of that character. To which we may add, that this agreement or disagreement, not admitting of degrees, all virtues and vices wou'd of course be equal.
>
> (*T* 460)

Finally, should the rationalist counter that immorality is grounded not in regular factual error but in 'mistakes about *right*', Hume replies that to make a mistake about X is to presuppose that the criteria for X have already been established. It begs the question to say that immorality consists of an 'error of right', since this presupposes a prior criterion of moral rightness, independent of these mistaken judgements, about which the mistake has been made. Hence, even if such errors are possible, they cannot be the ultimate source of moral distinctions.

> I would answer, that 'tis impossible that such a mistake can ever be the original source of immorality, since it supposes a real right

> and wrong; that is, a real distinction in morals, independent of these judgments. A mistake, therefore, of right may become a species of immorality; but 'tis only a secondary one, and is founded on some other, antecedent to it.
>
> (*T* 460)

Hume brings out the circularity of the rationalist position nicely in the Second *Enquiry*. To say that morality consists not in the relations between actions themselves, but 'in the relation of actions to the rule of right', is already to grant privileged status to the rule of right. If one says that we apprehend this rule by reason alone, 'which examines the moral relations of actions', then one has argued in a circle. The relations between actions are explained by reference to their relation to this rule, which in turn is explained in terms of the relations between actions.

> No, say you, the morality consists in the relation of actions to the rule of right; and they are denominated good or ill, according as they agree or disagree with it. What then is this rule of right? In what does it consist? How is it determined? By reason, you say, which examines the moral relations of actions. So that moral relations are determined by the comparison of actions to a rule. And that rule is determined by considering the moral relations of objects. Is not this fine reasoning?
>
> (2*E* 288–9)

Hume introduces his own theory of the basis of moral distinctions towards the end of the following passage, the most commonly quoted remark of all his writings on morality, where he claims that in examining any event we judge to be immoral, the *understanding* can detect no fact in which vice consists. Rather, the vice is only identified when we view the scene as *whole persons*, rather than as disembodied dispassionate intellects. When we do so, we become aware of an impression of pain on seeing or contemplating such an action. This is the source of moral disapproval, which fully emerges with the correction of this initial affective response.

> Take any instance allow'd to be vicious: Wilful murder, for instance. Examine it in all lights, and see if you can find that matter of fact, or real existence, which you call *vice*. In which-ever way you take it, you find only certain passions, motives, volitions and thoughts. There is no other matter of fact in the case. The vice entirely escapes you, as long as you consider the object. You never can find it, till you turn your reflexion into your own breast, and find a sentiment of disapprobation, which arises in you, towards this action. Here is a matter of fact; but 'tis the object of feeling, not of reason. So when you pronounce any action or character to be vicious, you mean nothing, but that from the constitution of your nature you have a feeling or sentiment of blame from the contemplation of it. Vice and virtue, therefore, may be compar'd to sounds, colours, heat and cold, which, according to modern philosophy, are not qualities in objects, but perceptions in the mind.
>
> (*T* 468–9)

Hume is not denying that were a psychologically normal person to actually witness a brutal murder, they would be appalled by such an act, and be unable not to respond in such a manner. His point is rather that there is no a priori connection between such a perception and the subsequent response. They are distinct and separable, in theory if not in practice. But this is just to make a point about human nature: that as a brute matter of fact, certain observations or thoughts are constantly conjoined with certain moral judgements. So Hume agrees that if I were to witness a murder, I would see it *as* wrong just as I would see it *as* killing; but I only do so because of the interaction between reason and passion that leads to the moral judgement itself. By contrast, in the first part of the passage quoted above, Hume has invited the reader to perform a thought experiment in which all affective aspects of their detective apparatus are blocked, and the event perceived through the rational capacities alone. It is under these contrived conditions that the vice would fail to be perceived.

Hume's intention is not to deny that morality is founded in matters of fact, but only to oppose the claim that it consists in facts *that the understanding alone can discover*. He explicitly tells us that 'Here is a matter of fact', but one requiring a particular nature involving human sentiments, a sympathetic capacity for interpreting others and empathizing with them in order to detect, in the same way as a particular kind of visual system is needed for colour perception.

What kind of facts are these? Certainly not facts that are objectively 'out there' in the sense of being independent of all possible human perceptual capacities. Nor, to go to the other extreme, are they to be identified with our subjective responses, as a decontextualized reading of the quotation's last sentence might encourage. Rather, moral evaluation involves a particular type of sentiment, resulting from the correction of the initial passionate reactions by reason. This 'feeling of sentiment or blame' is not to be equated with one's *personal* like or dislike of an action, but with the response made when we separate from the partiality of our individual perspective.

He draws an analogy between the sensing of moral properties and secondary qualities such as colour. When the common man, unacquainted with the new science, perceives a red book, he assumes that the redness is 'in' the book in an objective mind-independent manner. On the contrary, the sensations of red are caused by effects of the object's primary qualities on our particular modes of sense-perception. If all the book's properties were kept the same, yet humans all became colour-blind, then the book would not be red, except in a dispositional sense; that is, had there been anyone with the 'old' human sense-organs, they would see it as red (under standard lighting conditions). Ascription of secondary qualities thereby involves an unavoidable reference to human ways of seeing.

When Hume says 'you mean nothing, but that from the constitution of your nature you have a feeling or sentiment of blame from the contemplation of it', he is not trying to describe the action as you yourself conceive of it, or how you would describe or explain it. Neither is he alluding to any thesis about the term's standard usage within the community. Rather, he is saying that the capacity to cause this feeling of approbation is what the vice actually consists in. To give it any more objectivity than that is to commit an error analogous to those who see colours as being mind-independent properties.

In conclusion, the source of morals does not reside in the realm of reason, in ideas nor the relations between them. Rather, it is grounded in *secondary impressions*. But nothing so far has denied some role to reason in the discovery of moral distinctions. That is, nothing denies that its involvement is a necessary condition for moral evaluation, only that it is necessary and sufficient for it.

'Is' and 'ought'

> I cannot forbear adding to these reasonings an observation, which may, perhaps, be found of some importance. In every system of morality, which I have hitherto met with, I have always remark'd, that the author proceeds for some time in the ordinary way of reasoning, and establishes the being of a God, or makes observations concerning human affairs; when of a sudden I am surpriz'd to find, that instead of the usual copulations of propositions, *is*, and *is not*, I meet with no proposition that is not connected with an *ought*, or an *ought not*. This change is imperceptible; but is, however, of the last consequence, For as this *ought*, or *ought not*, expresses some new relation or affirmation, 'tis necessary that it shou'd be observ'd and explain'd; and at the same time that a reason should be given, for what seems altogether inconceivable, how this new relation can be a deduction from the others, which are entirely different from it.
>
> (*T* 469–70)

Over the past decade or so, most discussion of Hume's moral theory has focused on what I have called the 'motivational argument', and the ontological status of moral properties. However, it is instructive to recall that in the 1950s and 1960s, centre stage was given to this short passage on whether an 'ought' can be derived from an 'is'; that is, whether any claim about what one is morally obligated to do can be inferred from statements of fact alone. Hume was commonly interpreted as denying that any such deductive inference was valid, and this thesis was elevated to the status of 'Hume's law'. However, this interpretation was not unanimous, and a lively controversy developed regarding Hume's intentions. For example, should we read him as meaning that the derivation of an 'ought' from an 'is' really *is* impossible, or take him literally as saying merely that it just *seems* impossible, before showing how it can be done? I agree with Jonathan Harrison on the former interpretation, since otherwise 'he would, surely, have merely concluded that pointing out that it was involved *seemed to* subvert the vulgar systems of morality' (Harrison 1976: 70; my italics).

Contrary to the usual interpretation, Geoffrey Hunter argued that Hume meant that it is inconceivable how an inference from an 'is' to an 'ought' can be done, because *no inference is needed.* This, he says, is because Hume *identified* ought-statements with certain is-statements. He makes this interpretation on the basis of certain passages, such as 'when you pronounce any action or character to be virtuous, you mean nothing, but that from the constitution of your nature you have a feeling or sentiment of blame from the contemplation of it' (*T* 469). Hunter sees Hume as a subjectivist, who takes moral judgements to report the occurrence of these sentiments. However, it is surely clear that this passage does not concern what one 'means', in the sense of what information one intends to communicate. That is, Hume is not giving what Paul Grice called the 'utterer's meaning' of moral judgements. Neither is he saying that one's audience would standardly interpret them as being about one's subjective state. Hume is not offering any semantic theory at all, engaging neither in definitions nor conceptual analyses of moral language, but is pursuing his scientific, naturalistic account of what is actually going on when one makes a moral judgement.

Another controversy related to the interpretation of 'deduction'. For example, Alasdair MacIntyre (1955) points out that the eighteenth-century usage of this term was wider than our own, including not just what Hume would call demonstrative inference but also induction. However, it is essential to keep the precise location of Hume's remarks in mind. They occur at the end of a chapter devoted to a sustained critique of moral rationalism. In fact, the passage itself ends with an explicit reference to such theories, and his view that 'the distinction of vice and virtue is not founded merely on the relations of objects, nor is perceived by reason'. It is therefore reasonable to assume that such theories are the target of this passage. So I am fairly comfortable with the usual interpretation of Hume as saying that within the rules of deductive reasoning, no moral judgement can be logically derived from any set of factual statements. I take him to be making a brief aside, having already refuted rationalism by a series of arguments, most importantly the argument from motivation. He is saying that while we actually do move from factual to moral judgements – and it is perfectly legitimate to do so – we utilize our motivationally active passions as well as our reasoning capacities.

There is, of course, a trivial way to validly derive a moral 'ought' from an 'is', by means of the natural deduction rule of Disjunction–Introduction. Thus, from *Snow is white*, I can infer *Either snow is white or one ought to always tell the truth*. Of course, one might reply that this conclusion is not *itself* an ought-statement, but a complex statement which *includes* an ethical statement. Second, one could point out that from these two premises above, one cannot infer the genuinely ethical claim that one ought to always tell the truth.

Another logical manoeuvre relies on the fact that any statement can be inferred from a contradiction. So, let 'S' stand for *Snow is white*, and 'T' represent *One ought to always tell the truth*.

1	S & ~S	
2	S	1, Conjunction Elimination
3	S v T	2, Disjunction Introduction
4	~S	1, Conjunction Elimination
5	T	3,4, Disjunction Elimination

Clever though this is, it does not touch the deeper point that Hume is trying to make. First, one might say that even on its own terms it does not succeed because a contradiction does not state a possible fact. As Wittgenstein put it in the *Tractatus*, contradictions and tautologies are the formal limits of factual discourse, but do not themselves lie within those limits. Hence it is not a genuine case of deriving an 'ought' from an is', since a contradiction is not an 'is'. However, the more important point, as with the previous example, is that no substantive moral conclusions can be drawn in such a way. A clear way to see this is to notice that the very same method would allow you to infer *absolutely anything* as a disjunct, including *One ought not always tell the truth*.

The moral sentiments

I will only present what I take to be the full picture regarding Hume's moral theory in the final chapter, having taken into account not only the entire *Treatise* but also the Second *Enquiry*, plus his essay 'Of the Standard of Taste'. For the moment, I will briefly summarize the position as he presents it in *T* 3/1/2. Believing himself to have refuted rationalism in showing that moral properties or distinctions are not discovered within relations among ideas, nor from facts that the understanding alone can identify, Hume concludes by elimination that they are discovered 'by means of some impression or sentiment they occasion', and hence that morality 'is more properly felt than judg'd of' (*T* 470). He adds that this fact has not been recognized due to the *calmness* of the moral sentiment, which 'is commonly so soft and gentle, that we are apt to confound it with an idea, according to our common custom of taking all things for the same, which have any near resemblance to each other' (*T* 470).

He then turns to the task of specifying the nature of these impressions, and the causal mechanisms leading to their production. As to the first matter, he immediately identifies one essential characteristic, namely that 'the impression arising from virtue, to be agreeable, and that proceeding from vice to be uneasy' (*T* 470). Regarding the second, he identifies *personal character* as the object of the sentiments. 'To have a sense of virtue is nothing but to *feel* a satisfaction of a particular kind from the contemplation of character. The very *feeling* constitutes our praise or admiration' (*T* 471).

He adds that the determination of virtue is not, ultimately, the work of reason, in that we 'do not infer a character to be virtuous, because it pleases: But in feeling that it pleases after such a particular manner, we in effect feel that it is virtuous' (*T* 471). This is another of those passages which, if taken out of context, can make Hume seem like a naive subjectivist. This error is avoided by keeping in mind that Hume is certainly not denying that reason plays an essential, if ultimately subsidiary, role in moral judgement. As we shall see, coming to make a moral judgement is the culmination of a complex process in which reason refines and corrects our initial indirect passions. To make a moral judgement is, by that very fact, to have one's affective responses rationally informed. His point in this particular passage is that in making a moral judgement, one assumes a certain stance in which these refined passions are felt, and there is no extra move of rational inference, of 'I have a feeling of moral approval towards this person, therefore he has a virtuous character'. He need not deny that such an inference can *ever* take place, but this would be a result of already having made a moral evaluation, not a cause of one. This restricting the moral sentiments to actions emerging from personal character is sufficient to avoid a problem that wrecked rationalism, namely that any purportedly moral or immoral relation of ideas could apply to non-rational beings or inanimate matter.

We can now be a little more specific about the conditions under which moral evaluations can be made. First, these conditions always involve *persons*, either oneself or others. In particular, there requires the 'double relation of impressions and ideas' that marked the presence of indirect passions.

> Pride and humility, love and hatred are excited, when there is anything presented to us, that bears a relation to the object of the passion, and produces a separate sensation relating to the passion. Now virtue and vice are attended with these circumstances. They must necessarily be plac'd either in ourselves or others, and excite either pleasure or uneasiness; and must therefore give rise to one of these four passions.
>
> (*T* 473)

The second factor distinguishes moral sentiments from the indirect passions. Whereas the cause of an indirect passion is some quality relating to a person, the object of the passion is the particular person herself. I may be caused to hate someone by recognizing her as a manipulative liar. By contrast, the object of a *moral* sentiment is always the aspect of character *per se* – the universal rather than the particular – such as *being a liar*. It is essential to the particular species of pain or pleasure involved in moral sentiments that ''Tis only when a character is considered in general, without reference to our particular interest, that causes such a feeling or sentiment, as denominates it morally good or evil' (*T* 472).

For example, as I write these words, I feel hatred towards a neighbour (call him Buck), for allowing his cretinous dogs to bark day in day out, disturbing my equanimity and wrecking my concentration as I try to write this book. Here, Buck himself is the object of my indirect passion. As yet, this is insufficient to constitute a moral disapproval. This requires me to abstract away from Buck and, more importantly, from my own involvement in the issue, to consider the general practices involved. The object of my moral disapproval, then, is not *Buck's* inconsiderate behaviour towards *me*, but the general character trait causing such actions as *being inconsiderate to one's neighbours*.

So, contrary to subjectivism, the primary bearers of virtue or vice are traits of those *judged*, rather than of those *judging*. When A judges B's *actions* vicious, he is really attributing the vice to B's *character*. B's behaviour is a reliable indicator of this vice, causing the initial unpleasant sentiment in A, which can, after refinement, lead to moral disapprobation and a true ascription of vice in B. The initial link in this causal chain is some real aspect of B's character.

In making this distinction between moral judgements and the indirect passions, Hume makes another point that distinguishes him from a naive subjectivist, namely that the notion of *error* can apply to moral judgements. For example, we can mistake non-moral indirect passions for moral judgements, due to their subjective resemblance: 'It seldom happens, that we do not think an enemy vicious, and can distinguish betwixt his opposition to our interest and real villainy or baseness. But this hinders not, but that the sentiments are, in themselves, distinct' (*T* 472). Another source of error is that we may be responding to two different tokens of the same type of action or trait in different ways, depending on such variable factors as proximity in time or place. Reason can identify this error, and recommend that this practice be corrected by abstracting away from particulars and partialities.

In sum, the presence of an indirect passion is a necessary condition of making a moral judgement, or equivalently, having a moral sentiment. But these should not be considered as a species of indirect passions, because (1) their object is always a character trait considered as such, rather than a particular person, and (2) a passion only becomes essentially moral when it emerges from the 'general point of view'.

Having gone some way to distinguish the moral sentiments from other passions, the next question that arises is to determine the particular kinds of character traits that cause moral approval or disapproval. '*From what principles is it derived, and whence does it arise in the human mind?... Why any action or sentiment upon the general view or survey, gives a certain satisfaction or uneasiness*' (*T* 473). As with his general discussion of the passions, he remarks that it would be absurd to say that 'in every particular instance, these sentiments are produc'd by an *original* quality and *primary* constitution' (*T* 473). That is, it would be just as absurd to say that nature has given us a separate affective response for the disapproval of lying, of theft, of cruelty and so on, as it would to ascribe a separate physical principle for the falling of leaves, or apples, or books. The scientific enterprise is to find common principles underlying these particulars. So the aim is to 'find some more general principles, upon which all our notions of morals are founded'. This task is undertaken in the third Part of Book 3.

Further reading

For introductions to Hume's moral theory, see J.L. Mackie (1980) and Jonathan Harrison (1976), and the articles by Norton and Terence Penelhum in Norton (1993). For more detailed treatments, I recommend Bricke (1996) and Snare (1991), together with Ardal (1989: chs 5–6) and Baier (1991: chs 7–8).

Raphael (1991) and Schneewind (1990) both contain selections from various rationalists, along with moral sense theorists and others. For commentary, see Darwall (1995) and Schneewind (1998).

A.N. Prior (1949) discusses various historical attempts to derive normative statements from factual ones. W.D. Hudson (1983) is a clear summary of the more recent 'is–ought' controversy, and Hudson (1969) includes the main papers. For an influential attempt to derive an 'ought' from an 'is', see Searle (1964).

Chapter 6

The virtues

For the natural virtues, *Treatise*, Book 3, Part 3; 2nd *Enquiry*, chs 2, 6–8

For the artificial virtues, *Treatise*, Book 3, Part 2; 2nd *Enquiry*, chs 3–5, Appendix 3

For Hume's criticism of egoism, 2nd *Enquiry*, Section 5, Appendix 2

chapter 6

The four sources of personal merit

In the *Treatise*, Hume discusses the artificial virtues before the natural virtues. I will not follow him in this, since a brief account of the natural virtues will help to bring out the problems he had to overcome in explaining the origin of the artificial virtues.

A way into Hume's theory of the natural virtues is through a principle presented in his discussion of justice, namely the 'undoubted maxim' '*that no action can be virtuous, or morally good, unless there be in human nature some motive to produce it, distinct from a sense of its morality*' (2*E* 479). The natural virtues are the character traits at the basis of actions we morally approve of, where this approval is fully 'natural', not dependant on any human convention. He applies his scientific method to identify these virtues, observing the kinds of acts which elicit our approval, together with the character traits constantly conjoined with them; he then looks for common principles uniting these traits. He places special reliance on *introspection*, since he believes that the universality of human nature will ensure a certain convergence of views on these matters. In fact, he later went so far as to suggest that the philosopher

> can never be considerably mistaken in framing the catalogue, or incur any danger of misplacing the objects of his contemplation: he needs only enter into his own breast for a moment, and consider whether or not he should desire to have this or that quality ascribed to him, and whether or not such an imputation would proceed from a friend or an enemy.
>
> (2*E* 174)

Given his full awareness of the controversy of his views, and the effort he had to make to persuade rival philosophers of their truth, this looks rather optimistic of Hume, and contrary to his recognition of the difficulty of making reliable moral evaluations.

His investigations reveal four primary sources of moral approval: 'Personal Merit consists altogether in the possession of mental qualities, *useful* or *agreeable* to the *person himself* or to *others*' (2*E* 268). That is, virtuous character traits benefit either oneself or others, where this good is either intrinsic, or a means towards some other good. While the *Treatise*'s discussion of these virtues is relatively short, each of the four main categories is allotted its own chapter in the Second *Enquiry*, in a way that glosses over the natural–artificial distinction that played such a significant role in the *Treatise*. So we have:

1 Those *useful to society*, such as 'fidelity, justice, veracity, integrity' (2*E* 204), together with the 'social virtues' of 'meekness, beneficence, charity, generosity, clemency, moderation, equity' (*T* 578). He adds that social utility is 'also the source of a considerable part of the merit ascribed to humanity, benevolence, friendship, public spirit, and other social virtues of that stamp' (2*E* 204), although some of the merit afforded to these traits is also due to their intrinsic appeal.

2 Those *useful to the agent himself*, including '*prudence, temperance, frugality, industry, assiduity, enterprize, dexterity...generosity and humanity*' (*T* 587).
3 Those *intrinsically pleasing to those who encounter or consider them*, such as wit, eloquence, ingenuity, decency and decorum.
4 Those *intrinsically pleasing to the agent himself*, including cheerfulness, serenity and contentment.

In developing this catalogue of virtues, he pits himself against two main opponents. The first is another empirically based naturalistic theory, namely the egoism of Hobbes and Mandeville, which will be discussed in the following section. The second is the puritanical forms of Christianity that exercised such power and influence in the British culture of those times. By contrast with his treatment of the egoists, he does not employ much philosophical argument here, assuming that an appreciation of his own theory will enable the sensible reader to see the useless, anhedonic and literally unnatural character of the 'monkish virtues'.

Of the four natural sources of virtue, the most important is *social utility*. The 2nd *Enquiry* places *benevolence* at the head of these 'social virtues'. The *Treatise* presents benevolence as an indirect passion consequent on *love*, and consisting in a desire for the well-being of those whom one loved. In the 2nd *Enquiry*, with its playing down of the double association of ideas and impressions, it is understood in a broader and looser manner, as consisting in the disinterested concern for the welfare of others:

> no qualities are more intitled to the general good-will and approbation of mankind than beneficence and humanity, friendship and gratitude, natural affection and public spirit, or whatever proceeds from a tender sympathy with others, and a generous concern for our kind and species. These wherever they appear seem to transfuse themselves, in a manner, into each beholder, and to call forth, in their own behalf, the same favourable and affectionate sentiments, which they exert on all around.
>
> (2*E* 178)

It is undeniable, Hume thinks, that we naturally approve of those with a marked propensity for benevolence, particularly those who can extend it not just to their immediate family, but to anyone who happens to come their way. Benevolence is 'infectious', generating corresponding feelings in others, sympathetically setting off a dynamic of mutual reinforcement. Our approval for this tendency clearly comes from its benefit to all who come into contact with it, as well as its intrinsic agreeableness.

> The merit of benevolence, arising from its utility, and its tendency to promote the good of mankind has been already explained, and is, no doubt, the source of a *considerable* part of that esteem, which is so universally paid to it. But it will also be allowed, that the very softness and tenderness of the sentiment, its engaging endearments, its fond expressions, its delicate attentions, and all that flow of mutual confidence and regard, which enters into a warm attachment of love and friendship: it will be allowed, I say, that these feelings, being delightful in themselves, are necessarily communicated to the spectators, and melt them into the same fondness and delicacy.
>
> (2*E* 257)

With all this reference to utility, we must distinguish Hume from the utilitarianism of Jeremy Bentham and John Stuart Mill, despite his undoubted influence on them, since they differ significantly in their philosophical aims. Bentham and Mill were primarily concerned with a criterion of right action, claiming that an action (or kind of action) is right just in case it increases the overall amount of happiness in society, more than any other available option. Any theory of the morally good *agent* is derivative from this, such a person being one who performs acts generally conducive to happiness. By contrast, Hume's primary aim is to discover the structure of human nature, and thereby determine the human traits underlying actions we approve of. Nowhere does he explicitly offer a normative theory of right action. Secondly, as Hume's list of virtues shows, any such criterion that could be derived from this catalogue would not be equivalent to the Greatest Happiness Principle, but would, at best, resemble it. While granting that the lion's share of the foundations of moral approval goes to socially useful character traits, he resists fully reducing virtue to social utility.

Against egoism

Hume begins the 2nd *Enquiry* by commenting on the 'irksomeness' of debating those 'entirely disingenuous, who really do not believe the opinions they defend, but engage in the controversy, from affectation, from a spirit of opposition, or from a desire of showing wit and ingenuity, superior to the rest of mankind' (2*E* 169). Ironically, Hume himself has been placed in this category in the past, as being merely a shallow but clever man more interested in stirring controversy than offering a sincerely held position. Hume's targets are those who argue that all actions are ultimately grounded in 'self-love'; that is, purely egocentric interest, and that therefore all common distinctions between egoism and altruism, selfish and disinterested action, are mere illusion, such that:

> all *benevolence* is mere hypocrisy, friendship a cheat, public spirit a farce, fidelity a snare to procure trust and confidence; and that while all of us, at bottom, pursue only our private interest, we wear these fair disguises, in order to put others off their guard, and expose them the more to our wiles and machinations.
>
> (2*E* 295)

I will call this theory *egoism*, in contrast to Humean 'selfishness and confin'd generosity', wherein the natural sphere of our concern extends beyond the individual to close relations, particularly of blood. It is worth noticing Hume's accusation that egoists 'have denied the reality of moral distinctions' (2*E* 269), which shows that he regarded himself as attempting to put morality on solid foundations, in contrast to the moral sceptic he is often accused of being. His criticism of fellow naturalists of egoistic stamp is that their theory fails to fit the empirical facts, arguing by detailed accumulation of examples that such a theory is definitively refutable. He suggests that anyone accepting egoism must either possess 'the most depraved disposition', or be a 'superficial reasoner' who has carelessly overgeneralized from the fact that *many* actions involve deliberate deceit, to the conclusion that *all* behaviour is like this.

The basis of psychological egoism lies in the claim that we are naturally selfish beings who enter into so-called moral relations out of enlightened self-interest, seeing it to be to our long-term advantage to restrain our immediate impulses when others do so. Whereas Hume concluded that the entire natural basis of our approval of the 'social virtues' lies in their public utility, egoists take a more jaundiced view of the matter, holding 'that all moral distinctions arise from education, and were, at first, invented, and afterwards encouraged, by the art of politicians, in order to render men tractable, and subdue their natural ferocity and selfishness, which incapacitated them for society' (2*E* 214).

That is, they claim that all moral distinctions are founded *solely* on 'education', that is, social pressure and conditioning, as a cynical device to obscure the fact that all actions ultimately derive from self-love. In his highly popular book *The Fable of the Bees*, Bernard de Mandeville (1670–1733) had suggested that politicians realize that people cannot handle this truth, so have to be fooled into doing what is in their own interest by disguising it in a cloak of altruism. In response, Hume grants that 'education' plays a significant part in the acquisition of moral distinctions. Indeed, he explains the inevitability of such a process, via the sympathy mechanism. However, he insists that the ultimate basis of moral distinctions lies in our natural tendencies for the well-being of both ourselves and family, and others whom sympathy puts within our reach. Without the natural capacity to make moral distinctions, and be motivated to act upon them, methods of education will be ineffective: 'The social virtues must, therefore, be allowed to have a natural beauty and amiableness, which, at first, antecedent to all precept or education, recommends them to the esteem of uninstructed mankind, and engages their affections' (2*E* 214). In fact, a pure egoist could not acquire nor understand the distinctions of moral discourse.

> Had nature made no such distinction, founded on the original constitution of the mind, the words, *honourable* and *shameful*,

> *lovely* and *odious*, *noble* and *despicable*, had never taken place in any language; nor could politicians, had they invented these terms, ever have been able to render them intelligible, or make them convey any idea to the audience.
>
> (2*E* 214)

Hume draws our attention to the preponderance of observable facts which would seem impossible to derive from self-love, such as when we morally approve of things irrelevant to our self-interest:

> But notwithstanding this frequent confusion of interests, it is easy to attain what natural philosophers, after Lord Bacon, have affected to call the *experimentum crucis*, or that experiment which points out the right way in any doubt or ambiguity. We have found instances, in which private interest was separate from public; in which it was even contrary: And yet we observed the moral sentiment to continue, notwithstanding this disjunction of interests.
>
> (2*E* 219)

We approve of many acts that could not possibly have any causal connection to us, like those of antiquity 'where the utmost subtilty of imagination would not discover any appearance of self-interest, or find any connexion of our present happiness and security with events so widely separated from us' (2*E* 216). Second, we can still admire deeds hostile to our self-interest, such as the heroic act of an aggressor. Third, in cases in which some act, generally considered moral, happens to converge with our perceived self-interest, we have no difficulty in distinguishing these two species of approval in ourselves.

He then turns to a more abstract and theoretical argument in favour of egoism. Given that, when *correctly* perceived, self-interest and the common good are seen to converge, so that actions done from one motive would be virtually co-extensive with those performed from the other, some philosophers have 'found it simpler to consider all these sentiments as modifications of self-love; and they discovered a pretense, at least, for this unity of principle, in that close union of interest, which is so observable between the public and each individual' (2*E* 218–19).

In other words, there is a clear sense in which egoism is a *simpler* theory than Hume's, in that it postulates one prime motivational factor rather than several. However, Hume responds that this is just one dimension of simplicity. Another consideration is the ease with which actions can be explained by either theory, and he has shown that there are many actions to which an egoistic explanation would be, at best, extraordinarily complex and contrived. In such cases, Ockham's Razor would still be satisfied, since simplicity of proof would compensate for the extra ontological commitments.

> But farther, if we consider rightly of the matter, we shall find that the hypothesis which allows of a disinterested benevolence, distinct from self-love, has really more *simplicity* in it, and is more conformable to the analogy of nature than that which pretends to resolve all friendship and humanity into this latter principle.
>
> (2*E* 301)

He then considers another form of egoism, that

> whatever affection one may feel, or imagine he feels for others, no passion is, or can be, disinterested; that the most generous friendship, however sincere, is a modification of self-love, and that, even unknown to ourselves, we seek only our own gratification, while we appear to be the most deeply engaged in schemes for the liberty and happiness of mankind.
>
> (2*E* 296)

This hypothesis differs from the basic egoistic stance in claiming not that all actions come *directly* from selfish motives, but that they emerge from a variety of motives which are 'modifications' or transformations of some original egoism. That is, in the beginning there was egoism. As a result of training and social pressure, this evolved and mutated, generating a variety of different impulses, such as benevolence, which are ultimately grounded in self-love.

> An epicurean or Hobbist readily allows, that there is such a thing as a friendship in the world, without hypocrisy or disguise; though he may attempt, by a philosophical chymistry, to resolve the elements of this passion, if I may so speak, into those of another, and explain every affection to be self-love, twisted and moulded, by a particular turn of imagination, into a variety of appearances.
>
> (2*E* 296–7)

Hume responds that this theory still affords a clear distinction between actions which directly emerge from selfish motives, and those performed through benevolence. In other words, even granting the premise of this 'modified egoism', the distinction between selfish and altruistic motives and actions holds, and 'this is sufficient even according to the selfish system to make the widest difference in human characters, and denominate one man virtuous and humane, another vicious and meanly interested' (2*E* 297).

Hume offers another argument, similar to Joseph Butler's famous refutation of psychological egoism (which was, in fact, first presented by Francis Hutcheson a year previously). With regard to 'bodily wants or appetites', the derivation of pleasure from the satisfaction of a desire logically presupposes that the original desire was already there to be satisfied. These wants are mode-specific: if I am thirsty I want a drink; if I am hungry I want food, and drink will not suffice. So the 'end' of these desires is some particular kind of thing or activity. As a result of getting what I want, I (hopefully) experience pleasure. Of course, Hume is not saying here that my experience is of two separate things, for example, food plus pleasure. Rather, I experience pleasure in eating the food, and satisfaction in having eaten. This ensuing pleasure can, in future events, itself become the 'end' or 'object' of some desire; I may want that pleasure again. However, pleasure is an object of desire in a 'secondary' way, since it is grounded in primary needs and satisfactions.

The same model applies in the case of 'mental passions', where we 'are impelled immediately to seek particular objects, such as fame or power, or vengeance without any regard to interest; and when these objects are attained a pleasing enjoyment ensues, as the consequence of our indulged affections' (2*E* 301). We have a basic desire for social recognition and status, which, if satisfied, is experienced with pleasure; this pleasure both reinforces the original desire, and becomes an object of desire in its own right. But, as before, the pleasure is subsequent and secondary. Without the basic natural impulse to vanity, fame would not matter to me, and I could take no pleasure in it, any more than someone without any sexual drive could take pleasure in the act. Likewise with benevolence: it is an observable fact that people perform altruistic acts, and derive satisfaction from doing so, which would be impossible without a basic natural inclination towards altruism.

> Now where is the difficulty in conceiving, that this may likewise be the case with benevolence and friendship, and that, from the original frame of our temper, we may feel a desire of another's happiness or good, which, by means of that affection, becomes our own good, and is afterwards pursued, from the combined motives of benevolence and self-enjoyments?
>
> (2*E* 302)

Turning to character traits that are useful to oneself, egoism cannot account for the fact that I may approve of some character trait that is useful to its bearer, whether or not it benefits *me*. 'No force of imagination can convert us into another person, and make us fancy, that we, being that person, reap benefit from those valuable qualities, which belong to him' (2*E* 234). By contrast, Hume has a ready explanation of this phenomenon, deriving from the sympathy mechanism: on seeing his talents, and the pleasure that their exercise brings him, I sympathetically feel pleasure, leading to attitudes of liking and approval towards him. We value *our own* riches, apart from the pleasure they bring, because of the esteem directed towards us due to them; we esteem *another's* riches because of the pleasure they bring to the owner; and in which we then sympathetically participate.

Justice as an artificial virtue

The main subject of the second Part of Book 3 is *justice*, and Hume's purpose is to show it to be an artificial virtue, the product of 'human contrivance'. As he discussed in *T* 3/1/2, we can distinguish three senses of 'natural', depending on whether it is contrasted with the *miraculous*, the *unusual* or the *artificial*. The first is inapplicable to the discussion of virtue and vice, since all actions and events are natural except, he mischievously adds, '*those miracles on which our religion is founded*' (*T* 474). Nor is the second sense any more appropriate since 'if ever there was any thing, which could be call'd natural in this sense, the sentiments of morality certainly may; since there never was any nation of the world, nor any single person in any nation, who was utterly depriv'd of them' (*T* 474).

We are left with the contrast between the natural and the artificial. A mental process or character trait is *natural* if we possess it purely by being a normally functioning human being. The holding of these capacities is independent of any contingencies relating to our environment or culture. Likewise, an activity or practice is natural if it is fully explicable from these natural processes and traits. A character trait is a *natural virtue* when our *approval* of it is equally explicable from this basis. As we have seen, we approve of these traits because they are *useful* or *intrinsically pleasing*, either to the *agent* himself, or to *society at large* or some relevant section of it. An *artificial virtue*, while sharing this natural foundation, also requires the intervention of 'artifice' in order to emerge and to be approved of. Something is artificial if it is the product of *convention*, that is, of human rules and/or institutions. So 'artificial' is a purely descriptive term, with no pejorative connotations. Justice is no less of a virtue than its natural brethren.

One important difference between the natural and artificial virtues is that the former *always* produce good, and are *always* approved of, when the motive or subsequent action is considered in itself, devoid of all context. That is, the benefit and approval are inextricably bound to it. Each naturally virtuous act is a discrete event, complete and self-contained, and can be understood as such purely from a knowledge of human nature. The unconditional value we confer on the natural virtues is a direct result of this 'naturalness', their emergence from permanent facets of human nature. By contrast, the very existence of the artificial virtues rests on various contingencies of the human condition, such as a limited and uncertain supply of material goods requisite for our wants and needs. We might not approve of some just act when we consider it itself, since it need not directly benefit anyone involved. Rather, the benefit, and therefore the virtue, derives from the conventionally governed general practice of such acts. That of individual instances is only revealed when seen against this wider background.

Hume introduces the subject of justice by reviewing some results established in preceding sections. He reminds us that an action derives its virtue from being a sign of, and an effect of, a virtuous motive, where this in turn emerges from a stable character trait. It follows that no action can be virtuous without there being already some motive to do it other than because of its virtue. But what makes a motive a *virtuous* one? It cannot be that one intends to 'do a virtuous action', since that would be obviously circular, being to already assume that the virtue existed prior to the motivation. That is, it would be to say that one recognizes the virtue of some course of action, and is thereby motivated to act on this discovery. Hume's solution to the threatened paradox is to reject the assumption that morality is a self-standing phenomenon, lacking any non-moral foundation. He is thereby led indirectly to the conclusion that morality is founded upon our natural desires and affective responses: 'In short, it may be establish'd as an undoubted maxim, *that no action can be virtuous, or morally good, unless there be in human nature some motive to produce it, distinct from a sense of its morality*' (*T* 479).

While Hume grants that one can do something because it's 'the right thing to do', he insists that this is a complex and derivative type of case which depends on the prior existence of some other motive, apart from the sense of duty, that *normally* motivates actions of this kind, or else it would not be a duty at all. He gives the example that our criticism of a negligent father for failing in his duty is ultimately derived from his not acting in accordance with *natural* affection for one's children. So suppose that such a man recognizes his deficiency in this natural impulse; this knowledge provokes *humility*, which will be increased by his experiencing or imagining the disapproval of others.

As a consequence, he acquires a desire to rectify the situation. This desire motivates him to act as duty would demand, in order that repetition of such behaviour might cause it to become habitual. Such a strategy would be an indirect attempt to change his character, where the basic motivation came from the indirect passion of humility, and reason supplying the method of alleviating this pain.

Hume wants to show that the sole grounds for our approval of justice lies in its *social utility*, and his task is to explain how this can be so, given the preponderance of just acts which would seem to benefit no-one. He also needs to explain, within the constraints of his moral psychology, how one could be motivated to act for the sake of justice. This project will include an account of how such a practice could have got off the ground in the first place.

Starting from his 'undoubted maxim' that every virtuous action requires a motivation separate from a sense of its morality, he considers what might be the natural basis for performing just acts *per se*. The problem is the seemingly counter-productiveness of many of these acts. For example, suppose I borrow money, promising to repay it. What could motivate me to keep my promise? He has argued that an act is honest if it is done through an honest motive; but what constitutes the honesty of a motive? It would be circular to say that an honest motive consists in the intention to perform honest actions *per se*.

While *we* might obey the law because it's the law, how did this practice of obeying the law for its own sake ever come to be established? While *we* may feel the force of the law on our behaviour, we cannot appeal to this force to explain the *origin* of the law, nor the original allegiance to it. This 'sense of duty' derives from these laws themselves, and therefore cannot explain them. As we shall see shortly, it is not that a pre-societal person would find any appeal to justice unintelligible when he asks why he should *keep his promise* to return someone else's *property*. Rather, the very ideas of property and promising would be equally unintelligible to him, since they come into existence only as a result of human convention.

Given the sheer variety of the rules of justice, our conduct cannot be explained in terms of *instinct*. He dismisses this option quickly in the *Treatise*, but gives it greater attention in the 2nd *Enquiry*. If the idea of justice is innately grasped via a 'simple original instinct', then so must all dependent or related ideas such as that of *property*; but then one is driven to the implausible view that a multitude of concepts are innate.

> For when a definition of *property* is required, that relation is found to resolve itself into any possession acquired by occupation, by industry, by prescription, by inheritance, by contract, &c. Can we think that nature, by an original instinct, instructs us in all these methods of acquisition?...Have we original innate ideas of praetors and chancellors and juries?
>
> (2*E* 201–2)

As Hume sarcastically remarks, 'But who is there that ever heard of such an instinct? Or is this a subject in which new discoveries can be made?' (2*E* 201). Such a discovery, he thinks, is as likely as that of discovering a new sense that we never knew we had.

Nor can natural *self-interest* suffice to motivate all just acts. At most, it could encourage those coinciding with personal advantage, but not cases in which selfishness would seem to conflict with the demands of justice. In fact, unconstrained self-interest is the primary *obstacle* to justice: 'But 'tis certain, that self-love, when it acts at its liberty, instead of engaging us to honest actions, is the source of all injustice and violence; nor can a man ever correct those vices, without correcting and restraining the *natural* movements of that appetite' (*T* 480).

Neither can concern for the public interest, or *public benevolence*, motivate all just actions. Not only would it be inert in 'secret' cases that the public were unaware of, but such a motive is 'too remote and too sublime to affect the generality of mankind, and operate with any force in actions so contrary to private interest as are frequently those of justice and common honesty' (*T* 481). In fact, Hume's psychology allows no room for any desire for the public interest as such, since there is no passion of a 'love of mankind' as such. Our desires and affections always concern individuals or specific groups. We only love or hate others if there is something particular about them causing these responses, and being a person *per se* is not enough. This is not contradicted by Hume saying 'perhaps a man would be belov'd as such, were we to meet him in the moon' (*T* 482), because then he would not be merely 'a man as such', but one's only companion in a remote place. This would just be an extreme case of how hardship pushes people together who, under other circumstances, would not form any relationship. There appears to be a slight change of attitude on this matter between the *Treatise* and the 2nd *Enquiry*, where he allows such impersonal concern as a calm passion, while continuing to insist that it lacks the force to be the prime motivation to just actions.

Finally, there are too many counter-examples against the claim that *private benevolence*, concern for the interests of those directly affected, could motivate all just actions:

> For what if he be my enemy, and has given me just cause to hate him? What if he be a vicious man, and deserves the hatred of all mankind? What if he be a miser, and can make no use of what I wou'd deprive him of? What if he be a profligate debauchee, and wou'd rather receive harm than benefit from large possessions? What if I be in necessity, and have urgent motives to acquire something to my family? In all these cases, the original motive to justice wou'd fail, and consequently the justice itself, along with it all property, right, and obligation.
>
> (*T* 482)

Like all moral obligation, justice is impersonal, requiring us to act well towards those for whom we have no naturally benevolent impulses. By contrast, unchecked passions such as private benevolence are partial. Secondly, private benevolence could not explain why the obligation to respect another's property is greater than the obligation to give him something of equal value that he lacks. Rather, the difference between these cases rests on the fact that in the former case we are *taking his property*. But, of course, the whole point was to explain the origin of the practices that bring property into being.

So justice seems to threaten Hume's 'undoubted maxim', since no *natural* motive seems to be available from which to explain this original motivation for, and approval of, just acts. The rules are too varied to be accounted for by *instinct*; public benevolence is either non-existent or, at best, too weak; and there are too many counterexamples to *narrow selfishness*. In sum, any attempt to explain the origin of our approval of justice that is restricted to natural motives will be either circular or blatantly false. Hume takes these results to show that justice cannot be a natural virtue, and that the rules of justice are artificial in being human contrivances.

> From all this it follows, that we have naturally no real or universal motive for observing the laws of equity, but the very equity and merit of that observance; and as no action can be equitable or meritorious, where it cannot arise from some separate motive, there is here an evident sophistry and reasoning in a circle. Unless, therefore, we will allow, that nature has establish'd a sophistry, and render'd it necessary and unavoidable, we must allow, that the sense of justice and injustice is not deriv'd from nature, but arises artificially, tho' necessarily from education, and human conventions.
>
> (*T* 483)

However, being *artificial* does not mean that these rules are totally *arbitrary*. In fact, they can even be said to be *natural* in that some such rules were inevitable, given our natural ingenuity in the face of the challenge presented by our natural circumstances. In this sense, the rules of justice can be considered 'Laws of Nature'.

In *T* 3/2/6 Hume offers more arguments for the artificiality of justice. One is based on the claim that all natural properties, including natural virtues, *admit variations of degree*, whereas matters of justice do not. That is, 'rights, and obligations, and property, admit of no such insensible gradation, but that a man either has a full and perfect property, or none at all; and is either entirely oblig'd to perform any action, or lies under no manner of obligation' (*T* 529). So X never literally has 'more of a right' to something than does Y. He may have a stronger claim, or more factors in support of his claim to a right, but the right itself is all or nothing. Likewise, X could be closer than Y to attaining a right; but once held, the right is total. This argument is weak, since the same point can be made about some natural conditions. For example, either one is or is not a virgin. Again, while you can be further along in pregnancy than someone else, you are not thereby literally more pregnant.

Hume adds that changes in rights happen instantly, such as through transfer of possession, whereas natural processes occur gradually: 'however the use may be bounded in time or degree, the right itself is not susceptible of any such gradation, but is absolute and entire, so far as it extends. Accordingly we may observe, that this right both arises and perishes in an instant' (*T* 529–30). But my previous counter-examples apply here. Similarly, while *dying* may be gradual, *death* is instantaneous. This seems entirely analogous to the fact that although a court case to ascertain property rights may be long and drawn out, the victor immediately acquires full property rights once a decision is made.

Another argument contrasts the *inflexibility* of laws of justice with decision procedures based on natural virtues. Natural means–ends reasoning provides reliable rules of thumb for achieving our goals. On confronting particular cases where these rules give unappealing results, we are willing to make an exception. Hume gives the example of a case in which one had to decide to whom to allocate an estate, where one party was a friend and 'poor, a man of sense, and has a numerous family', and the other candidate not only an enemy, but 'rich, a fool, and a batchelor'. In such a case, the natural passions alone would favour the former, 'whether I be actuated in this affair by a view to public or private interest' (*T* 530). In other words, a naturally based decision would only consider the particulars of the case at hand. However, a general practice of such partial and particular judgements would lead to chaos, and we would recognize the need for more inflexible rules, to be applied even in cases where the outcome seems to satisfy no-one.

The origin of justice and property

Section 3/2/2 of the *Treatise* explains how rules of justice are *established*, and how we come to *approve* of them. He separates these two issues, arguing that the original motive for entering into what we would regard as just practices derives from self-interest. To be more precise, it comes from the belief that such practices will be of overall benefit to oneself and one's closest relations. By contrast, the moral approval of justice derives from the social utility of the practice as a whole. '*Self-interest is the original motive to the establishment of justice: but a sympathy with public interest is the source of the moral approbation which attends that virtue*' (*T* 499).

This account does not aspire to historical accuracy. Rather, Hume's aim is to make the emergence and approval of justice causally explicable in terms of his theory of human nature. Very briefly, the idea is that prior to the establishment of rule-governed societies, people lived in small familial groups. Recognizing the inevitability of encountering outsiders, they knew that they could only avoid the conflict that would inevitably result from the competition for limited resources if everyone's behaviour was restricted by common rules. On realizing this, they voluntarily placed themselves under these restraints, on condition that others did so as well. After the initial forming of the conventions, the only motive for keeping to them was long-term self-interest in restraining immediate drives, backed up by the threat of ostracism through not being trusted again. However, once this practice was entered into by enough people for long enough, participants came to see the advantage of its continuance, causing them to morally approve of acts that accorded with the rules, and disapprove of intransigence. I will now discuss the features of this theory in greater detail.

We are motivated to form large social groups through regarding this as a reliable way of satisfying basic needs. Nature has put man in an unfortunate position due to 'the numberless wants and necessities, with which she has loaded him, and in the slender means, with which she affords to the relieving these necessities' (*T* 484). In other animals, 'these two particulars generally compensate each other' in that they have few and simple needs which are easily satisfied. Society provides a remedy for three specific kinds of problem, relating to *force*, *ability*, and *security*. First, self-sufficiency is extremely time-consuming, and we lack the power to adequately fulfil our own needs when we work in isolation or in competition with each other. Second, the sheer number of skills involved in having to provide all one's own food, protect oneself from the elements and each other, and so on, are a tax on even the most able of us. Third, even if one could temporarily achieve this self-sufficiency, one would then be at the mercy of those less capable, who could band together and take the results of one's efforts.

> Society provides a remedy for these *three* inconveniences. By the conjunction of forces, our power is augmented: By the partition of employments, our ability encreases; And by mutual succour we are less expos'd to fortune and accidents. 'Tis by this additional *force*, *ability*, and *security*, that society becomes advantageous.
>
> (*T* 485)

'Society' constitutes a network of persons engaged in cooperative acts specifically designed to overcome these three obstacles. Efficiency is greatly increased by combining forces and talents with each at the service of all, not in a collective way but as a set of free exchanges. Restrictions are placed on behaviour, and sanctions put in place to back them up. While society will result in greatly increased expectations, and the development of new artificial desires (i.e., dependent on conventions), Hume maintains that the overall degree of satisfaction will increase.

> 'Tis by society alone he is able to supply his defects, and raise himself up to an equality with his fellow-creatures, and even acquire a superiority above them. By society all his infirmities are compensated; and tho' in that situation his wants multiply every moment upon him, yet his abilities are still more augmented, and leave him in every respect more satisfied and happy, than 'tis possible for him, in his savage and solitary condition, ever to become.
>
> (*T* 485)

In order that people be motivated to form societies, it is not enough that this *be* to their advantage; they need to 'be sensible of' these benefits, and pre-societal persons could not work this out a priori. However, this is another case in which nature comes to the rescue, stepping in to fill a void that reason is incapable of satisfying. Sexual attraction, plus subsequent drives for the protection of family, overcomes the impasse. In fact, the family not only provides an impetus for forming society, but is the *model* for it.

People make people. Thus, even before societies were formed, no one was born as a solitary individual, but emerged into a form of social setting, albeit involving only a few other persons. Through the desire for sex, and natural concern for the welfare of children, people fall into familial structures. Humans are 'naturally social' only regarding these small clan-like groups, within which the natural virtues are practised. Family life gives us the prototype for societal relations, providing the conditions under which we can conceive of wider social ties, and the benefits that would ensue from them. For example, having a partner provides a model for cooperation and a division of labour; being in a parent–child relationship gives you an example of obedience to authority and the idea of hierarchy. It should be emphasized that Hume does not commit himself to any specific hierarchy adopted within these pre-societal proto-families, such as matriarchy versus patriarchy. His point is merely that families provide crude analogues of rule-governed life, and of adjusting the demands of one's immediate passions to those rules. Given our associative mechanisms, we generalize and thereby extrapolate these relations onto wider groups.

These original families differ from those within society in that the latter are a result of the convention of marriage. The maintenance of this institution results in the creation of the artificial virtues of *chastity* and *modesty*. These are principally 'female virtues', due to the fact that a child's paternity can be doubted in a way that its maternity cannot. The 'length and feebleness of human infancy' (*T* 570) requires a child to be raised by both a man and a woman, but no man could be expected to make the sacrifices involved unless he was certain that the child was his. The most effective way of guaranteeing fidelity is to condition females from an early age against immodest behaviour, and indeed against sexual pleasure itself. (He never considers the possibility of so conditioning males.) This is supplemented by 'the punishment of bad fame or reputation' for adulteresses. Hume emphasizes that the only justification for the inculcation of these 'virtues' lies in their role in providing a stable environment for the raising of children.

Returning to the main narrative, Hume brings out the sexual foundation of society in the 2nd *Enquiry* by inviting us to imagine a 'species' of autogenetic hermaphrodites, each of whom were thoroughly self-contained and self-sufficient. The very idea of justice would not occur to these creatures, since they would lack the family model in which cooperative practices are established, and, more fundamentally, because they would have no need of others, nor therefore of societal rules.

However, the family ties that push us towards larger groups also generate factors which can impede these developments. As we have seen, Hume thinks that Hobbes has seriously exaggerated the degree of our egoism, and hence the problem it poses for the forming of society. However, Humean 'selfishness and confined generosity' creates as big a problem for the development of society as would Hobbesian egoism, since these personal concerns can conflict with the impersonal demands of justice.

> But tho' this generosity must be acknowledg'd to the honour of human nature, we may at the same time remark, that so noble an affection, instead of fitting men for large societies, is almost as contrary to them, as the most narrow selfishness. For while each person loves himself better than any other single person, and in his love to others bears the greatest affection to his relations and acquaintance, this must necessarily produce an opposition of passions, and a consequent opposition of actions; which cannot but be dangerous to the new-establish'd union.
>
> (*T* 487)

I will continue to use 'selfishness' in the Humean rather than the Hobbesian sense, taking it to consist not in holding one's own personal interest above all others, but where one's circle of immediate concern includes family members. Hume does not regard this selfishness as being *necessarily* a problem for justice, but only due to the relative scarcity of material goods and the 'easy transference' of possessions. As we shall see, Hume contrasts 'possession' with 'property', where the latter term is only intelligible within the context of societal rules. Possession, by contrast, is a natural relation, consisting in the *exclusive use* of a given object. (The relationship between possession and property is analogous to that between pre-societal families and those governed by the institution of marriage.) The aim of a system of justice is to put material possessions on the same stable level as bodily or mental goods.

The solution to our pre-societal problems involves the typical Humean division of labour between reason and passion, in which passion supplies the goal of the action, and reason directs it by suggesting means for the satisfaction of desires. The only difference in this case is that the process is intrinsically *interpersonal* rather than individualistic, due to the involvement of a social convention. In a lawless pre-societal situation, possessions are vulnerable to attack, and can be in short supply. The competition for these goods will inevitably lead to conflicts. We are smart enough to realize that we would all be better off in the long run if we could all work together, rather than wasting time and resources in destructive conflicts. But since we recognize ourselves to be selfish persons in a world of limited and insecure material goods, we know that our unregulated natural passions cannot solve this problem, since they are partly the cause of it. However, reason tells us that it is in our overall long-term selfish interest to cooperate with others, *on condition* that they reciprocate. We imaginatively see the benefit of living under a rule that would permit this situation, and this vision generates the motive to enter into such a conventional arrangement.

Recognition of society's long-term benefits can motivate us to change our external circumstances so that our self-interested passions will be redirected. While in nature, selfishness motivates us to take others' possessions, whereas conventions create circumstances under which it benefits us, in the long term, to curb these impulses. In saying that the understanding changes the direction of the passions, Hume means that no new motive is added; rather, a new means–ends solution is proposed, in the form of property conventions, to satisfy pre-existing needs for security, and so on.

> The remedy, then, is not deriv'd from nature, but from *artifice*; or more properly speaking, nature provides a remedy in the judgment and understanding, for what is irregular and

> incommodious in the affections. For when men, from their early education in society, have become sensible of the infinite advantages that result from it, and have besides acquir'd a new affection to company and conversation; and when they have observ'd, that the principal disturbance in society arises from those goods, which we call external, and from their looseness and easy transition from one person to another; they must seek a remedy, by putting these goods, which we call external, as far as possible, on the same footing with the fix'd and constant advantages of the mind and body. This can be done after no other manner, than by a convention enter'd into by all the members of the society to bestow stability on the possession of those external goods, and leave every one in the peaceable enjoyment of what he may acquire by his fortune and industry. By this means, everyone knows what he may safely possess, and the passions are restrain'd in their partial and contradictory motions. Nor is such a restraint contrary to the passions; for if so, it cou'd never be enter'd into, nor maintain'd; but it is only contrary to their heedless and impetuous movement. Instead of departing from our own interest, or from that of our nearest friends, by abstaining from the possessions of others, we cannot better consult both these interests, than by such a convention; because it is by that means we maintain society, which is so necessary to their well-being and subsistence, as well as to our own.
>
> (*T* 489)

Just acts are different from naturally virtuous acts, in that the merit of the latter is intrinsic to the acts themselves. That is, it can be seen merely by examining an action (and motive behind it) narrowly, devoid of context. By contrast, the virtue (and point) of *just* acts may not reveal itself from such a perspective. In the former case there is a direct, non-derivative connection between the action itself and either the individual or public interest. In the latter case, individual acts are always beneficial in an *indirect* way, through their place within a wider practice which is itself in the public interest.

Consider the payment of taxes. Neither my motivation to pay, nor my approval of doing so, can be understood from my natural inclinations and affections alone. The act is not intelligible in terms of my *intentions* if I am considered purely as an individual, but only makes sense when I am considered as a member of a society within which such payments are a recognized practice. Likewise, making my mortgage payments cannot be understood purely with reference to myself and the faceless consortium who receive my money. Naturally altruistic behaviour occurs only between family and friends, whereas society requires interaction with strangers to whom these attitudes will not be extended. While token acts, considered under non-conventional descriptions, may appear to lack natural grounding, this rationale is revealed when they are seen as *just* acts, since they embody and support institutions which are in every participant's interest.

> A single act of interest is frequently contrary to *public interest*; and were it to stand alone, without being follow'd by other acts, may, in itself, be very prejudicial to society...Nor is every single act of justice, consider'd apart, more conducive to private interest than to public...But...'tis certain, that the whole plan or scheme is highly conducive, or indeed absolutely requisite, both to the support of society, and the well-being of every individual.
>
> (*T* 497)

Although our informed self-interest can tell us of the benefits of living under rules of justice, we are tempted to break them due to the fact that a lesser good that is available right now will have more effect on the imagination, and consequently the will, than a greater benefit that lies in the future.

> Now as every thing, that is contiguous to us, either in space or time, strikes upon us with such an idea, it has a proportional effect on the will and passions, and commonly operates with more force than any object, that lies in a more distant and obscure light. Tho' we may be fully convinc'd, that the latter object excels the former, we are not able to regulate our actions by this judgment; but yield to the sollicitations of our passions, which always plead in favour of whatever is near and contiguous.
>
> (*T* 535)

However, reason can step in here and redirect self-interest. We can recognize that from an even more distant perspective, the temporal distance between the options will appear negligible, and the difference in their value be far clearer. We know that we are unlikely, by ourselves, to exercise enough strength of character to do what is in our best interests. However, the very acknowledgement of this fact can encourage us to *now* set up a system of external sanctions which will *later* provide the extra incentive that will 'tip the balance' in favour of our long-term interest. Hence the development of a legal system. *Government* also plays such a role: we elect people into a position where it is in their immediate interest that the rules of justice be enforced, and give them the power to enforce these rules, and to decide on controversial cases of interpretation or application.

> Here then is the origin of civil government and allegiance. Men are not able radically to cure, either in themselves or others, that narrowness of soul, which makes them prefer the present to the remote. They cannot change their natures. All they can do is change their situation, and render the observance of justice the immediate interest of some particular persons, and its violation their more remote. These persons, then, are not only induc'd to observe those rules in their own conduct, but also to constrain others to a like regularity, and inforce the dictates of equity thro' the whole society. (*T* 537)

In order to be viable, the rules must be fairly simple, with no endless *ceteris paribus* clauses. The inevitable price will be some cases in which the immediate results seem to benefit no-one. For example, a starving student caught stealing from a rich moneylender is still guilty of a crime against property, and must be punished. Even if mitigating circumstances are taken into account, and some leeway is given to judges, these must be kept under significant restraints if the legal system is to function. No two acts are identical in all their circumstances, and there needs to be some rule regarding the range of punishment appropriate for acts of certain kinds. The best we can do is to set up a system which, taken overall, combines social utility with viability in an optimal way.

> Public utility requires that property should be regulated by general inflexible rules; and though such rules are adopted as best serve the same end of public utility, it is impossible for them to prevent all individual hardships, or make beneficial consequences result from every individual case. It is sufficient, if the whole plan or scheme be necessary to the support of civil society, and if the balance of good, in the main, do thereby preponderate much above that of evil.
>
> (2*E* 305)

Hume clearly conceives of justice as primarily a set of rules for the protection of property. One reason for committing himself to what seems to be an excessively restrictive theory lies in this following passage:

> There are three different species of goods, which we are possess'd of; the internal satisfaction of our mind, the external advantages of our body, and the enjoyment of such possessions as we have acquir'd by our industry and good fortune. We are perfectly secure in the enjoyment of the first. The second may be ravish'd from us, but can be of no advantage to him who deprives us of them. The last only are both expos'd to the violence of others, and may be transferr'd without suffering any loss or alteration.
>
> (*T* 487–8)

His emphasis on property, rather than equally obvious factors such as protection from personal assault, is because out of the three kinds of goods existing in the state of nature, only material possessions can be transferred to someone else. While I can deprive you of the first two, I cannot then use them myself. (Hume was living before organ transplants were possible.) However, Hume has also claimed that *competition* is a cause of hatred and anger, so one might object that even though I cannot take your mind or your organs, my depriving you of their use could be to my benefit through putting you, my competitor, at a relative disadvantage. It would surely follow that there is a need for laws protecting the person. I agree with Jonathan Harrison (1981) that Hume does not take this line because he takes such violence to be a *natural* vice. That is, our disapproval of such acts is explicable without recourse to convention.

Still, it is common to criticize Hume for identifying justice with considerations of property, and ignoring 'the twin virtues of equity and impartiality'. However, I believe that such a charge is unfounded. Hume intends the relation between justice and property to be conceptual and substantive, laying a constraint on the *subject matter* of justice. Equity and impartiality, by contrast, are *formal* requirements of justice. A rule applied partially would thereby fail to be a rule of justice, since equity and impartiality are already built into the 'general point of view', the moral stance of which justice is a part.

I will now describe the nature of Hume's conventions in greater detail. When an individual first enters into the cooperative practices at the root of social institutions, his compliance is conditional. He has reason to comply only if he sees others doing so, and if such mutual compliance is in his interest. He will predict that others will reciprocate only if they regard it as being in *their* interests to do so. Given our largely shared psychology, he will assume that this is the case.

Nature will impose some restrictions on who will participate in these first conventions. One will be *spatio-temporal contiguity*, that is, between those whose actions have fairly direct consequences on each other. Second, membership will be restricted to *persons* in the standard Lockean sense of the term, that is, to those capable of understanding the complex higher-order communicative intentions mentioned above. Third, as he brings out in the 2nd *Enquiry*, it will be restricted to those with enough 'strength, both of body and mind' for their participation to *matter* from the point of view of others' self-interest. One's cooperation must make a difference, for good or bad; otherwise, what reason would other self-interested agents have to include you?

> Were there a species of creatures intermingled with men, which, though rational, were possessed of such inferior strength, both of body and mind, that they were incapable of all resistance, and could never, upon the highest provocation, make us feel the effects of their resentment; the necessary consequence, I think, is that we should be bound by the laws of humanity to give gentle

> usage to these creatures, but should not, properly speaking, lie under any restraint of justice with regard to them, nor could they possess any right or property, exclusive of such arbitrary lords. Our intercourse with them could not be called society, which supposes a degree of equality.
>
> (2*E* 190)

Hume denies that the establishment of this 'contract' is a *promise*, since the practice of promising is itself convention-based, and could not exist prior to societal institutions. Rather, cooperation proceeds incrementally, with the success of each small stage providing gradual momentum for the process to proceed. He gives the analogy of two men rowing a boat, gradually synchronizing their activity by a sequence of fine-tuned movements.

> Two men, who pull the oars of a boat, do it by an agreement or convention, tho' they have never given promises to each other. Nor is the rule concerning the stability of possession the less deriv'd from human conventions, that it arises gradually, and acquires force by a slow progression, and by our repeated experience of the inconveniences of transgressing it. On the contrary, this experience assures us still more, that the sense of interest has become common to all our fellows, and gives us a confidence of the future regularity of their conduct: And 'tis only on the expectation of this, that our moderation and abstinence are founded. In like manner are languages gradually establish'd by human conventions without any promise.
>
> (*T* 490)

Note that this does not involve explicit instructions and negotiations between the men. Rather, they employ 'sympathetic' capacities in a sort of synergistic feedback loop, getting in tune with each other by actually *doing it*, rather than planning it out first. Each step contributes to the creation of the convention, and increases the probability that future actions will accord with it. Hence the practice gets stabilized to the point that an explicit rule can be stated. This rule can then guide and reinforce future conduct. By analogy, property conventions will gradually become established in this implicit way, as people come to appreciate their benefits. I take Hume to be saying that a fully-fledged promise is future-directed, and involves the repayment or delivery of something that is presently absent. By contrast, the prior cases such as with the rowing analogy involves only present-tense conduct (or refraining) on both sides. This matter will be returned to shortly.

In fact, Hume takes the very concepts (or 'ideas') of 'property', 'promising', 'obligation' and so on to emerge only in the establishment of the rules of justice. 'The origin of justice explains that of property. The same artifice gives rise to both' (*T* 491). Only once the cooperative practices are up and running are these concepts intelligible. Prior to this, nothing in human nature can provide the resources to conceive of them. So, since we are trying to ascertain the origin of justice, we cannot do it by saying that the initial motivation involves respect for property rights, since these presuppose the notion of justice that we're trying the explain. Secondly, since property is itself a product of artifice, the idea of justice cannot be reductively defined in terms of it. Rather, the concepts are interdefinable.

> After this convention, concerning abstinence from the possessions of others, is enter'd into, and every one has acquir'd a stability in his possessions, there immediately arise the ideas of justice and injustice; as also those of *property*, *right*, and *obligation*. The latter are unintelligible without first understanding the former. Our property is nothing but those goods, whose constant possession is establish'd by the laws of society; that is, by the laws of justice. Those, therefore, who make use of the word property, or right, or obligation, before they have explain'd the origin of justice, or even make use of it in that explication, are guilty of a very gross fallacy.
>
> (*T* 490–1)

Of course, Hume was not the first to suggest the idea of a convention or contract in the establishment and legitimization of societal rules. However, his presentation of the idea is very different to previous writers such as Hobbes and Locke, who wanted to found civic obligation on explicit agreements or promises. The deepest difference lies in his *reversal of priority between practice and rule*. Hume denies that a general rule or principle could be established out of nowhere, prior to all practice. Rather, each individual recognizes that it will be beneficial to refrain from taking another's possessions only if others reciprocate this behaviour; given that we all have roughly the same psychology, significant numbers of persons will come to this conclusion separately, and be fairly assured that they are not alone in their understanding; they will begin to make tentative first moves, always checking for reciprocity; the longer this goes on, the more the practice gets established. While this is happening, their conscious awareness of the rule-qua-rule, or convention-qua-convention, becomes stronger. This developing form of life, this practice, has made them capable of explicitly formulating the idea of a convention. The convention emerges out of the practice, and only then can take on a life of its own. To put it in terms of Quine's (1972) useful distinction, the first cooperative moves may *fit a rule* – i.e., may look as if they derive from such an instruction – but actions are only explicitly *guided by a rule* once the practice is well established.

In conclusion, Hume's response to the first question with which he began *T* 3/2/2 is that:

> Here is a proposition, which, I think, may be regarded as certain, *that 'tis only from the selfishness and confin'd generosity of men, along with the scanty provision nature has made for his wants, that justice derives its origin*...[and that] *those impressions, which give rise to this sense of justice, are not natural to the mind of man, but arise from artifice and human conventions*.
>
> (*T* 495–6)

The original motive for justice is self-interest, but this end is pursued 'in an oblique and indirect manner', via the artifice of social rules.

Natural preconditions of justice

In the 2nd *Enquiry*, he strengthens his case by applying the 'method of difference' in a series of thought-experiments where different factors necessary for the emergence of justice, such as the limits on our benevolence or natural resources, are removed. For example, conventions of justice would not have arisen if our 'selfishness and confined generosity' were replaced by a more expansive altruism, since this would make the rules unnecessary.

> Why raise land marks between my neighbour's field and mine, when my heart has made no division between our interests; but shares all its joys and sorrows with the same force and vivacity as if originally my own? Every man, on this supposition, being a second self to another, would trust all his interests to the discretion of every man; without jealousy, without partition, without distinction.
>
> (2*E* 184)

In fact, Hume's point could be extended to say that the very idea of *morality* would never have arisen, since no gap would arise between what one ought to do and what one would do anyway. Like all moral obligations, the need for justice only arises because of a perceived conflict between self-interest and the good of all. Still, Hume is not quite correct, since we would surely still need rules to solve coordination problems, although we would not need enforcers for them. For example, while we would still need to teach everyone to drive on the same side of the road, speeding tickets or parking fines would be a thing of the past.

Second, imagine a situation in which we, with our actual limited benevolence, lived in a 'golden age' in which demand for material goods was always superseded by supply, so that whatever anyone needed was immediately at their disposal, without the need for the slightest effort. In such a case, the *natural* virtues would flourish, since the factors that usually block them, such as competition, fear, envy and so on, would be absent. However, there would be no need for 'the cautious, jealous virtue of justice'. As we have seen, Hume conceives of justice as a set of rules regarding the use of property, and that the notion of property consists of dividing objects into those that are 'mine' or 'another's', depending on who has the right to their exclusive use. But such a division would only arise if such goods were relatively scarce, at least to the extent that an object lost would not automatically be replaced.

> For what purpose make a partition of goods, where every one has already more than enough? Why give rise to property, where there cannot possibly be any injury? Why call this object *mine*, when upon the seizing of it by another, I need but stretch out my hand to possess myself to what is equally valuable? Justice, in that sense, being totally useless, would be an idle ceremonial, and could never possibly have place in the catalogue of virtues.
>
> (2*E* 184)

He makes the same point in considering the opposite extreme, in which the standard mechanisms of society could not satisfy even the most basic needs. The rules of justice would lose their grip on our practice and approval, since their only purpose is to provide a means to satisfy our material needs in an optimally viable way. If they manifestly fail to achieve this, they lose their justification. If the worst has already happened, and anything that justice is designed to protect has been lost, there is nothing to gain by placing oneself under these rules.

> The use and tendency of that virtue is to procure happiness and security, by preserving order in society; but where the society is ready to perish from extreme necessity, no greater evil can be dreaded from violence and injustice; and every man may now provide for himself by all the means, which prudence can dictate, or humanity permit.
>
> (2*E* 186)

Finally, suppose that our limited benevolence and resources were united with reasoning capacity sufficient to calculate one's own long-term self-interest, and to see that it was intricately bound up with the welfare of others. Suppose also that this reasoning ability were augmented by strength of character sufficient to make long-term interest always trump short-term gratification, so that one always acted on rationally informed calm passions. As before, rules of justice would be unnecessary under such circumstances, and so would not have evolved.

These thought experiments combine to reinforce Hume's original point that the institutions of justice arise from a delicate balance between several factors, both in human nature and external circumstances, applying to persons caught between egoism and altruism, between short-term gratification and long-term satisfaction, living in a world of finite and unstable resources.

> Thus, the rules of equity or justice depend entirely on the particular state and condition in which men are placed, and owe their origin and existence to that utility, which results to the public from their strict and regular observance. Reverse, in any considerable circumstance, the condition of men: Produce extreme abundance or extreme necessity: Implant in the human breast perfect moderation and humanity, or perfect rapaciousness and malice: By rendering justice totally *useless*, you thereby totally destroy its essence, and suspend its obligation on mankind.
>
> The common situation of society is a medium amidst all these extremes. We are naturally partial to ourselves, and to our friends; but are capable of learning the advantage resulting from a more equitable conduct. Few enjoyments are given to us from the open and liberal hand of nature; but by art, labour, and industry, we can extract them in great abundance. Hence the ideas of property become necessary in all civil society: Hence justice derives its usefulness to the public: And hence alone arises its merit and moral obligation.
>
> (2*E* 188)

More should be said on how we come to morally approve of just acts. As already explained, persons become aware that their pre-societal situation, in which wants and needs are being inadequately dealt with, can be overcome by entering into conventional agreements with reciprocating others. In the initial small local groupings, it will be relatively easy to see a direct connection between these rules and self-interest. The immediate effects of breaking the rules will be equally obvious. However, this connection becomes far more remote and amorphous as society gets bigger, generating apparent conflicts between private self-interest and the common good. Even though we appreciate the benefits of these rules, our tendency to want to make exceptions for short-term interest will increase in direct proportion to the size of the society, since the perceivable effects of one's just actions will seem increasingly remote. What counters this destabilizing influence is that each individual will still be highly conscious of the original connection when he is the victim of another's transgression. Secondly, even when he suffers no obvious hardship, such actions produce feelings of displeasure and disapproval, since he can sympathize with those affected. Once established, these conventions can be plugged into the sympathetic mechanism; we can see unpleasant consequences of unjust actions, and come to disapprove of them. Such sentiments will be *moral* when they are considered in an impersonal manner, as discussed in the previous chapter. In sum, '*Self-interest is the original motive to the establishment of justice: but a sympathy with public interest is the source of the moral approbation which attends that virtue*' (*T* 499–500).

While Hume recognizes the role of peer group pressure in inculcating the virtue of justice, he emphasizes the secondary and derivative role these can play. 'As publick praise and blame encrease our esteem for justice, so private education and instruction contribute to the same effect' (*T* 500). Nor does he deny that we are motivated to obey the law due to the desire to be approved of by others; in fact his psychology demands it: 'What farther contributes to encrease their solidity is the interest of our reputation, after the opinion, *that a merit or demerit attends justice or injustice*, is once firmly establish'd among mankind' (*T* 501). However, he stresses that someone could be influenced by such things only because she cared about others' opinion of her. Contrary to Hobbes and Mandeville, someone incapable of natural virtues would be incapable of acquiring artificial ones. Although she could act *as if* she had them, the internalization process would not take, and she would never come to *really* have them. Likewise, Hume admits the need for legal sanctions such as punishments, but only to *reinforce* public disapproval, to swing the balance in favour of honesty.

The acquisition and transfer of property

In *T* 3/2/1–2, Hume shows the necessity of developing *some* rules for regulating possessions. In *T* 3/2/3–4 he suggests how *particular* ways are chosen. These proposals are examples of his general preference for natural rather than rationalistic foundations, emphasizing what is viable given human nature, rather than what might be derived from some allegedly timeless principles existing outside it.

The recognition that only by placing ourselves under societal rules can we limit the disruptive effects of unchecked self-interest does not, by itself, force us into any particular arrangements. In fact, this underdetermination is now thought to be partially constitutive of being a convention at all. David Lewis (1969) has argued that it is built into the notion of a conventional solution to a coordination problem that there is at least one other way in which the matter could have been solved. On the contrary, if no alternative means existed, the issue would be resolved naturally.

Hume suggests that the actual rules chosen from these possible options will be those following most naturally from the associative principles governing the imagination. Recall that possession is a natural relation, existing prior to conventions of justice, and consisting in a history of exclusive use of the object in question. Property is the artificial analogue of possession. In laying out viable rules to inaugurate the *acquisition* of property, Hume takes advantage of its resemblance to possession. He then augments these with rules regulating the *transfer* of property. Only then does he introduce a third type of convention, relating to *promises*. Recall that he has already denied that the initial cooperative arrangements at the basis of society take the form of promises. As we shall see, this is because he conceives of promises as involving a higher degree of abstraction, and a degree of cooperation that could only be achieved once a certain prior foundation of trust had been established.

He insists that any attempt to establish rules of acquisition on some a priori basis, without regard to the facts of human nature and contingent human circumstances, will be disastrous. For example, he excludes any sort of rule allocating property in terms of merit, or who 'deserves' it most. Such a rule would cause more disagreement and trouble than the situation it was trying to alleviate, since there is no agreed method to ascertain who would thus qualify. As he puts it in the 2nd *Enquiry*, 'But were mankind to execute such a law, so great is the uncertainty of merit, both from its natural obscurity, and from the self-conceit of each individual, that no determinate rule of conduct would ever result from it' (2*E* 193).

A more appealing suggestion would be that one's possessions at the time of the convention become one's property, taking advantage of the already existing mental associations between particular individuals and their possessions, so that

> everyone continue to enjoy what he is at present master of, and that property and constant possession be conjoin'd to the immediate possession. Such is the effect of custom, that it not only reconciles us to any thing that we have long enjoy'd, but even gives us an affection for it, and makes us prefer it to other objects, which may be more valuable, but are less known to us.
>
> (*T* 503)

Such a rule would be augmented by the rule of *occupation* or 'first possession', wherein something that has never been possessed becomes the property of whoever claims it first. These rules would not be taken as exceptionless. For example, in cases where there has been a history of different possession, we might not be able to find out who was first. We would then allocate it by *prescription* to who has had it for a long time, regardless of whether they had it first. This would accord with the well-known tendency of the mind to give more weight to what is contiguous, over factors located in the distant past or future. Even if we knew that something was possessed by X in the distant past, this factor might be overruled if Y later acquired and kept it for some time up to the present.

Another immediately obvious principle would be that of *accession*, whereby we acquire something when it is closely connected with something else that is already our property. For example, I own the eggs laid by my chicken. When Hume says that these are 'esteem'd our property, even before possession' (*T* 509), he means that everyone would take them to be ours even before they exist. Everyone accepts that when my pear tree yields fruit next summer, it will be mine. Finally, we may acquire property by *succession*, that is, by inheritance. Here, the natural associative link is between the persons themselves, which is extended to their possessions.

Hume recognizes that these rules for the establishment and allocation of property need to be supplemented with rules for its transference. Not only do we need to be able to exchange goods we do not want or need for those we do, but we also need to exchange *services*. He therefore adds the condition that 'possession and property shou'd always be stable, except when the proprietor agrees to bestow them on some other person' (*T* 514).

He repeats many of these points in the 2nd *Enquiry*, emphasizing the utility of the chosen rules, without trying to derive them from his principles of association. One interesting development occurs in his discussion of the acquisition of property by prescription, where he comments that

> Sometimes both *utility* and *analogy* fail, and leave the laws of justice in total uncertainty. Thus, it is highly requisite, that prescription or long possession should convey property; but what number of days or months or years should be sufficient for that purpose, it is impossible for reason alone to determine
>
> (2*E* 196)

Hume differs from rationalists in seeing a significant disanalogy between the rules of justice and certain other fact-stating discourses. Whether they are attempting to derive moral rules from quasi-mathematical 'eternal relations', like Clarke, or from empirically checkable truths, as with Wollaston, rationalists assume that there is always an objective fact of the matter regarding the rightness or wrongness of any plan of action, independent of our acknowledgement of it. By contrast, Hume asserts that the laws of justice have gaps in their application. That is, they are devised according to present perception of how to satisfy our purposes; when a new unforeseen case crops up that the law cannot adjudicate on, we adjust it on an 'as needs' basis. But clearly such an act is one of *decision*, not *discovery*. Still less is it some a priori deduction. Likewise, there is a tacit recognition that such a process is essentially incompletable: 'In general, it may be safely affirmed that jurisprudence is, in this respect, different from all the sciences; and that in many of its nicer questions, there cannot be said to be truth or falsehood on either side' (2*E* 308). This important insight will be returned to in the final chapter.

Despite the conventionality of our laws, there is an undeniable difference between them and religious rules regarding food, hats and so on. This difference lies not in anything intrinsic to the practices themselves, but concerns whether or not these rules are *useful*; that is, does mankind actually benefit from having these rules? Hume's answer is a resounding 'Yes' in the case of justice, and an equally emphatic 'No' in the latter. 'But there is this material difference between *superstition* and *justice*, that the former is frivolous, useless, and burdensome; the latter is absolutely requisite to the well-being of mankind and existence of society' (2*E* 199).

The artificiality of justice does not weaken our obligation to it. Rather, our adherence to it is strengthened, since it has been given a coherent rationale in human wants and needs, without appeal to rationalistic obscurity. Given that only such a foundation can forge a connection to human motivation, no stronger validation can be given.

> These reflections are far from weakening the obligations of justice, or diminishing anything from the most sacred attention to property. On the contrary, such sentiments must acquire new force from the present reasoning. For what stronger foundation can be desired or conceived for any duty, than to observe, that human society, or even human nature, could not subsist without the establishment of it.
>
> (2*E* 200–1)

The artificiality of promises

> That the rule of morality, which enjoins the performance of promises, is not *natural*, will sufficiently appear from these two propositions, which I proceed to prove, viz. *that a promise wou'd not be intelligible, before human conventions had establish'd it; and*

> *even if it were intelligible, it wou'd not be attended with any moral obligation.*
>
> (*T* 516)

In denying that promising is natural, Hume means that it is not explicable from the psychology of individuals living prior to the conventions of society. That is, it is only intelligible within the psychology of *civilized* men, not men *per se*. For promising to be natural, it would have to consist in some *act of mind* that such a pre-societal person could perform, and from which its obligatory nature would derive. However, a survey of potential candidates proves that no such mental act exists.

Promising cannot consist in a *resolution*, since the mere act of resolving to do something need not put one under any obligation to stick to it. Thus, if I make a New Year's resolution to give up alcohol, my medicinal visit to the bar on the 2nd of January would not be taken as a sign of *moral* culpability, but, at most, as showing self-deception or weakness of will. Nor can promising be a *desire* to act in some way, since I can put myself under an obligation to do something merely by promising, whether or not I *want* to do it. A promise done grudgingly is still a promise.

Nor can a promise consist in *willing* to perform an action at some future date. Hume reminds us of the results of *T* 2/3/3, which refuted the rationalist conception of the will as something with its own power of agency, independent of that of the passions. He used these results in *T* 3/1/1 to prove that 'all morality depends on our sentiments'. It follows from these arguments that to come under a new obligation would require some change in the sentiments. However, since a new sentiment cannot be generated by a pure act of will, neither can a new obligation. Furthermore, recall from Book 1 that cause and effect are contiguous. Hence, the will is described in *T* 2/3/1 as *immediately* preceding action, and 'has an influence only on our present actions' (*T* 516). It follows that the idea of 'willing a future action' is incoherent, as it would involve 'action at a distance'.

He also shows the artificial nature of promising by re-running the argument of *T* 3/2/1 regarding the artificiality of justice: For an action to be naturally virtuous, individual psychology must supply a motive to do it, apart from the purported virtue itself. No action can be obligatory unless there is a natural passion to perform it, and a sense of duty cannot constitute such a motive, since it 'presupposes an antecedent obligation: And when an action is not requir'd by any natural passion, it cannot be requir'd by any natural obligation; since it may be omitted without proving any defect or imperfection in the mind and temper, and consequently without any vice' (*T* 518). But since there is no motive to keep promises apart from this sense of duty, 'it follows, that fidelity is no natural virtue, and that promises have no force, antecedent to human conventions' (*T* 519). He concludes that 'promises are human inventions, founded on the necessities and interests of society' (*T* 519), that is, our limited benevolence plus the instability of limited resources.

As mentioned earlier, the 'laws of nature' regarding the stability and transfer of ownership need augmenting by a third form of convention, as not all cooperative agreements can be completed immediately, but involve a temporal gap between what X gives to Y, and what Y gives or does in return. That is, these cases do not involve goods which are '*present* and *individual*' (i.e., exchanged there and then), but which are '*absent* or *general*'. For example, some deals involve 'absent' things not present at the time of agreement, such as if I, in Portland, promise to sell you my house in Glasgow. Again, some arrangements concern no specific items, but just something of a particular kind. If someone agrees to buy ten bushels of corn, he is usually not demanding any particular bushels. Finally, some agreements involve not goods but services, which can be both absent and general.

All these cases involve a delay between the benefit received by one party, and what he gives or does in return. However, given the selfish psychology of pre-societal man, his motive to keep what was given, and not deliver what he agreed to, will outweigh his motive to fulfil the bargain. So, left to their own devices, self-interest will ensure that everyone loses out. However, such individuals can reason that were they to have cooperated, everyone would now be better off. But they are, at this point, without any guarantee that the other will reciprocate, so have a disincentive to make the first move. Such a person would reason like this: If I do nothing, I lose out; but if I help him and he does not help me in return, I am in an even worse situation, having worked for nothing, and thereby increased his wealth and his advantage over me.

In nature, this is a catch-22 situation. We cannot directly will some new motivation, such as a new desire, to break the impasse. Nor, of course, can we act from reason alone. The only solution is 'to give a new direction to those natural passions, and teach us that we can better satisfy our appetites in an oblique and artificial manner, than by their headlong and impetuous motion' (*T* 521). As before, reason and imagination can identify the means towards a solution, and the motivation rests on the pre-existing selfish passions. We realize that it is in our best interest to be in a situation where people reciprocate services and goods; we know that this will not happen 'naturally' by itself; so we see that it is in our interest to change the outward circumstances, such that there is an incentive to reciprocate. This is done by means of a conventional choice of words (said, or in a written agreement), such as 'I promise', to represent the intention to perform a given act. The mutual understanding of this act puts one under an obligation, where failure to do so will result in penalties, whether legally sanctioned punishment, or the informal social penalty of no one trusting you in the future:

> there is a certain *form of words* invented...by which we bind ourselves to the performance of any action. This form of words constitutes what we call a *promise*, which is the sanction of the interested commerce of mankind. When a man says *he promises any thing*, he in effect expresses a *resolution* of performing it; and along with that, by making use of this *form of words*, subjects himself to the penalty of never being trusted again in case of failure. A resolution is the natural act of the mind, which promises express: But were there no more than a resolution in the case, promises wou'd only declare our former motives, and wou'd not create any new motive or obligation. They are the conventions of men, which create a new motive, when experience has taught us, that human affairs wou'd be conducted much more for mutual advantage, were there certain *symbols* or *signs* instituted, by which we might give each other security of our conduct in any

> particular incident. After these signs are instituted, whoever uses them is immediately bound by his interest to execute his engagements, and must never expect to be trusted any more, if he refuses to perform what he promis'd.
>
> (*T* 522)

Finally, the gradual appreciation of the benefit of this convention will generate moral approval for those who break it. As before, this will be reinforced by 'public interest, education, and the artifices of politicians'.

Hume uses his account of promising to criticize social contract theory, the 'fashionable' view that

> *All men…are born free and equal: Government and superiority can only be established by consent: The consent of men, in establishing government, imposes on them a new obligation, unknown to the laws of nature. Men, therefore, are bound to obey their magistrates, only because they promise it: and if they had not given their word, either expressly or tacitly, to preserve allegiance, it would never have become a part of their moral duty*.
>
> (*T* 542)

The idea that our present obligation to accept the authority of government rests on the making of some promise or contract to do so is implausible. While Hume grants it probable that some element of contract was involved in the initial establishment of government, this could not ground *our* allegiance, since we made no such promise. Rather, we are born into situations in which governmental authority is already a fact of life. Recall that Hume regards the making of a promise as an explicit activity. The idea that we have *tacitly* promised our obedience by the sheer fact of living under a government makes no sense. Second, such a view is refuted by the fact that even if I publicly announced that I did not consent to be governed, this would not free me from allegiance. The only valid basis for present allegiance to government is our belief that such a system remains in the public interest. Such a recognition generates our feelings of obligation to uphold and protect these rules, and a corresponding approval of such behaviour in others. As before, this is reinforced by peer group pressure.

Self-interest in its proper place

As mentioned at the beginning of this chapter, Hume's aim in presenting his catalogue of virtues is to break the grip of distorting theories, principally egoism and the 'monkish virtues' advocated by certain forms of Christianity. This raises the question of how such a simple and plausible theory as his own could have escaped everyone's notice. In response to this question, Hume suggests that adherence to the monkish virtues literally corrupts the mind so that these apparent truths are missed:

> it seems a reasonable presumption, that systems and hypotheses have perverted our natural understanding, when a theory, so simple and obvious, could so long have escaped the most elaborate examination...If we observe men, in every intercourse of business or pleasure, in every discourse and conversation, we shall find them nowhere, except in the schools, at any loss upon this subject.
>
> (2*E* 268–9)

In the Conclusion to the 2nd *Enquiry*, Hume deals briskly with those so afflicted in this splendid piece of invective which shows his literary skills at their finest:

> And as every quality which is useful or agreeable to ourselves or others is, in common life, allowed to be a part of personal merit; so no other will ever be received, when men judge of things by their natural, unprejudiced reason, without the delusive glosses of superstition and false religion. Celibacy, fasting, penance, mortification, self-denial, humility, silence, solitude, and the whole train of monkish virtues; for what reason they are everywhere rejected by men of sense, but because they serve to no manner of purpose; neither advance a man's fortune in the world, nor render him a more valuable member of society; neither

> qualify him for the entertainment of company, nor increase his power of self-enjoyment? We observe, on the contrary, that they cross all these desirable ends; stupify the understanding and harden the heart, obscure the fancy and sour the temper. We justly, therefore, transfer them to the opposite column, and place them in the catalogue of vices; nor has any superstition force sufficient among men of the world, to pervert entirely these natural sentiments. A gloomy, hair-brained enthusiast, after his death, may have a place in the calendar; but will scarcely ever be admitted, when alive, into intimacy and society, except by those who are as delirious and dismal as himself.
>
> (2*E* 270)

To anyone accepting Hume's account of human nature, the only defence of religion would be to show that it could be useful or agreeable to oneself or to others. However, by all accounts, Hume would regard such a project as doomed to failure, seeing religion as being at best useless and at worst harmful, both a major cause of human misery and an unnatural and corrupting influence on character.

Turning to egoism, while Hume disagrees with Hobbes in seeing self-love not as the true nature and foundation of morality, he grants its place as a vital part of morality, since virtue and self-interest are seen to coincide, when a long-term dispassionate view of one's welfare is taken, i.e., when one is controlled not by transient violent passions, but by calm passions informed by reason. After all, he asks, who would not choose to have a character formed around his table of virtues? 'No man was ever willingly deficient in this particular. All our failures here proceed from bad education, want of capacity, or a perverse and unpliable disposition' (2*E* 280). Who would not choose to have a sort of contagiously pleasant disposition that generates love in others?

> …let a man suppose that he has full power of modeling his own disposition, and let him deliberate what appetite or desire he would choose for the foundation of his happiness and enjoyment. Every affection, he would observe, when gratified by success, gives a satisfaction proportioned to its force and violence; but

> besides this advantage, common to all, the immediate feeling of benevolence and friendship, humanity and kindness, is sweet, smooth, tender, and agreeable, independent of all fortune or accidents. These virtues are besides attended with a pleasing consciousness or remembrance, and keep us in humour with ourselves as well as others; while we retain the agreeable reflection of having done our part towards mankind and society. As though all men show a jealousy of our success in the pursuits of avarice and ambition; yet we are almost sure of their good-will and good wishes, so long as we persevere in the paths of virtue, and employ ourselves in the execution of generous plans and purposes. What other passion is there where we shall find so many advantages united; an agreeable sentiment, a pleasing consciousness, a good reputation?
>
> (2*E* 281–2)

Hume ends the 2nd *Enquiry* with some reflections on the age-old worry about the extent of the self-interested person's motivation to obey general rules of morality and justice. A 'knave' might frame the issue like this: I can understand how everyone, including myself, is better off when the rules of justice are generally adhered to. It follows that it's clearly in my interest that *everyone else* obeys them; but would not I be even better off if I disobeyed them when it was to my advantage, if I could get away with it, and if such actions made a negligible dent in the overall beneficial effect of the rules of justice?

Hume replies that even if such a strategy worked, such a 'successful knave' would have won the battle but lost the war. His position is a secular version of the Biblical admonition about what does it profit a man to gain the whole world but lose his soul. His point is that this man would have wasted his life on ephemera, to the inevitable detriment of his character; in particular, his humanity, which would have to be denied and repressed in order to take advantage of others.

> But were they ever so secret and successful, the honest man, if he has any tincture of philosophy, or even common observation and reflection, will discover that they themselves are, in the end, the greatest dupes, and have sacrificed the invaluable enjoyment of a

> character, with themselves at least, for the acquisition of worthless toys and gewgaws. How little is requisite to supply the *necessities* of nature? And in a view to *pleasure*, what comparison between the unbought satisfaction of conversation, society, study, even health and the common beauties of nature, but above all the peaceful reflection on one's own conduct; what comparison, I say, between these and the feverish, empty amusements of luxury and expense. These natural pleasures, indeed, are really without price; both because they are below all price in their attainment, and above it in their enjoyment.
>
> (2*E* 283–4)

Further reading

On the artificial virtues, see Jonathan Harrison (1981) and David Miller (1981) for full-length treatments; also Knud Haakonsen in Norton (1993). On the natural virtues, see Ardal (1989: ch. 7) and Baier (1991: ch. 9). For background on psychological egoism, see Darwall (1995: ch. 3), and Schneewind (1998: chs 4–5).

Chapter 7

The moral stance

Treatise, Book 3, particularly Part 3; 2nd *Enquiry*, ch. 9, Appendixes 1 and 4; 'Of the Standard of Taste'

Chapter 7

Sympathy and its correction

This final chapter will elaborate on Hume's thesis that moral evaluation consists in the appraisal, from a 'steady and general point of view', of traits which we naturally approve due to their usefulness or intrinsic appeal, or condemn for their unpleasantness or disutility. The initial pre-moral attitudes are delivered by sympathy and are then corrected by a variety of means, both individual and societal. The former resources include reason and imagination, and the latter involve peer group pressure and the acquisition of moral vocabulary. I will call the successful adoption of this corrective process 'entering into the *moral stance*'. The discussion will begin with the relevant passages from the *Treatise* and the 2nd *Enquiry*, after which I turn to the later essay 'Of the Standard of Taste'.

Hume begins Section 3/3/1 of the *Treatise* by reminding us of sympathy's foundational role in the transmission of passions:

> The minds of all men are similar in their feelings and operations, nor can any one be actuated by any affection, of which all others are not, in some degree, susceptible. As in strings equally wound up, the motion of one communicates itself to the rest; so all the affections readily pass from one person to another, and beget correspondent movements in every human creature. When I see the *effects* of passion in the voice and gesture of any person, my mind immediately passes from these effects to their causes, and forms such a lively idea of the passion, as is presently converted into the passion itself. In like manner, when I perceive the *causes* of any emotion, my mind is convey'd to the effects, and is actuated with a like emotion.
>
> (*T* 575–6)

However, he has already acknowledged that the natural operation of sympathy is intrinsically partial, dependent on one's proximity (whether personal or merely spatio-temporal) to the person under consideration. Any indirect passions resulting from this sympathy will be equally variable in strength. By sharp contrast, it is constitutive of the moral stance that these relational factors do not determine assessment of someone's character. It follows that while indirect passions are part of the causal basis of moral sentiments, the latter evaluations cannot be equated with nor reduced to the immediate products of sympathy.

The inner separation from personal preferences and immediate emotional reactions required to enter into the moral stance involves the cooperation of reason and imagination. We have already seen how reason can indirectly exert its influence by identifying factors relevant to the pursuit of our goals, and hence that an action can be judged unreasonable if based on empirical error or faulty reasoning. In arriving at the moral stance, reason also exercises this normative function by indicating the unreliability of basing character assessments on immediate emotional responses. The actual process of abstracting away from an exclusive focus on our personal situation is the work of *imagination* rather than reason: 'the imagination adheres to the *general* view of things, and distinguishes the feelings they produce from those which arise from our particular and momentary situation' (*T* 587). That is, we go beyond what we *do* feel about some situation, and consider what we *would* feel from a distance, or from different perspectives. Reason draws conclusions from this counterfactually-based data. In recognizing the potentially misleading effects of untreated sympathy, we are motivated to revise our immediate judgements, and to act upon these revisions.

> Sympathy, we shall allow, is much fainter than our concern for ourselves, and sympathy with persons remote from us much fainter than that with persons near and contiguous; but for this very reason it is necessary for us, in our calm judgements and discourse concerning the characters of men, to neglect all these differences, and render our sentiments more public and social. Besides, that we ourselves often change our situation in this particular, we every day meet with persons who are in a situation different from us, and who could never converse with us were we to remain constantly in that position and point of view, which is peculiar to ourselves. The intercourse of sentiments, therefore, in society and conversation, makes us form some general unalterable standard, by which we may approve or disapprove of characters and manners.
>
> (2*E* 229)

He compares the development of the moral stance to our capacity to distinguish the idea of an object's 'real' shape from the passive deliverances of our senses. For example, as I type, my computer screen occupies a relatively small proportion of my visual field, which grows as I move closer to it. However, I do not infer that the screen itself is actually getting bigger, since past experience has shown me that appearances vary with distance. Although it now occupies more of my visual field than the sun, I am not led to construct extravagant cosmological theories on that account. As I dine, I see my plate as being round, while my guest sitting opposite me sees it as elliptical. I know that if I were sitting there, that is how I would see it. In a similar manner, I can work out how the plate would appear from a variety of different viewing positions, so that its apparent shape will vary with my viewing position. I can distinguish which aspects of my present sense-impressions are due to the object itself (its primary qualities, we might say) and those due to contingencies of personal perspective. That is, we can learn to consider situations objectively, in an idealized form irreducible to the output of any single perspective. The advantages of having this capability are obvious. If we acted purely on the basis of objects' momentary appearance, we would be unable to predict future stimuli, nor explain the occurrence of past or present experiences, and so would be unable to regularly satisfy our needs. In fact, we would not last five minutes.

In a similar manner, the moral stance requires the capacity to separate from one's own immediate position, and come to a judgement about someone's character that is informed and tempered by consideration of how others might see it under various conditions. In some cases, the primary task in achieving the moral stance will be to step back from one's own personal involvement in the issue under consideration. Other cases, such as when we consider events from the distant past, may involve projecting oneself into the situation to imagine how it would feel to be directly affected by it. I emphasize that this latter exercise would only occur as part of *reaching* the moral stance, and not as part of that stance itself. The moral stance does not consist in simulating the attitudes to someone's character that would be felt by those around him, since these responses will be biased and personal.

In his critique of moral rationalism, Hume pointed out a significant difference between the drawing of conclusions in moral and mathematical reasonings, in that the former only took place *once all the facts were in*. That is, a moral evaluation is a response to all the relevant natural facts. Some of these facts concern responses to someone's character, when it is considered from a variety of positions. The aim of developing a specifically *moral* sentiment requires that we try to take all these perspectives into account. Our own initial opinion is not ignored in this enterprise, but takes its place as one position among many. The resulting judgement emerges from the complex process of mutual readjustment between the different perspectives. So, unlike Kant, Hume's response to the unreliability of the affections is not to bar sentiment from involvement in moral judgement, but to *extend* its input, so that it can participate in its own correction.

Another use of the imagination is shown in what are sometimes called cases of 'virtue in rags' (see *T* 584). Hume considers the objection that if our moral judgements were ultimately based on sympathy, we would only approve of those persons whose actions *actually* caused us to feel that unique species of pleasure that prefigured moral judgement; whereas we also extend our approval in cases where we see that someone is prevented from exercising virtuous traits. As before, Hume's explanation rests on our imaginative capacity to consider counterfactuals in the assessment of character. That is, we know that had these external restrictions been absent, this person would have acted in a way that would cause this approval. We are also assisted by our adherence to *general rules*: we know that we typically approve of these contingently impeded traits, and have a mental association between them and the pleasure grounding moral approval, so we are naturally led to extend that approval to this anomalous case. In all these cases we actively manipulate the imagination in order to ascertain (or evoke) the pleasure caused by appreciation of the person's conduct and character when seen *objectively*. In other words, the aim is to come to an assessment that is not attached to a single perspective, but which is the result of the mutual adjustment of a variety of viewpoints. So objectivity is conceived not so much as a 'view from nowhere', but more like a 'view from everywhere'.

From our initial standpoint of limited benevolence and confined generosity, the benefits of entering into the moral stance would be clear, since acting purely on the basis of uncorrected sympathy is a recipe for chaos. If mutual character assessment was determined by moment-by-moment feelings, the capacity not only to communicate, but to even make sense of ourselves and each other, would be seriously compromised. Suppose that you were emotionally close to someone, but later grew apart due to geographical distance. The only resources available with which to describe your change in attitude would be in some non-normative vocabulary, such as merely noticing the *change* in your feelings. You would be unable to *explain why* these feelings had changed, or decide whether such a change was *justified*:

> Our situation, with regard both to persons and things, is in constant fluctuation; and a man, that lies at a distance from us, may, in a little time, become a familiar acquaintance. Besides, every particular man has a peculiar position with regard to others; and 'tis impossible we could ever converse together on any reasonable terms, were each of us to consider characters and persons, only as they appear from his peculiar point of view. In order, therefore, to prevent those continual *contradictions*, and arrive at a more *stable* judgment of things, we fix on some *steady* and *general* points of view; and always, in our thoughts, place ourselves in them, whatever may be our present situation. In like manner, external beauty is determin'd merely by pleasure; and 'tis evident, a beautiful countenance cannot give so much pleasure, when seen at a distance of twenty paces, as when it is brought nearer us. We say not, however, that it appears to us less beautiful: Because we know what effect it will have in such a position, and by that reflexion we correct its momentary appearance. Such corrections are common with regard to all the senses; and indeed 'twere impossible we cou'd ever make use of language, or communicate our sentiments to one another, did we not correct the momentary appearances of things, and overlook our present situation.
>
> (*T* 581–2)

As the previous quotation suggests, the development of moral sentiments is aided by the acquisition of a peculiarly moral vocabulary. When I employ the 'language of self-love', such as when I call someone 'my enemy' or 'my rival', I am taken to be only describing my personal attitudes, from a position of vested interest, with no more objective evaluation implicated. By contrast, when someone

> bestows on any man the epithets of *vicious* or *odious* or *depraved*, he then speaks another language, and expresses sentiments, in which he expects all his audience are to concur with him. He must here, therefore, depart from his private and particular situation, and must choose a point of view, common to him with others.
>
> (2*E* 272)

That is, I am taken to be not just expressing my opinion, but also to imply that any reasonable person who was aware of the relevant facts would come to the same conclusion. As David Wiggins puts it:

> In the process of learning the sense of the public language in which there is talk of good and bad, fair and foul, beautiful and ugly, they have to learn to depart from their private and particular situation and see things not only from thence but also from the point of view that shall be common between one person and another. The only way in which one can come to speak the public language of praise and blame or attain to any agreement with others in judgments is to learn to see his judgments and responses as answerable to that common point of view.
>
> (Wiggins 1991: 301)

The aspiration to objectivity leads to calm passions of moral approval or disapproval. What makes these passions *moral* is their impersonality, that is, their coming from the general and stable viewpoint; what makes them *passions* is their motivational force. In the 2nd *Enquiry*, Hume names the central moral sentiment as *humanity*, where this is a calm impersonal form of benevolence, that is, a disinterested desire for the benefit of any person purely on account of our shared humanity. I should add that the *object* of the passion of humanity will still be a specific person or group of persons. Hume is insistent that there is no motivationally active concern for humanity-as-a-whole. It is always directed to individuals, but individuals as viewed *qua human beings*.

We are now in a better position to understand the strength of influence that calm passions can exert. One factor is that they are *corroborated by reason*. Hume has already pointed out the tendency for desires to disappear, or lose force, if they are seen to be based on errors of fact or inference. Since moral evaluations are produced through the refinement of the pre-moral passions by reason (together with imagination), they have already passed this test. A related factor is that since moral sentiments result from the broadening of perspective beyond that of personal involvement, this exercise may lead to the realization that one's pre-moral likes and dislikes are based on contingent factors, and that they would be utterly different had one's situation or history been other than it is. So the development of the moral stance involves the attribution of error to the pre-moral sentiments; the mistake of granting them a validity they do not deserve, through placing unjustified emphasis on contingencies of time, place or relationship.

Another source of the strength of calm passions lies in their being *approachable from any position*; that is, starting from any set of partial or personal details. Tying in with this is the fact that although in each individual, the motivational force of his humanity is weak compared to that of self love, the combined force of humanity can overrule an individual's selfish impulses. This is because while each individual's self-love is pulling in a different direction to that of another, being incompatible and antagonistic, those same persons' humanity, being essentially equivalent (or at least converging), can combine their strength. When this is applied throughout society, the aggregate force of humanity can overpower self-love.

> What wonder then, that moral sentiments are found of such influence in life; though springing from principles, which may appear, at first sight, somewhat small and delicate? But these principles, we may remark, are social and universal; the form, in a manner, the *party* of humankind against vice or disorder, its common enemy. As the benevolent concern for others is diffused, in a greater or less degree, over all men, and is the same in all, it appears more frequently in discourse, is cherished by society and conversation, and the blame and approbation, consequent on it, are thereby roused from that lethargy into which they are probably lulled, in solitary and uncultivated nature. Other passions, although perhaps originally stronger, yet being selfish and private, are often overpowered by its force, and yield the denomination of our breast to these social and public principles.
>
> (2*E* 275–6)

Hume's moral stance has strong similarities to Ideal Observer theory. The central point uniting versions of this theory is that moral judgements are constituted out of the responses of an 'ideal observer' (or 'true judge', as Hume sometimes puts it), where this hypothetical person is shorn of all factors that can distort judgement. So to say that some action is morally wrong is not to say that I, or you, disapprove of it, but that an ideal observer would condemn it. This ideal observer will be adequately informed: he will have enough true beliefs and no false beliefs about the matter in hand; he will reason well, both regarding deductions and causal inferences; and he will not be in the grip of distorting passions such as prejudice or vested interest.

The main appeal of such a theory is that it allows a satisfactory compromise between, on the one hand, simplistic forms of subjectivism which identify moral judgements with initial emotional responses, leading to a relativism in which no standard of adjudication is possible, and in which there is no difference between *being* morally right and *seeming* that way to X or Y; and, on the other hand, the metaphysical excess of theories asserting the existence of facts pertaining to moral properties, holding independently of all possible human cognition or sensibility. Hume attempts to derive a regulative standard from within the contingent facts of human responses, taking it to consist in rationally refined sentiment. As we have seen, the objectivity of moral evaluations is to be construed as *intersubjectivity*; that is, as a stance that delivers judgements that can be reached by any competent person, and from a variety of starting points. While Hume does not equate moral judgements with the *beliefs* of the ideal observer (since beliefs cannot motivate action), he does say that true beliefs are an essential component of such judgements. However, these beliefs must be combined with the refinement of *sensibility*, in the creation of moral sentiments. With this point in mind, we can see how Hume escapes the objection that appeal to an ideal observer is inconsistent with other aspects of his theory.

Barry Stroud argues that if we accept Hume's definition of virtue as 'whatever mental action or quality gives to the spectator the pleasing sentiment of approbation' (2*E* 289), then this 'implies that vice and virtues are objective features of an action or character'; but then 'we could come to discover by reasoning and observation alone whether a particular action has that quality'. That is, we could empirically discover that we approve of utility, and that certain acts are useful. Hence 'we could arrive at moral judgements by reason and observation alone. That is what Hume explicitly denies; it would destroy the whole point of his moral theory' (Stroud 1977: 182–3).

But while Hume can agree that reason could discover these facts, as part of the scientific study of human nature, this would not yet fully constitute what I have called his moral stance. While moral approval *includes* an impartial judgement that something is either useful or pleasing, the moral stance also requires that we come to have a sentiment of moral approval alongside these factual judgements. Reason can tell us that a person possesses some trait that evokes moral approval, through noting a constant conjunction between the property and the subsequent feeling. However, this recognition, by itself, has no motivational force. The following passage makes Hume's position clear.

> But though reason, when fully assisted and improved, be sufficient to instruct us in the pernicious or useful tendency of qualities and actions; it is not alone sufficient to produce any moral blame or approbation. Utility is only a tendency to a certain end; and were the end totally indifferent to us, we should feel the same indifference towards the means. It is requisite a *sentiment* should here display itself, in order to give a preference to the useful above the pernicious tendencies. The sentiment can be no other than a feeling for the happiness of mankind, and a resentment of their misery; since these are the different ends which virtue and vice have a tendency to promote. Here therefore *reason* instructs us in the several tendencies of actions, and *humanity* makes a distinction in favour of those which are useful and beneficial.
>
> (2*E* 286)

Rachel Cohon emphasizes the importance of Hume's remark that 'these two particulars are to be consider'd as equivalent, with regard to mental qualities, virtue and the power of producing love or pride, and vice and the power of producing humility or hatred. In every case, therefore, we must judge the one by the other' (*T* 574–5). In 'judging the one by the other', that is, holding that something is a virtue just in case it has the power of producing love or pride, it follows that 'in making moral judgments we always simultaneously make *objective*, *causal* judgments about the traits we evaluate' (Cohon 1997: 841). As we have seen, such evaluations involve verifiable beliefs about our affective responses in certain possible situations.

Similar considerations show that Hume escapes J.L. Mackie's claim of a conflict between the moral stance and the motivationally active nature of moral judgements.

> The only sentiment that could directly influence action would be one which the agent himself actually had at the time of acting. How, then, would a judgment that referred to a sentiment of a speaker, if he is not the agent, or of a representative impartial spectator, or to merely possible sentiments which one or other of these would have if he thought further in certain ways, help to direct action?
>
> (Mackie 1980: 68)

In other words, Mackie objects that the adoption of the 'general point of view' would make moral judgements *cognitive*, being the result of beliefs about what such a hypothetical impartial agent would feel from this rarefied viewpoint. But then, he continues, the mere fact that this ideal observer would disapprove of something would give *me* no motivation not to do it. Hence, Hume's account of coming to the moral stance conflicts with his internalism. However, if my interpretation is correct, Hume avoids this criticism by requiring that I *become* the impartial spectator. In other words, when reason and imagination refine and correct my original sentiments, it transforms them into new, impartial sentiments, which can thus motivate me to action.

A standard of taste

I will now turn my attention to 'Of the Standard of Taste', using Hume's parallel between the development of moral and aesthetic sensibilities to bring out the various conditions that must be in place before moral evaluations can be made.

Despite the 'great variety of taste' prevailing in the world, 'It is natural for us to seek a *Standard of Taste*; a rule by which the various sentiments of men may be reconciled; at least a decision afforded confirming one sentiment, and condemning another' ('Of the Standard of Taste' [ST] 229). That is, we try to bring some order to our evaluative discourses by developing criteria to resolve disputes. However, one 'species of philosophy' would rule out this possibility, by asserting a fundamental and unbridgeable difference between judgement and sentiment. Such a naive subjectivism sees all aesthetic judgements as being of equal status because they do not refer to properties in objects themselves, but merely make explicit our reaction to them. Consider two cases, where I say that (1) a certain painting was done in the seventeenth century; and (2) that it is beautiful. My former claim is unproblematically true or false, since it 'has a reference to' a matter of fact beyond the judgement itself. That is, it is true if the painting actually was created in that century; otherwise it is false. So, if you say that it was done in 1723 and another takes it to be a recent forgery, then, out of the three of us, at most one is correct. With (2), this species of philosophy suggests, the situation is radically different. Here, if we disagree (for example, suppose I regard it as a masterpiece, you are indifferent to it and a third person thinks it wretched) then one judgement is just as good as the other, in that distinctions between right and wrong, true and false, do not apply. That is, none are true in the same way that my claim about the date of the painting can be true, because there is no fact of the matter for the competing claims to correspond to.

> All sentiment is right; because sentiment has a reference to nothing beyond itself, and is always real, wherever a man is conscious of it. But all determinations of the understanding are not right; because they have a reference to something beyond themselves, to wit, a real matter of fact; and are not always conformable to that standard. Among a thousand different opinions which different men may entertain of the same subject, there is one, but only one, that is just and true, and the only difficulty is to fix and ascertain it. On the contrary, a thousand different sentiments, excited by the same object, are all right; because no sentiment represents what is really in the object. It only marks a certain conformity or relation between the object and the organs

> or faculties of the mind, and if that conformity did not really exist, the sentiment could never possibly have being.
>
> (ST 230)

So, this theory continues, beauty is not a genuine property of objects, but is merely a way in which we happen to see things; however, these responses vary among different people, and there is no way of adjudicating such disagreements. As Hume was aware, one might be tempted to draw such a conclusion from a careless reading of his arguments of *T* 2/3/3 and 3/1/1. In this later essay, he agrees that no criterion *external to human nature* can enable us to resolve such disputes, but denies that it follows that all judgements are of equal worth, since a normative standard can be established from *within* aesthetic practice.

Although our everyday thinking on these matters reveals a strongly subjectivist strain, this is countered by a different line of thought which accepts distinctions between informed and uninformed judgements, and between refined and coarse sensibilities. While some cases compare items of roughly equal merit, such that two competent persons could disagree and make nothing of that disagreement, other cases involve a difference in quality so great that a contrary judgement would be regarded as equally culpable and open to ridicule as in disputes over numerically quantifiable matters. 'Whoever would assert an equality of genius and elegance between Ogilby and Milton, or Bunyan and Addison, would be thought to defend no less an extravagance, than if he had maintained a mole-hill to be as high as Tenerife, or a pond as extensive as the ocean' (ST 230–1). An aesthetic theory must acknowledge and explain the fact that while great differences of taste exist, some aesthetic judgements are regarded as beyond dispute.

Hume insists that the resolution of evaluative disagreements does not rely on a priori rules. Rather, our criteria are discovered through systematic observation of actual human practice, which reveals a high degree of regularity in aesthetic response, deriving from basic facts of human nature:

> It is evident that none of the rules of composition are fixed by reasonings *a priori*, or can be esteemed abstract conclusions of the understanding, from comparing those habitudes and relations of ideas, which are eternal and immutable. Their foundation is the same with that of all the practical sciences, experience; nor are they any thing but general observations, concerning that what has been universally found to please in all countries and in all ages.
>
> (ST 231)

Hume is making a general claim, applying to ethics, aesthetics and all modes of evaluation, that human nature is such that certain properties provoke pleasure and approbation, whereas others produce a negative reaction. Hence, agreement can be attained in aesthetic and moral judgements, despite the ontologically 'secondary' nature of beauty or goodness, due to this naturally guaranteed convergence. This is augmented by our reflective capacity to critique our immediate responses, together with our training in the languages of aesthetics or morals, with their recognition of the difference between immediate and considered responses.

> It appears, then, that amidst all the variety and caprice of taste, there are certain general principles of approbation or blame, whose influence a careful eye may trace in all operations of the mind. Some particular forms or qualities, from the original structure of the internal fabric are calculated to please, and others to displease.
>
> (ST 233)

Aesthetic disagreement is due to the fact that these rules could only be completely applied by an *ideal* judge, one in whom a host of different factors were functioning optimally, enabling the delicate 'finer emotions' constitutive of a true aesthetic response to shine through. We can at best approximate to that ideal. A response may diverge due to malfunction within the system, analogous to the way that jaundice may affect colour perception. Contrary to the naive subjectivist opinion that 'To seek the real beauty, or real deformity, is as fruitless an inquiry, as to pretend to ascertain the real sweet or real bitter' (ST 230), we regard an object's 'true and real colour' as that observed by healthy persons under standard lighting conditions. Hence it is clear that the jaundice sufferer has erred, and that his error is explained by the malfunction of his visual system. This verdict is confirmed by the virtually complete agreement of those appropriately situated. Clearly, if disagreements over colour perception can be explained in this manner, the room for error will be far greater in the case of aesthetic judgements, since colour vision depends on factors given 'for free' by nature, whereas aesthetic evaluations also involve a variety of educational or circumstantial contingencies. In fact, one might say that the two cases are disanalogous, since accurate colour perception is the norm, whereas Hume admits the difficulty of making true aesthetic judgements.

We can specify what a well-functioning visual system consists in, independently of any particular judgements on colours. It is important that something comparable be done for aesthetics, otherwise Hume will be open to the charge of circularity, of saying both that refined sensibilities make true aesthetic judgements, and that these judgements are made by those with refined sensibilities. He avoids this trap by appealing to several well-understood factors which could result in inadequate aesthetic appreciation. The presence or absence of these factors in any particular case will be a straightforward matter of fact. The prevailing 'great variety of taste' is due to the fact that few persons manage to fully avoid these traps:

> Those finer emotions of the mind are of a very tender and delicate nature, and require the concurrence of many favorable circumstances to make them play with facility and exactness, according to their general and established principles.
>
> (ST 232)

Errors in judgement can be due to (1) lack of delicacy; (2) lack of good sense; (3) prejudice; and (4) ignorance. To avoid these sources of error, we need *practice* and the capacity to make appropriate comparisons between cases.

It is well understood that *prejudice* interferes with the operations of the understanding. Since proper reasoning is a prerequisite for accurate aesthetic (and moral) judgement, prejudice thereby impedes these evaluations as well. The distorting influence of prejudice ties into the fact that *durability of approval* is a reliable indicator of aesthetic worth. In assessing new works of art, it can be hard to extricate the intrinsic merit of the work from one's personal feelings about the artist himself, whether this may be envy from afar, or bias due to personal acquaintance. It is utterly crucial to see the work of art as it is in itself, not filtered through the distorting lens of our personal preferences. The parallel to the virtues is clear, and has already been discussed.

> Authority or prejudice may give a temporary vogue to a bad poet or orator; but his reputation will never be durable or general…On the contrary, a real genius, the longer his works endure, and the more wide they are spread, the more sincere is the admiration which he meets with. Envy and jealousy have too much place in a narrow circle; and even familiar acquaintance with his person may diminish the applause due to his performances; but when these obstructions are removed, the beauties, which are naturally fitted to excite agreeable sentiments, immediately display their energy; and while the world endures, they maintain their authority over the minds of men.
>
> (ST 233)

Hume's model for *delicacy* in aesthetic judgement is that of a refined or sensitive palate. This consists in the capacity to discriminate and focus attention on small and subtle features that might be overlooked in favour of more salient properties. He describes this skill as delicacy of *imagination*, since it involves reconfiguring one's actual experience, selectively focusing on certain features over others, and bringing them to the forefront of attention. The moral analogy should be obvious. It is clearly no indicator of a developed moral sensibility that you regard Hitler as evil, since anyone but a monster can agree on this. The real test comes with more subtle and complicated cases.

He illustrates delicacy by a story from *Don Quixote*, in which

Sancho Panza tells of two relatives known for their expertise in wine. When asked for their opinion on a hogshead, they were ridiculed for judging that an otherwise excellent wine was tarnished by a slight taste of leather and of iron. They were vindicated when an old key, with a leather thong attached, emerged from the container as the last of the wine was poured.

This example has been used to propose that Hume was amending his position, granting aesthetic (and, by extension, moral) properties an objectivity that his previously stated theory could not support. For example, Anthony Savile takes the story to suggest that the 'true judge' is responsive to factors that are *there to be seen*, and which both cause and justify his evaluation. That is, Sancho's kinsmen taste the leather and metal not only because of their refined discriminatory powers, but because these faculties were detecting leather and metal that were actually there to be tasted. Similarly, the fact that true judges tend to agree in their judgements of taste is explained by their convergence on real properties that exist independently of their sensibilities. Likewise, disagreement can be resolved by indicating these properties. Hence, contrary to the interpretation of Hume presented in the previous section, the responses of true judges do not *constitute* aesthetic or moral virtue, but merely *indicate its presence*. That is, they provide evidence for the presence of the properties in which virtue consists. So, even if we ought to defer to experts in such cases, these experts ultimately defer to the world.

I disagree that Hume is recanting from the view that the judgement (or 'joint verdict') of true judges constitutes the standard of taste. Consider this passage, immediately following the Sancho example:

> Though it be certain that beauty and deformity, more than sweet and bitter, are not qualities in objects, but belong entirely to the sentiment, internal or external, it must be allowed, that there are certain qualities in objects which are fitted by nature to produce those particular feelings. Now, as these qualities may be found in a small degree, or may be mixed and confounded with each other, it often happens that the taste is not affected with such minute qualities, or is not able to distinguish all the particular flavors, amidst the disorder in which they are presented. When the organs

> are so fine as to allow nothing to escape them, and at the same time so exact as to perceive every ingredient of the composition, this we call delicacy of taste, whether we employ these terms in the literal or metaphorical sense. Here then the general rules of beauty are of use, being drawn from established models, and from the observation of what pleases or displeases, when presented singly and in a high degree; and if the same qualities, in a continued composition, and in a smaller degree, affect not the organs with a sensible delight or uneasiness, we exclude the person from all pretensions to this delicacy.
>
> (ST 235)

This passage employs Locke's distinction between primary and secondary qualities (or Hume's interpretation of it) whereby sweetness and bitterness are not self-standing sensibility-independent properties intrinsic to objects, but ways in which we experience the other more basic properties that are in objects. (Actually, Hume's attitude to this distinction is ambiguous, given that he rejects it in the *Treatise* 1/4/4, but makes constant use of it elsewhere in explicating his moral and aesthetic theories.) His point in this present case is that even if secondary qualities are ways in which we respond to objects, nonetheless there are properties genuinely in objects which regularly and systematically produce these effects on persons, subject to the abovementioned standard conditions. Hume suggests that beauty and deformity have the same ontological status as these secondary qualities.

Hume says explicitly that 'beauty and deformity, more than sweet and bitter, are not qualities in objects, but belong entirely to the sentiment'. By contrast with these secondary qualities, 'there are certain qualities in objects which are fitted by nature to produce those particular feelings'. In other words, objects possess other properties – primary qualities – which are such as to produce certain impressions, sensory or sentimental, in creatures like ourselves. I think the confusion has been caused by the fact that the Sancho example does not fit Hume's position; but the fault lies in the example rather than the theory itself. In the story, the experts tasted the leather and iron because of the presence of leather and iron, existing independently of any possible detection. However, in the case of the finer sentiments of aesthetic and moral appreciation, no such resembling property exists to be discovered.

Returning to the preconditions of true aesthetic judgement, *good sense* seems to be a balanced and informed appreciation of the *point* of the work in question. It requires an understanding of the audience whom the artist was intending to reach, and the context in which he was putting his message across. Clearly, *ignorance* of these matters would prevent sound judgement, in the same way as a lack of appreciation of context will inevitably cause us to misread someone's actions and their moral character. So good sense is more a matter of understanding than of sensibility, since only reason can determine the efficacy of means–ends relationships. Given the sheer amount of data which can be involved in such contextualization, and the difficulty in assessing their truth, the possibility of error is always present.

While there are natural differences in our degree of aesthetic appreciation, all can be improved by *practice*, without which one is unable to distinguish superficial responses from more settled ones. In the same way as there is all the difference in the world between disliking someone and morally disapproving of them, there is a huge difference between merely 'liking' a work of art (it may excite you, you may think it 'cute', and so on) and appreciating it with a genuine aesthetic sense. Instructive practice involves making appropriate *comparisons* with other works. For example, we must be able to distinguish different genres of art, so that one does not unfairly condemn, or mistakenly approve of, some work because of false assumptions about what sort of thing it is. Second, one needs to be able to compare it to different examples of the same genre. One cannot see of something as a *good* example of some kind unless one has seen plenty of the kind in question. For example, if you have never heard Indian classical music, you will be unable to judge whether a given performance is exemplary or unique, or whether it is mundane, derivative or formulaic. You will not know where to look or listen; the subtle nuances that would be apparent to a connoisseur will totally pass you by. In order to come to the point of discrimination, you will need experience of a variety of different cases, which will give you the background to make the appropriate comparisons.

This reference to 'comparison' must not be confused with the 'principle of comparison', invoked in the *Treatise* to explain the emergence of non-basic indirect passions such as envy or malice. Those passions were the result of considering someone not as he is in himself, but in comparison to oneself, such as being 'richer than me', and so on. Hume made it clear that these comparisons were intrinsically distorting. Here in this later essay, he is making the different and compatible point that the making of relevant comparisons is a necessary condition of appropriate aesthetic (and, by analogy, moral) judgement. In such cases, Hume is clear that the works must be considered in their own right, not in terms of any relation to me or anyone else. The critic must 'allow nothing to enter into his consideration, but the very object which is submitted to his examination'. If I bear any relationship to the artist, 'I must depart from this situation, and, considering myself as a man in general, forget, if possible, my individual being, and my peculiar circumstances'. So, while making appropriate comparisons are a precondition of seeing the work of art in its true colours, the work so conceived is not considered in relation to anything else.

Hume summarizes the essay's conclusions in the following passage:

> Thus, though the principles of taste be universal, and nearly, if not entirely, the same in all men; yet few are qualified to give judgment on any work of art, or establish their own sentiment as the standard of beauty. The organs of internal sensation are seldom so perfect as to allow the general principles their full play, and produce a feeling correspondent to those principles. They either labour under some defect, or are vitiated by some disorder; and by that means excite a sentiment, which may be pronounced erroneous. When the critic has no delicacy, he judges without any distinction, and is only affected by the grosser and more palpable qualities of the object: the finer touches pass unnoticed and disregarded. Where he is not aided by practice, his verdict is attended with confusion and hesitation. Where no comparison has been employed, the most frivolous beauties, such as rather merit the name of defects, as the object of his admiration. Where he lies under the influence of prejudice, all his natural sentiments

> are perverted. Where good taste is wanting, he is not qualified to discern the beauties of design or reasoning, which are the highest and most excellent. Under some or other of these imperfections, the generality of men labor; and hence a true judge in the finer arts is observed, even during the polished ages, to be so rare a character: strong sense, united to delicate sentiment, improved by practice, perfected by comparison, and cleared of all prejudice, can alone entitle critics to this valuable character; and the joint verdict of such, wherever they are to be found, is the true standard of taste and beauty.
>
> (ST 241)

He ends with a cautionary remark that not every aesthetic dispute can be settled, even when all the disputants are 'entirely blameless' and cannot be faulted in their information, their inferences, their empathic capacities, nor anything else. He indicates two sources of divergence which can still hold under such conditions, and which may be ineliminable from the human condition, and regarding which normative comparisons do not apply. 'The one is the different humors of particular men; the other, the particular manners and opinions of our age and country' (ST 243). An example of the former is the fact that an individual's taste may change over time, but in such a way that no stage can be regarded as better or more refined than the other.

> A young man, whose passions are warm, will be more sensibly touched with amorous and tender images, than a man more advanced in years, who takes pleasure in wise, philosophical reflections, concerning the conduct of life, and moderation of the passions. At twenty, Ovid may be the favorite author, Horace at forty, and perhaps Tacitus at fifty. Vainly would we, in such cases, endeavor to enter into the sentiments of others, and divest ourselves of those propensities which are natural to us. We choose our favorite author as we do our friend, from a conformity of humor and disposition. Mirth or passion, sentiment or reflection; whichever of these most predominates in our temper, it gives us a peculiar sympathy with the writer who resembles us.
>
> (ST 244)

However, this example can be interpreted in different ways. One would be as a case in which ideal observers differ in their judgements. Another way of taking the example, which differs from Hume's own but which suits his theory better, would be to treat this not as a dispute between three true judges of Ovid, Horace or Tacitus, but involving only one true judge per author, the other two being barred by temperament from enjoying maximal appreciation of the other two's favourites. In other words, we add more constraints to the specification of the 'true judge' and say, with Anthony Savile, that one can only be a true judge regarding 'an area *appropriate to his interests, his character, and his background*' (Savile 1996: 135). Hence, 'the criterion of good taste in respect of one author or another will be the sentiment of someone whose interests, temperament and background naturally draw him to works of the kind in point and whose responses are most appropriately chosen for the writer in question' (Savile 1996: 136). This will ensure more uniformity between those fitting the added requirements, moving the incommensurability onto the temperaments themselves.

Hume is right not to lose any sleep over this sort of case. Given that these men really are 'true judges' of their favourite authors, they are likely to possess the more general skills and refinements that would afford a high level of appreciation of the other two writers. It is clear that Hume implies no disagreement over whether Tacitus is *any good*, but, at most, whether he is better than Ovid or Horace. Such innocent and trivial disputes, on which nothing important depends, crop up in all evaluative contexts. For example, while two football experts could reasonably disagree over whether Johan Cruyff was a *better* player than George Best, any pundit who denied that both were *superb* players would never be taken seriously again.

A standard of morals

> To understand the genealogy of morals is to understand not only *how much* but also *how relatively little* room there sometimes is for the actual standard to be varied.
>
> (Wiggins 1991: 308)

Of the many weaknesses of Hume's rationalist opponents, one of the most important was their failure to explain the prevalence of error and disagreement in moral matters. If morality is grounded in objective facts or relations which Divine Providence has equipped us with reasoning capacity sufficient to discern, how do such fundamental and seemingly intractable disputes remain? As we have seen, rationalists were forced to account for this in terms of the perverse and wilful denial of self-evident facts. At the other extreme, it is now well understood that naive subjectivism cannot even make sense of the notion of moral disagreement, let alone account for the phenomenon. Hume, by contrast, in appreciating both the powers and limitations of reason and sentiment, provides a solid basis for understanding not only the cause of moral disagreements, but also how and when they can be resolved.

One cause relates to the complexity of the natural pre-moral basis of moral judgement, whereby four kinds of character traits elicit approval, namely those either useful or pleasing, to the bearer or to others. As I discussed in the previous chapter, while Hume stresses the hedonistic roots of moral judgement, and places special emphasis on social utility, nowhere does he endorse a single criterion of right action, such as the utilitarians' Greatest Happiness Principle. In fact, he never advocates *any* criterion of right action, since his project was one of moral psychology, namely to provide a naturalistic account of how we could come to make moral judgements *at all*. However, to the extent that a normative theory could be reconstructed from his scientific project, it could not be a straightforwardly utilitarian one. In the eyes of Bentham and Mill, the theoretical and practical benefit of a unitary source of value was that it could resolve all moral disputes. In endorsing a pluralistic basis, you thereby pay the price of accepting that coming to a moral decision will often involve a complex trading off between several incompatible goods, with no formal procedure to tell you what to do.

A second source of moral disagreement comes from the fact that although the moral stance itself is 'general', the primary motivation to enter it comes from self-interest, where this is taken to include specific personal loyalties and obligations. Hume is fully aware of the difficulty of distinguishing such personal considerations from the impartial feeling of 'humanity'. To be precise, this would not be a case of disagreement occurring within the moral stance, but the problem of ascertaining whether one is really judging from that perspective. However, nothing in Hume's moral stance necessarily forbids personal loyalties that entail duties over and above those to other individuals. So, unlike the utilitarians, the Humean picture leaves open the possibility of disputes over the relative weighting of personal and impersonal considerations.

Finally we have the fact that we are creatures of limited rationality. Two strands should be emphasized here. First, as we have seen, a great deal of reasoning may be needed in order to achieve the moral stance, and we may fail to meet the challenge. Second, we can be seduced by more salient and immediate benefits, overruling the calm perspective of long-term interest which Hume regards as congruent with altruism.

However, despite all these sources of difficulty, Hume has the resources to explain how persons like ourselves, fairly rational, self interested but imbued with fellow feeling, can very often come to agree on the right thing to do, and recognize that, in David Wiggins's apt phrase, 'there is nothing else to think' regarding the matter in hand. In making moral evaluations, and even in employing moral language, we acknowledge a difference, and a potential divergence, between what we may *want* to do and what we *ought* to do. That is, we regard our immediate responses as being up for appraisal against factors independent of our wishes. Recall the case of the negligent father. Hume would insist that this man could come to see that he ought to help his children. Granted, he does not have any *direct* motive to act, purely on the basis of his unreconstructed passions. However, assuming that he is an otherwise normal man, he has other resources at his disposal. Even though he feels no natural inclination to support his children, he would be aware of the unnecessary suffering his neglect was causing. He would no doubt disapprove on being confronted with *other* such cases of neglect, and would have sufficient intelligence to see the comparison between such behaviour and his own, and to make the appropriate inferences. He would also have enough insight to notice the peculiarity of his own indifference, and to recognize the disapproval that would come his way as a result of it. This would give him the incentive to acquire parental concern by the indirect strategy of acting *as if* he were so motivated, in the hope that the practice would become habitual and thereby second nature to him. Finally, and most relevant to the present topic, if this man were to attempt to justify his behaviour, he surely could not avoid factual error, bad arguments or self-deception.

This is not to say that the man would be willing to enter into such a dialogue, or any of the other strategies mentioned above. Hume is not naive enough to say that people can always be brought to see the errors of their ways, let alone change them. Such a belief wouldn't fit the facts of this cruel world. His point is rather that anyone who *did* utilize all the resources at his disposal would be brought to see that basic non-negotiable facts of human nature put him under a categorical obligation to look after his children. Such a non-conditional demand is not, of course, derived from a Kantian a priori rule applying to all rational agents *per se*, but is a natural consequence of the wants and needs of human beings. While this duty is grounded in natural human responses, it still applies to him even if he does not feel the natural affection, since he is still *capable* of recognizing his obligation.

But to repeat, nothing guarantees that one will actually come to see a situation from the moral stance in any particular case. Coming to do so involves a complex interaction of empathic, imaginative and rational skills, each of which could fail to operate satisfactorily. Second, even if this stance is reached, this alone does not guarantee that one will *act* on its deliverances, since nothing guarantees that this newly activated calm passion of humanity will not be overruled by a stronger violent self-centred passion.

Of course, not all moral issues are so straightforward as that of the 'deadbeat dad'. In particular, there will be some in which the sheer quantity of the information requisite to a reliable judgement, and the difficulty of obtaining it, will ensure that no party can reasonably claim exclusive occupancy of the moral stance. This will be particularly the case in matters of justice, where the relevant data goes beyond an individual case, concerning an entire practice. Consider an issue such as capital punishment, and the difficulty one faces in acquiring reliable information on whether the death penalty actually deters violent crime. This problem exists even if, for practical purposes, both parties decided to base their decision purely on the ground of social utility. The complexity of the relevant data makes any easy conclusion impossible. Hume's position shows how it is possible that intelligent, informed and humane persons could disagree on the matter.

Second, and analogous to the 'different humors' at the root of the Ovid–Horace–Tacitus case, moral disagreements may occur due to different 'weightings' or prioritizations of the different goods that must be considered in any complex moral judgement, such that the good will of all 'blameless' parties may be powerless to fully resolve them. However, I share Hume's apparent lack of concern regarding the possibility of such cases since, as I have argued, such 'ideal observers' will agree on virtually all important matters. There will be no possibility of a stalemate among true judges over Nazism, for example, or enforced genital mutilation, since such positions could only be endorsed through either (1) intellectual error, whether straightforwardly empirical or based on some bizarre metaphysical theory, or (2) through excessive self-interest or the hardness of heart that comes from impaired sympathy or failure to utilize the imagination. The existence of these defects will be matters of fact, holding whether or not the disputant recognizes it himself.

One example of the latter form of defect would be what are now commonly known as 'hate crimes'. As discussed earlier, sympathy involves the transformation of an idea of someone's inner state to a corresponding impression, through perceiving that person as being 'similar to oneself' in some relevant way. As we have seen, this mechanism operates more or less effectively depending on the degree of identification felt towards the individual under consideration. The *correction* of sympathy involves expanding the scope of one's identification, tuning into our common humanity and letting this bond take precedence over contingent affinities. In the case of hate crimes, it seems that the initial sympathy never takes, since the victim is seen primarily as someone as explicitly 'other' and different to oneself. Appreciation of common humanity never gets off the ground.

While Hume allows the possibility of two or more incompatible options that cannot be criticized on the grounds of inadequacies of understanding or sensibility, such an apparent stalemate will be tempered by the mutual recognition that another equally smart, informed and decent person can take an opposing viewpoint. This acknowledgement will diffuse the potential for conflict, as both parties will be thus reminded of the complexity of the issue, and be deterred from the dangerous consequences of a doctrinaire line.

Second, as discussed earlier, Hume disputed the rationalist analogy between mathematical and moral judgements on the grounds that moral evaluation is both subsequent to and dependent on all the relevant non-moral facts. In such an 'apparent stalemate' situation, true judges may appreciate that one can never be certain that *all* the facts have been considered. There is always the possibility that something has been overlooked, or that new facts could arise which might justify a reversal of judgement. It might seem, in the light of all this understanding, that the only thing to do would be to practise tolerance, while continuing the dialogue with such a worthy opponent.

In the meantime, however, there will be cases where utility demands a conventional solution, in which what matters is that everyone acts in the same way, even though other solutions may have equal support. (It is a moot point whether societies can bear such knowledge, or whether we will require the intervention of 'education and politicians' to guarantee adherence to these rules by inventing stronger foundations for them.) Hume acknowledged this in saying that the laws of justice have gaps in their application. In such disputes between different 'true judges' or, alternatively, where incommensurable differences in temperament prevent anyone from fully embodying this ideal, perhaps we have to say that there just is no fact of the matter regarding which of them is right. However, I repeat that this would be no cause for alarm, since this indeterminacy would exist only regarding the *relative* merits of incompatible options which, *considered in their own right*, would be beyond reproach. Suppose that X and Y cannot be criticized in any of the ways that Hume allows. In that case, while 'is X a better option than Y?', or 'ought we to do Y rather than X?', would be empty questions, the issue of whether X and Y, taken singly and judged on their intrinsic merits, are perfectly honourable and adequate choices could be answered straightforwardly in the positive.

Always remember that Hume is primarily doing moral psychology rather than normative theory. While his system demonstrates that we have the resources to resolve many disputes, his aim is to describe these resources rather than to solve the disputes himself. His task as a 'scientist of human nature' is to explain what is going on when we *do* act on the moral stance, and when we do not; how consensus is possible, and how it can fail to be reached. This he achieved more than anyone before, or indeed after him.

Further reading

See references to Chapter 5; also, Rachel Cohon (1997), R.M. Sainsbury (1998) and David Wiggins (1991). For 'Of the Standard of Taste', see Simon Blackburn (1984: ch. 6), and, for an opposing interpretation, Anthony Savile (1996).

Bibliography

Anscombe, G.E.M. (1957) *Intention*, Oxford: Blackwell.
Ardal, P.S. (1989) *Passion and Value in Hume's 'Treatise'*, Edinburgh: Edinburgh University Press, 2nd edn; 1st edn 1966.
Baier, A. (1991) *A Progress of the Sentiments: Reflections on Hume's 'Treatise'*, Cambridge, MA: Harvard University Press.
—— (1994) *Moral Prejudices*, Cambridge, MA: Harvard University Press.
Beattie, J. (1770) *An Essay on the Immutability of Truth; In Opposition to Sophistry and Scepticism*, Edinburgh.
Beauchamp, T.L. and Rosenberg, A. (1981) *Hume and the Problem of Causation*, Oxford: Oxford University Press.
Biro, J. (1993) 'Hume's New Science of Mind', in D.F. Norton (ed.), *The Cambridge Companion to Hume*, Cambridge: Cambridge University Press, pp. 33–63.
Blackburn, S. (1984) *Spreading the Word*, Oxford: Clarendon Press.
—— (1990) 'Hume and Thick Connexions', in *Philosophy and Phenomenological Research*, vol. L; repr. in Blackburn's *Essays in Quasi-Realism*, Oxford: Clarendon.

Boswell, J. (1962) 'An Account of My Last Interview with David Hume, Esq.', in D. Hume, *Dialogues concerning Natural Religion*, ed. N. Kemp Smith, Indianapolis: Bobbs-Merrill.

Bricke, J. (1996) *Mind and Morality*, Oxford: Clarendon.

Chazan, P. (1998) *The Moral Self*, London: Routledge.

Clarke, S. (1738) *A Discourse concerning the Unchangeable Obligations of Natural Religion, and the Truth and Certainty of the Christian Revelation*, in *Works*, vol. II, London; repr. New York, 1978; selections in Schneewind (1990), vol. I.

Cohon, R. (1997) 'The Common Point of View in Hume's Ethics', *Philosophy and Phenomenological Research*, vol. 57, pp. 827–50.

Dancy, J. (1993) *Moral Reasons*, Oxford: Blackwell.

Darwall, S. (1995) *The British Moralists and the Internal 'Ought', 1640–1740*, Cambridge: Cambridge University Press.

Davidson, D. (1976) 'Hume's Cognitive Theory of Pride', *Journal of Philosophy*, vol. 73, pp. 744–57; repr. in *Essays on Actions and Events*, Oxford: Clarendon, 1980, pp. 277–90.

Fogelin, R. (1985) *Hume's Skepticism in the 'Treatise of Human Nature'*, London: Routledge.

—— (1993) 'Hume's Scepticism', in D.F. Norton (ed.), *The Cambridge Companion to Hume*, Cambridge: Cambridge University Press, pp. 90–116.

Garrett, D. (1997) *Cognition and Commitment in Hume's Philosophy*, Oxford: Oxford University Press.

Grice, H.P. (1957) 'Meaning', *Philosophical Review*, vol. 66, pp. 377–88.

Haakonsen, K. (1993) 'The Structure of Hume's Political Theory', in D.F. Norton (ed.), *The Cambridge Companion to Hume*, Cambridge: Cambridge University Press, pp. 182–221.

Harrison, J. (1976) *Hume's Moral Epistemology*, Oxford: Clarendon.

—— (1981) *Hume's Theory of Justice*, Oxford: Clarendon.

Hobbes, T. (1991) *Leviathan*, ed. R. Tuck, Cambridge: Cambridge University Press.

Hudson, W.D. (ed.) (1969) *The Is–Ought Question*, London: Macmillan.

—— (1983) *Modern Moral Philosophy*, New York: St Martin's Press.

Hume, David (1978), *A Treatise of Human Nature*, ed. L.A. Selby-Bigge and P.H. Nidditch, Oxford: Clarendon Press.

—— (1975) *Enquiries Concerning Human Understanding and Concerning the Principles of Morals*, ed. L.A. Selby-Bigge and P.H. Nidditch, Oxford: Clarendon.

—— (1985) *Essays, Moral, Political and Literary*, ed. E.F. Miller, Indianapolis: Liberty Classics.

—— (1993) *My Own Life*, reprinted in D.F. Norton (ed.), *The Cambridge Companion to Hume*, Cambridge: Cambridge University Press.

—— (1985) '*Of the Standard of Taste*', in *Essays Moral, Political and Literary*, ed. E.F. Miller, Indianopolis: Liberty Classics

Hunter, G. (1963) 'Hume on *Is* and *Ought*', *Philosophy*, vol. 38; repr. in W.D. Hudson (ed.), *The Is–Ought Question*, London: Macmillan.
Hutcheson, F. (1755) *A System of Moral Philosophy*, 2 vols, London.
—— (1787) *A Short Introduction to Moral Philosophy*, Dublin.
—— (1938) *An Inquiry into the Original of our Ideas of Beauty and Virtue*, London.
—— (1969) *An Essay on the Nature and Conduct of the Passions, with Illustrations on the Moral Sense*, ed. P. McReynolds, Gainesville.
—— (1971) *Illustrations on the Moral Sense*, ed. B. Peach, Cambridge: Cambridge University Press.
—— (1994) *Philosophical Writings*, ed. R.S. Downie, London: Everyman.
Kemp Smith, N. (1941) *The Philosophy of David Hume*, London: Macmillan.
Lewis, D.K. (1969) *Convention: a Philosophical Study*, Cambridge, MA: Harvard University Press.
MacIntyre, A. (1955) 'Hume on "Is" and "Ought"', *Philosophical Review*, vol. 68; repr. in W.D. Hudson (ed.), *The Is–Ought Question*, London: Macmillan.
—— (1988) *Whose Justice, Which Rationality?*, Notre Dame, IN: Notre Dame University Press.
Mackie, J. L. (1977) *Ethics: Inventing Right and Wrong*, Harmondsworth: Penguin.
—— (1980) *Hume's Moral Theory*, London: Routledge.
Mandeville, B. de (1924) *The Fable of the Bees*, ed. F.B. Kaye, Oxford: Oxford University Press.
Miller, D. (1981) *Philosophy and Ideology in Hume's Political Thought*, Oxford: Clarendon.
Mossner, E. (1980) *The Life of David Hume*, Oxford: Clarendon, 2nd edn.
Norton, D.F. (1982) *David Hume, Common Sense Moralist, Sceptical Metaphysician*, Princeton, NJ: Princeton University Press.
—— (ed.) (1993) *The Cambridge Companion to Hume*, Cambridge: Cambridge University Press.
—— (1993) 'An Introduction to Hume's Thought', in D.F. Norton (ed.), *The Cambridge Companion to Hume*, Cambridge: Cambridge University Press, pp. 1–32.
—— (1993) 'Hume, Human Nature, and the Foundations of Morality', in D.F. Norton (ed.), *The Cambridge Companion to Hume*, Cambridge: Cambridge University Press, pp. 148–81.
Pears, D.F. (1990) *Hume's System: An Examination of the First Book of his 'Treatise'*, Oxford: Oxford University Press.
Penelhum, T. (1975) *Hume*, London: Macmillan.
—— (1993) 'Hume's Moral Psychology', in D.F. Norton (ed.), *The Cambridge Companion to Hume*, Cambridge: Cambridge University Press, pp. 117–47.

Prior, A.N. (1949) *Logic and the Basis of Ethics*, Oxford: Oxford University Press.

Quine, W.V. (1972) 'Methodological Reflections on Current Linguistic Theory', in D. Davidson and G. Harman (eds), *Semantics of Natural Languages*, Dordrecht: Reidel.

Raphael, D.D. (ed.) (1991) *British Moralists: 1650–1800*, 2 vols, Indianapolis: Hackett.

Reid, T. (1764) *An Inquiry into the Human Mind, on the Principles of Common Sense*, Edinburgh.

Rorty, A.O. (1990) '"Pride produces the idea of self": Hume on Moral Agency', *Australasian Journal of Philosophy*, vol. 68, pp. 255–69.

Rosenberg, A. (1993) 'Hume and the Philosophy of Science', in D.F. Norton (ed.), *The Cambridge Companion to Hume*, Cambridge: Cambridge University Press, pp. 64–89.

Russell, B. (1990) *The Problems of Philosophy*, Indianapolis: Hackett.

Russell, P. (1995) *Freedom and Moral Sentiment*, Oxford: Clarendon.

Sainsbury, R.M. (1998) 'Projections and Relations', *The Monist*, vol. 81, no. 1, pp. 133–60.

Savile, A. (1996) 'Of the Standard of Taste', in S. Lovibond and S.G. Williams (eds), *Essays for David Wiggins: Identity, Truth, and Value*, Oxford: Blackwell.

Sayre-McCord, G. (1994) 'Why Hume's "General Point of View" Isn't Ideal – and Shouldn't Be', *Social Philosophy and Policy*, vol. 11, no. 1.

—— (1995) 'Hume and the Bauhaus Theory of Ethics', *Midwest Studies in Philosophy*, vol. 20, pp. 280–98.

—— (1997) 'Hume's Representation Argument against Rationalism', *Manuscrito*, vol. 20.

Shaftesbury, Anthony Ashley Cooper, Third Earl of (1900) *Characteristics of Men, Manners, Opinions, Times, etc.*, ed. J.M. Robinson, London; *Inquiry concerning Virtue, or Merit* is to be found in vol. I.

Schneewind, J.B. (ed.) (1990) *Moral Philosophy from Montaigne to Kant*, 2 vols, Cambridge: Cambridge University Press.

—— (1998) *The Invention of Autonomy*, Cambridge: Cambridge University Press.

Searle, J.R. (1964) 'How to Derive an "Ought" from an "Is"', *Philosophical Review*, vol. 63, pp. 43–58.

Smith, M. (1994) *The Moral Problem*, Oxford: Blackwell.

Snare, F. (1991) *Morals, Motivation, and Convention: Hume's Influential Doctrines*, Cambridge: Cambridge University Press.

Strawson, G. (1989) *The Secret Connexion: Causation, Realism, and David Hume*, Oxford: Clarendon.

Stroud, B. (1977) *Hume*, London: Routledge.

Wiggins, D. (1991) 'Categorical Requirements: Kant and Hume on the Idea of Duty', *The Monist*, vol. 74, pp. 297–330.

Wittgenstein, L. (1961) *Tractatus Logico-Philosophicus*, trans. D.F. Pears and B.F. McGuinness, London: Routledge.
Wollaston, W. (1726) *The Religion of Nature Delineated*, London; selections in Raphael (1991), vol. I, pp. 239–58.

Index